FOOTBALL

AIMS FOR THE

STARS

FOOTBALL
AIMS FOR THE
STARS

How the constellations can affect planet football

AK AYRE

Matador
5 Weir Road
Kibworth Beauchamp
Leicester LE8 0LQ, UK
Tel: (+44) 116 279 2299
Fax: (+44) 116 279 2277
Email: books@troubador.co.uk
Web: www.troubador.co.uk/matador

ISBN 978 184876 4576

British Library Cataloguing in Publication Data.
A catalogue record for this book is available from the British Library.

Typeset in 11pt Palatino by Troubador Publishing Ltd, Leicester, UK
Printed and bound in Great Britain by TJI Digital, Padstow, Cornwall

Matador is an imprint of Troubador Publishing Ltd

To the spirit of football

CONTENTS:

ACKNOWLEDGEMENTS

Many thanks to my partner Christine Chalklin for her encouragement and inspiration throughout the writing of this book; thanks to my sons Joe and George for their advice and support; thanks to my friends Stewart Skidmore, Julian Ellis and Mark Cropley for proof reading and sharing their expertise, and to Caroline Davies for her silky computer skills; I am also grateful to Penny Jones, Merrell Hardy, Pete Mountford and Tom Evans for their helpful comments.

All errors of judgement, and lack of good form, are mine.

FOREWORD

The truth is always strange, stranger than fiction.
Lord Byron

On the 1st January 2010 the top of English football was dominated by foreign managers; Arsene Wenger at Arsenal: Mancini at Manchester City: Benitez at Liverpool: Chelsea had sacked Mourinho in 2007, replaced him with Avram Grant, then Luis Felipe Scolari, then Guus Hiddink and then in 2009, Ancelotti: Martinez at Wigan: Avram at Portsmouth: Zola at West Ham, and, with the sacking of Gary Megson, there was a vacancy at Bolton Wanderers. In 2002 Scolari won the World Cup with Brazil; in 2006 France and Italy contested the World Cup final under the management of Raymond Domenech and Marcello Lippi, respectively; in 2007 England sacked Steve McLaren and appointed Fabio Capello. What was going on?

It is an open secret that royalty, politicians, and financial institutions make use of astrology: American magnate, JP Morgan, proclaimed, *millionaires don't use astrology, billionaires do!* Forward-thinking business leaders use the ancient wisdom to innovate and build high-performance teams; many winemakers in France, Germany, and Chile are successfully producing Biodynamic wines using cosmic cycles; and even on planet Football some influential figures are tuning into the wisdom of the stars to get better results. But - you may be asking - what competitive advantage could they possibly get from astrology?

- In *Football Aims for the Stars* we will take a light-hearted look at the mysterious connections between the stars in football and the stars in the sky.

- As the ancient texts say, *character is destiny.* Although, knowing yourself is just the first step on the path to fulfilling your potential: after all, football is a team game.

- As Fabio Capello says, *it is not possible to win anything without good players,* but as he has demonstrated with most of his teams, and as other top managers have shown, it is much better to have the 'right' players than the best players.

- If you have ever wondered why a player, or a coach, can be a star at one club and flop at another then what follows will be enlightening; and, why do so many talented youngsters fall by the football wayside, whilst many less skilful lads go on to stardom? Is it because they joined the wrong club and had the wrong coach?

- If you are a football fanatic, find out what you have in common with your heroes.

- Finally, you do not need to have any prior knowledge of astrology to get some value from this book: all you need is a fascination with football and an open mind.

INTRODUCTION

After many years during which I saw many things
what I know most surely about morality and
the duty of man I learned from football.
Albert Camus

All football clubs are different. They have their own heritages, their own legends, songs, mascots, colours and their traditional adversaries; they have their bogey teams (the teams they never have any luck against), and the teams they always seem to beat. In fact everything about them is different, except in this respect: from the owners, sponsors, directors and investors, to the managers, players and fans, everyone hopes to be successful and a successful club is built on a winning team.

Every manager and every player is also different, and every era produces its own legends and stars. They are all unique and it is impossible to compare heroes from long ago with legends of today. Nevertheless, we will consider the characters and careers of players and managers past and present, highlighting as we go curious similarities in temperaments and a strange replaying of experiences. Times change, the game moves on, tactics, fitness and formations evolve; everything changes, but it seems that some things only appear to be different.

Football has a long history. The ancient Chinese played a form of the game. Over 500 years ago the Aztecs and Mayans of Mexico and Guatemala played a sophisticated style of football; they had a thriving industry vulcanising rubber to make high-tech balls and every town and city had its own stadium. They had their own stars, mascots, and their own patron saint of the beautiful game: Venus (appropriately). When the Spanish invaded in 1518 they were so impressed with the South Americans' ball skills that, once the Conquistadors were in control, they took a team back home to entertain the King. In the 1470s, King Edward IV banned the playing of football in England to encourage young men to take up archery and help defend his realm. However, in spite of his best efforts, the game continued to be popular until the mid 1830s when the Highways Act, banning street football, drove the game to the brink of extinction: only a handful of Public Schools, a few Cambridge Dons, the professional classes in Sheffield, tiny enclaves around Alnwick, and parts of the Scottish Lowlands kept the flame alive until the 1850s when the game of 'association' football emerged. In 1857 Sheffield Football Club was founded; in 1862 Notts County was formed. In 1863, a gathering of club representatives from Barnes, Surbiton, Crystal Palace, Perceval House, the War Office and Crusaders met in London to get organised: they called themselves the Football Association, and the FA was born. In 1865 Nottingham Forest came into being, and then Aston Villa, Bolton Wanderers, the Corinthians, and the Old Etonians soon followed. By 1871 there was enough interest to agree a simple set of rules and establish the game as a distinct sport: the FA launched a nationwide 'Challenge Cup' (the FA Cup), and, gradually, the framework of the modern game was put in place. Amateur clubs drew their players from officers and gentlemen, whilst the professional clubs recruited from the working classes. In the 1880s the top amateur club, Corinthians, showed that they were more than a match for the professionals when they beat the FA Cup holders, Blackburn, and then provided 9 of the England side who played Scotland in 1886.

By the 1920s football was the dominant sport in England, and it was becoming increasingly commercialised: in 1923 over 120,000 spectators were crammed into the Empire Stadium to watch the FA Cup final. In 1930 the first World Cup competition was staged in Uruguay. By the 1950s association football was a global game and England, the dominant force. But many believed England had grown complacent, that there had been no innovation, that the players were badly led - the England team was still picked by committee on the basis of current fitness and form, the manager was little more than an administrator, there was no conception of team-building, of developing effective partnerships, varying the pattern of play or of paying any regard to the opposition and local conditions. A series of humiliating defeats at the feet of the USA, Hungary, and Sweden caused a stir among the powers that be and as the austere 1950s swung into the 60s, the times, and the mood, were changing: in 1961 Jimmy Hill led the unionised players against the owners of the game and they agreed to abolish the maximum wage: in 1962 Alf Ramsey demanded the right to pick the England team and, they conceded. In 1967 Jock Stein blended 11 Scots and won the European Cup (European Champions Clubs' Cup - forerunner of the Champions League Cup), in 1968 Matt Busby led Manchester United to their first European trophy, and in the 1970s Bob Paisley and Brian Clough blazed the European trail.

In the 1990/2000s, a second wave of commercialisation, globalisation, and player freedom took hold. On the 11th January 2009, over a billion viewers world-wide tuned in to watch Manchester United play Chelsea. Whilst in July, United granted Cristiano Ronaldo's wish to join Real Madrid for a world record £80M. But for all the changes some things remain the same - it is still a beautifully simple game: there are still 11 players versus 11 on the pitch: the goal is still to score more than your opponent, and sometimes the club with the better players is still beaten by a better team. Although, according to Giovanni Trapattoni, even the best manager can only hope to improve the performance of a side by 5%, however, if you think that 5% is poor value for money, then think again: with around 5% improvement Reading would not have been relegated in 2008 and would have been more than £40 million better off. Nonetheless, many believed that Trapattoni was being too conservative with his percentages: was the difference made by Matt Busby, Alf Ramsey, Jock Stein, Helmut Schoen, Sebes, Hogan, Chapman, Lippi, Clough, Shankly, Paisley, and Bobby Robson 5%? And what about Alex Ferguson, Arsene Wenger, and Jose Mourinho?

Football Aims for the Stars takes a sideways glance at planet Football. It is not a statistical analysis of the game, neither is it scientific, unless you feel that Bill Shankly was being scientific when he claimed, *the supporters on the Spion Kop are worth a goal start*. Was it as far-fetched as it seemed, or was Bill ahead of his time? Years later in the weird world of quantum systems some scientists seemed to agree with him. They discovered that, in the sub-atomic world, light responds to the mind of the observer. Really? If the experimenter believed that light was made up of particles, it was, and then if s/he imagined it was made up of waves, it obligingly changed, or in other words the Kop was worth a goal start to Bill. Henry Stapp, a physicist at the University of California, also discovered that particles can continue to be connected to each other even when separated by long distances; in the weird world of football systems some pioneering managers have made a connection between the stars in the sky and the stars on the pitch (we will consider this cosmic phenomenon in Part 2).

The astrological principles in the book are kept simple so, even if you think that you don't know anything about astrology, you will be able to understand the main themes: there are 12 signs of the zodiac and they are grouped together according to the qualities of the 4 Elements in nature: FIRE, EARTH, AIR and WATER. For example, if you were born when the Sun was in Aries, Leo, or Sagittarius you have a fiery temperament. If you were born when the Sun was in one of the EARTH signs - Taurus, Virgo, Capricorn - you are more pragmatic and 'down to earth'. AIR sign people are more detached and thoughtful. WATER sign people are more emotional and motivated by their feelings (see Figure 1, page xxi). In Part 1, we look at the characters and careers of famous managers and players from the perspective of their birth signs and reveal some curious similarities. But - you may also ask - is there any philosophical basis for making such comparisons? The pioneering psychologist, CG Jung, wrote in 1931:

Time far from being an abstraction is a concrete continuum which contains qualities or basic conditions manifesting themselves simultaneously in various places in a way not to be explained by causal parallelisms. In other words whatever is born or done this moment of time, has the qualities of this moment.

Astrology is a symbolic language that helps us interpret those qualities as they manifest through character. Jung goes on:

Astrology is assured of recognition from psychology, because it represents the summation of all the psychological knowledge of antiquity.

Let us go on. Whilst there are 11 stars or heavenly bodies in our solar system, for simplicity, we will only consider 2 - the Sun and Mars.

Why the Sun and Mars? Because the Sun relates to your essential character and Mars shows how you instinctively play football (The Sun – is: Mars – does. The Sun visualises: Mars executes. In the Roman myths, Mars, the warrior son of the Sun, set out to do battle for his dad - on planet Football his battlefield is the pitch).

The Sun/Mars relationship is not only evident in you - in the way you approach the game and play - the same principle works throughout a football club. Really? Yes, take partnerships: let's briefly consider the manager (Sun) / captain (Mars) relationship: the manager (Sun) devises a tactical plan and the captain (Mars) takes responsibility for carrying it out on the field. For the plan to work well the captain should be on the same wavelength - both on and off the field - as the manager. Pardon? To illustrate: Alf Ramsey appointed Bobby Moore captain of England. Ramsey came under the zodiacal sign of Aquarius (born between approx 20th January and 19th February), so we would expect him to be on the same wavelength as someone with either the Sun or Mars in Aquarius. Moore was born at 3.00 am on the 12th April 1941 in London, when the Sun was in Aries and Mars was in Aquarius (refer to Bobby Moore's horoscope: Figure 2, page xxiv). Whereas when Fabio Capello (Sun

Gemini) was appointed England manager his first captain was Steven Gerrard (Sun Gemini), but for some reason he changed his mind, appointed John Terry (Sun Sagittarius) and then demoted him.

The illustration can be taken further: when Alf played as a right back for Spurs and England, his career was helped by having a good understanding with key players around him. At Spurs the right half back was Bill Nicholson - Bill had both the Sun and Mars positioned in Aquarius. Alf also enjoyed a good rapport with his England captain Billy Wright - Billy had the Sun positioned in Aquarius. Alf also shared an uncanny partnership with Stanley Matthews (Sun Aquarius Mars Aquarius). As you will see, Ramsey had the kind of understanding with Nicholson, Wright, Matthews and Moore that is often found in a successful career. The reverse is also true; many talented youngsters have fallen by the football wayside, not because of any lack of ability, but because they are at the wrong club, because they are not on the same wavelength as the coach, because they don't click with the rest of the team or because they are in the wrong place.* And it is not just the youngsters, sometimes star players flop at new clubs for similar reasons.

So with that at the back of your open mind, let's investigate the mysterious side of football.

* The issue of location (astrolocality) - why some people do better in one place rather than another - is not considered in this book.

FIGURE 1

SIGN*	ELEMENT**	SUN ***	MARS ****
ARIES 20th March-21st April	FIRE	Pioneer/ Dynamic/ Assertive	Hard hitting Powerful header
LEO 23rd July- 23rd August	FIRE	Dramatic/ Leader	Big match performer
SAGITTARIUS 22nd Nov- 22nd December	FIRE	Adventurous/ Inspirational	Flying winger Sharp shot
TAURUS 21st April- 21st May	EARTH	Creative/ Practical	Solid tackler Reliable
VIRGO 23rd Aug- 23rd September	EARTH	Tactical/ Technical	Relentless runner Versatile
CAPRICORN 22nd Dec- 20th January	EARTH	Responsible/ Disciplined/ A Rock	A tower of strength
GEMINI 21st May- 22nd June	AIR	Mercurial genius	Quick intelligent feet
LIBRA 23 Sept-24th October	AIR	Strategic/ Artistic	Midfield general
AQUARIUS 20th Jan- 19th February	AIR	Unconventional/ Intuitive	Expect the unexpected
CANCER 22nd June- 23rd July	WATER	Protective/ Godfather	Play with feeling
SCORPIO 24th Oct- 22nd November	WATER	Powerful/ Intense	Destructive tackler Clinical finisher
PISCES 19th Feb- 20th March	WATER	Visionary/ Romantic	Sublime passes Hollywood shots

*SIGN: The approximate dates when the Sun appears to enter and leave the signs of the zodiac.. For example, between approximately the 20th March and 21st April the Sun is in Aries, from approximately the 21st April to 21st May the Sun is in Taurus, from approximately 21st May to 22nd June the Sun is in Gemini.

**ELEMENT: Each of the 12 signs has characteristics in common with one of the 4 elements in nature: FIRE / EARTH / AIR / WATER.

***SUN: Key words to describe the character according to the zodiac sign. For example, if you were born when the Sun was in Aries you are pioneering, dynamic and assertive, if you were born when the Sun was in Pisces you are a visionary and have a romantic streak.

****MARS: Key words to describe how a footballer plays according to the zodiac sign. For example, if you were born with Mars in Gemini you will have quick 'intelligent' feet.

HOW TO USE THIS TABLE: For example, Sir Alex Ferguson was born on 31st December 1941 when the Sun was in Capricorn and Mars was in Aries. He is a responsible, sound and self-disciplined character, who was a hard-hitting centre forward with a powerful header.

COMPATIBILITY

This is an important consideration in creating effective partnerships and building successful teams. as a general rule all the signs within the same element are compatible: for example, Aries is compatible with Leo and Sagittarius. Fire signs are on a similar wavelength to Air signs, and Earth and Water signs usually click.

However, there is a creative tension when the other elements are mixed together. For example, a Fire sign person can make the blood boil of someone from a Water sign; conversely, a torrential downpour can extinguish a forest fire. Care, therefore, needs to be taken to get the right balance between compatible and complementary elements when selecting players for a team.

PLEASE NOTE: It appears to take Mars almost 2 years to travel through the 12 signs of the zodiac, so the list of approximate dates does <u>not</u> apply to Mars: for example, on the 1ˢᵗ January 2000 the Sun was in Capricorn but Mars was in Aquarius.

For a full list of dates for the zodiacal positions of Mars, from 1900 - 2050, refer to The American Ephemeris (Editions 1 and 2) by Neil F Michelsen, published by ACS Publications. Alternatively, visit www.astro.com and click on ephemeris. For further cosmic insights go to:

www.thefootballastrologer.co.uk

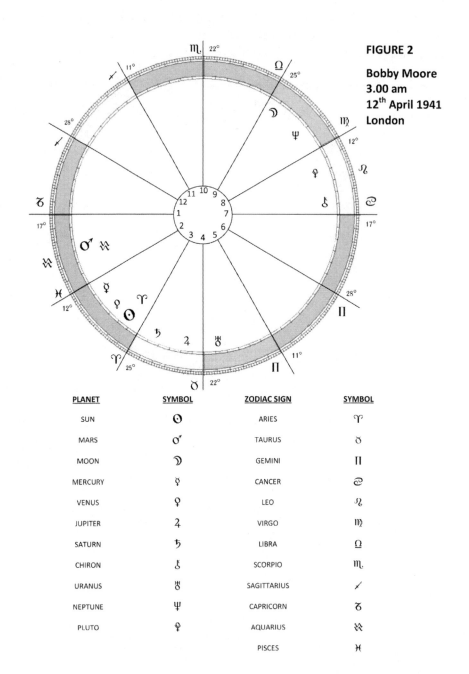

FIGURE 2

Bobby Moore
3.00 am
12th April 1941
London

PLANET	SYMBOL	ZODIAC SIGN	SYMBOL
SUN	☉	ARIES	♈
MARS	♂	TAURUS	♉
MOON	☽	GEMINI	♊
MERCURY	☿	CANCER	♋
VENUS	♀	LEO	♌
JUPITER	♃	VIRGO	♍
SATURN	♄	LIBRA	♎
CHIRON	⚷	SCORPIO	♏
URANUS	♅	SAGITTARIUS	♐
NEPTUNE	♆	CAPRICORN	♑
PLUTO	♇	AQUARIUS	♒
		PISCES	♓

PART
1

The 12 paths to success;

a cosmic journey through the Who's Who of football: 1909 – 2009

ARIES

Players lose you games, not tactics.
Brian Clough

There are many paths to success,
you have to do what fits your personality.
Marcello Lippi

Aries is a FIRE sign ruled by the god of war, Mars. The long accepted belief that there is life on Mars comes from the red planet's similarities with Earth: it has solid ground, a similar pattern of day and night, and it revolves on its axis at a similar speed – pure magnetite has also been found on its surface and that is only produced by aquatic bacteria. It takes 687 of our days to orbit the Sun and at its closest point it comes within 35 million miles of us – almost touching distance in the grand scheme of things. Mars has 2 moons appropriately named Phobos and Deimos – Fear and Panic. The brightest star in Aries is Hamal (from the Arabic for lamb); Aries' ancient symbol is the ram: the same ram that inspired the myth of the Golden Fleece and the best team ever assembled.*

Arietians are dynamic, pioneering, and assertive; they are brave and when riled, can be impulsive firebrands. In medical astrology, Aries has always been associated with the head and those born under its sign can also be headstrong. They are natural leaders and are happy to assume the captaincy of a team or be the head of a club. Yet, although they throw themselves headlong into life, never take a backward step, and are always willing to pick up the gauntlet, deep down they are not as sure of themselves as they would have you believe.

---

*Team Argo included captain courageous, Jason; with Hercules, the strongest man in the world, up front alongside the sharp-shooting Phalerus; down the wings were Calais, the fastest man in the world, and the tricky Periclymenus; Atalanta was hunting in midfield flanked by Orpheus, the enchanter, and the visionary Amphiaraus; at the heart of a solid defence were the Spartans – Polydeuces, the bare-knuckle boxing champion, and tough-guy Castor; Bootes, the bee keeper, was in goal, and with the support of a strong bench they overcame a 50ft dragon, fire breathing bulls, drones, people from outer space, umpteen armies, and returned with the 'Cup'.

THE RAMS

CHAIRMAN
ELTON JOHN Watford

DIRECTOR OF FOOTBALL
BARRY FRY Peterborough

COACHES
BRIAN CLOUGH Nottingham Forest
RAFA BENITEZ Liverpool
ARRIGO SACCHI AC Milan
WALTER WINTERBOTTOM England
HELENIO HERRERA Inter Milan
MARCELLO LIPPI Italy

GOALKEEPERS
ANDY GORAM Glasgow Rangers
GARY SPRAKE Leeds United

DEFENDERS
TOMMY SMITH Liverpool
ROBERTO CARLOS Real Madrid
ROY McFARLAND Derby County
ROBERTO AYALLA Valencia
BOBBY MOORE West Ham United
CARLES PUYOL Barcelona
SERGIO RAMOS Real Madrid

MIDFIELD
FRANCK RIBERY Bayern Munich
LOTHAR MATTHAUS Bayern Munich
MIKEL ARTETA Everton
CLARENCE SEEDORF AC Milan
JAMES McFADDEN Birmingham City

FORWARDS
TREVOR FRANCIS Nottingham Forest
FERENC PUSKAS Real Madrid
ROBBIE FOWLER Liverpool
RONALDINHO Barcelona
TOM FINNEY Preston North End
JOHN HARTSON Arsenal
TEDDY SHERINGHAM Nottingham Forest
AARON LENNON Spurs
KEVIN DAVIES Bolton Wanderers
JOE ROYLE Everton
JOHN TOSHACK Liverpool
DEAN WINDASS Hull City

INSPIRATIONS
SEVE BALLESTEROS
ERIC CLAPTON
VINCENT VAN GOGH
CAPTAIN KIRK
JASON

Ferenc Puskas

In the 1950s European football was led into a new era by Hungary's Magical Magyars. Their legendary captain, and inspiration, Ferenc Puskas (Sun Aries Mars Gemini) was born in Budapest on 2nd April 1927. Puskas established himself in his local side Kispest aged 16 and by 18 he was a star. He went on to score 83 goals in 84 internationals and rammed in 357 in 354 games for his club. He was stocky and powerful with deceptively quick acceleration and, with Mars in Gemini, had a particularly intelligent left foot. In his prime the opposition were often beaten before the game got started, and those that weren't were beaten by half time. His philosophy was simple:

The ball should be moved early, preferably with the first touch. To run with it wastes valuable attacking time.

In the Spring of 1950 Hungary were humbled by the Austrian Wunderteam, but in the return fixture they turned the tables and embarked on a remarkable winning streak: beating Yugoslavia 2-0, Italy 3-0, and then going another 28 games without defeat. When they came to Wembley in 1953 they were widely believed to be invincible – a belief not shared by the English; England had many more world-class players than Hungary including: Stanley Matthews, Tom Finney, Stan Mortensen, Nat Lofthouse, Billy Wright, and Ramsey, and so, no special arrangements were made to contain their star player. Nonetheless, the reputation of Puskas was a cause for concern in the dressing room, but as the England players lined up in the tunnel and saw Ferenc scoffing pie and mash they wondered what all the fuss was about, then when they saw him warming-up and noticed that he couldn't kick with his right foot, they breathed a collective sigh of relief. Two minutes later England were 0-1 down; twenty minutes rapier passing, swift interchanges and punishing potshots later it was 2-0, and by half time England had conceded 4. In the second half time stood still as Puskas received the ball in the England penalty area...darted away from goal....slipped his marker....braked....planted his right foot....dragged the ball with his left...*a golden–haired streak slid past*...swivelled...and rammed the ball home. The next day a reporter for the *London Times* compared the attempted sliding tackle of Billy Wright to a fireman rushing to the wrong fire. It was a landmark victory at a time when Britannia ruled the waves and England ruled football; indeed, only weeks before Wright wrote in his newspaper column,

I remain convinced that we still lead the world in technical know-how.

As it turned out it was an invitation to the Fates; some commentators insensitively compared Billy's boast to a claim made forty years earlier by sea captain Edward Smith:

When asked to describe my experience of nearly 40 years at sea, I merely say uneventful. Of course there have been gales, storms, fogs and the like, but in all my experience, I have never been in an accident of any sort worth speaking about. I have seen but one vessel in distress in all my years at sea. I never saw a wreck and have never been wrecked.

A few weeks later he captained the Titanic.

In the days following the humbling of the pride of English football, Puskas expressed his surprise at how calmly the English public had taken it – the nation had been stunned by sublime beauty. Sir Stanley Rous of the FA, however, certainly wasn't and quickly arranged a return match to re-assert England's authority. With Tom Finney (Sun Aries Mars Sagittarius) back from injury, the direct running and accurate crossing of the Preston plumber would complement the tricky dribbling runs of the wizardly Matthews – or so the public thought. In fact, Matthews and Ramsey were dropped and apart from those changes, no special arrangements were made to counter the threat of Puskas and the

Hungarians' innovative system. After 20 minutes England were a shambles:

It was as if we were playing a team from 'outer space'.
Syd Owen (England)

The 1956 'Hungarian Uprising' put paid to the magic: the team was broken up, Puskas made his way to Spain and signed for Real Madrid. Aged 31, he re-launched his career, formed a devastating partnership with Alfredo di Stefano (Mars Aries), had a good understanding with Luis Del Sol (Sun Aries Mars Libra), and helped Real dominate Europe for the next 5 years. When Puskas' playing career ended he tried his hand at management; but it took a while to find the right club; after travelling half way around the world he eventually settled at Panathinaikos and led them to the European Cup final, only to be beaten by Johan Cruyff's (Mars Aries) Ajax. In his later years, Puskas was welcomed home as the conquering hero and helped promote the national sport.

Bobby Moore

When Alf Ramsey finished playing he turned to management, first to Ipswich, with great success, then to England. Key to his success was having the right captain: Bobby Moore (Sun Aries Mars Aquarius) was the embodiment of Alf's football philosophy, *constructive defence*.

Bobby was born on the 12th April 1941 in the East End of London, aged 17, he signed for West Ham United and at 22 he was England captain. In 1964, Moore captained the Hammers to the FA Cup, beating Preston North End in the final, and beating cancer on the way. The following year he led West Ham to victory in the European Cup Winners Cup. He was a courageous, warm-hearted and charismatic leader. On the football field he was majestic, unhurried, inventive, and inspirational and although not the quickest, with Mars in intuitive Aquarius, he had good anticipation which gave him a head-start over faster opponents. Bobby was independent, wilful, and didn't always show the respect that those in authority expected. At times he contended with Ramsey and on occasions mocked his, alleged, gypsy heritage, but Alf seemed to accept it all in good humour – unlike Bob's West Ham manager Ron Greenwood:

There was a gulf between us: he was aloof and in team talks he either ignored me or looked around the room with glazed eyes, as if to say that he had nothing to learn from me. I just couldn't get close to him.

Bobby played the way Ramsey wanted his captain to play: solid in defence, but when he received the ball his first instinct was to go forward. In the 1966 World Cup final, 3-2 ahead and with seconds remaining: Bobby received the ball just outside the penalty area – *get rid of it* – screamed big Jack....controlled it – *get rid of IT* – looked up and, with Hurst in space, launched a decisive counter-attack.

Moore continued to deliver impeccable passes and complete immaculate tackles for the rest of his career:

Bobby Moore was the best defender I ever played against.
Pele

He achieved what he did because of who he was.
John Bond (West Ham teammate)

Walter Winterbottom

Ramsey made Moore England captain, but it was his predecessor, the ex-RAF wing commander, PE teacher and longest reigning England manager, Walter Winterbottom (Sun Aries Mars Pisces), who gave Bobby his first cap.

Winterbottom was appointed England manager in 1946. The war had changed the world but English football was still running on empire lines when it came to team selection. Teams were chopped and changed by the International Selection Committee and Walter didn't have much input. His record was patchy – at the start it was average, it was lamentable in the middle, but towards the end it was quite good. Indeed, Walter was responsible for one of England's most humiliating defeats: 0-1, v USA at the 1950 World Cup, not to mention the Magical Magyars. However, in Walter's defence: he didn't pick the team, he deployed England's time-honoured classic formation – WM – with Mannion, Mortensen, and Mullen up front and Wright at the heart, plus the pitch was bumpy, the air was thin, and the USA had the, *rub of the green* – at least that was one story. Neutrals said that England had the better players, but the USA had the better team.

Still, with Mars in the mysterious sign of Pisces, behind the scenes Winterbottom was fighting the FA for the organisational changes that he believed were necessary. Nevertheless, even diplomatic and fair-minded Bobby Charlton was dismissive of Walter's efforts: for a start, Bobby didn't believe Winterbottom had played the game at a high enough level to manage top-class players like him, and, secondly, he felt Wally was inept at communicating with them, *they were cogs in a machine.* Matthews felt the same way, even though Walter had actually played for Manchester United. Anyway, having recognised it was a problem, he set on the astute judge of character, Bill Nicholson, to engage with the lads. When Nick needed to concentrate more on his Spurs side,

Walter appointed Jimmy Adamson (Sun Aries Mars Cancer) and team spirit, and results, continued to improve: at the 1962 World Cup Finals, England beat the favourites Argentina 3-1 and were unlucky to be eliminated in the quarter-finals. By the end of his reign, he had restored national pride in the football team – won 78 games, drew 33, and alienated the media.

Brian Clough, Gary Sprake

It wasn't only Ramsey and Pele who thought Moore was the best defender, Brian Clough (Sun Aries Mars Libra) also thought he was immaculate. Cloughie tried to sign Bobby, when he was managing the Rams, with the intention of partnering him with a young, future England centre half Roy McFarland (Sun Aries Mars Leo), *what a partnership they would have been.*

Brian Howard Clough was born in Middlesbrough on the first day of Spring 1935. The ram is an apt symbol for Aries, it is the symbol for the Derby tups, and an apt symbol for the man who made a huge impact at the Baseball Ground. Brian was a warm-hearted, courageous, charismatic, and at times outrageous leader. As befits a child with Mars in Libra – the sign of beauty and grace – his boyhood heroes were all warriors who fought with style and good manners including John Wayne and Robin Hood. He was in awe of no-one, except Muhammad Ali:

Ali is the only person to have made me feel inferior.

He admired Ali's courage, magnetic power, charisma, humour, faith, and good manners, moreover, he loved his catchphrase:

Float like a butterfly and sting like a bee.

That's how Cloughie wanted his teams to play: with style and grace, with a delicate touch, and a stinging end product. He wanted his teams to play beautiful football, but also inflict pain. He played 222 games and scored 204 goals for Middlesbrough, at Sunderland he scored 63 goals in 74. Winterbottom recognised his talent and capped him for England, however, aged 26 his playing career was effectively finished by injury. He started early in management, but didn't find any success until he arrived at Derby. Brian felt at home in the Peak District and with his former teammate, and complementary character, Peter Taylor, he transformed the club. Brian fired the players up and Peter calmed them down. Peter identified the characters the team needed and Brian signed them. Derby were in the Second Division when they arrived, heading towards relegation, but remarkably within 5 years they had won the First Division title and reached the semifinal of the European Cup. Regardless, his turbulent relationship with the directors boiled over in 1973, headstrong and impulsive as ever – he resigned. Old Big 'ead immediately regretted it and did so for the rest of his life.

Brian went to Brighton but didn't settle. He frightened the players, *they froze on the pitch; they were hopeless,* and dreamed of Derby. He wished he was back up north, and soon his wish came true. Leeds United had lost their manager to England and, inexplicably, the Leeds directors offered Revie's post to the Don's biggest critic: Cloughie accepted. Taylor, however, refused to join him and advised against such lunacy, *there is no way that Leeds lot will ever forgive and forget.* They didn't: Cloughie was sacked after 44 days. He consoled himself with a generous financial settlement and then in 1975 they were re-united at Nottingham Forest. Forest were sliding towards the Second Division trapdoor at the time and yet within 5 years they had won the European Cup twice. What was his secret? Perhaps being in the right place at the right time, having the right assistant, and doing what fitted his personality – not dabbling in tactics,

About 10 percent of my time is spent on thinking about the opposition.

He concentrated on his own team. He selected players with character. He didn't bother with a player's weaknesses, it was his strengths he was interested in – that, and how he fitted into the team. He wanted a balanced side; he didn't want his teams ever to look ragged. He always had a player who could kick with his left foot, he always had someone to command the air, someone who could pass the ball, a player who could keep possession, a solid tackler and, oh yes, the most important – a goalscorer. Talent was important, yes, but it came second to character:

The art of management is knowing your players, really knowing them: understanding what sort of characters you have on your hands. Both on and off the pitch timing is important; you have to know when to be silent, when to leave well-alone, and when to blast 'em. And always remember....players can only play when they are relaxed, without fear.

He once said that without Taylor he was nothing,

I learnt early on that two heads are better than one, even if one is a sheep's `ead. We may have fought like cat and dog, but I needed Pete.

When he arrived at Derby the first thing he did was assess the players. Some weren't good enough, some didn't fit in, and others were too old. The veteran goalkeeper Reg Matthews was one of those showing his age:

He's too old...he's shot it...he's finished...he costs too much. He has to go!
    Hang on, Brian! He's experienced...he's courageous...he'd walk through a brick wall if you asked him to. He sets the right example.

Reg had his contract extended.
    It was Taylor's job to assess the needs of the team and he thought Derby needed a battle hardened powerhouse at the heart of defence, *we need Dave Mackay!* Clough set off on what seemed like an impossible

14

mission to White Hart Lane to get him. He arrived unannounced. Mackay was training. Bill Nicholson didn't recognise Cloughie:

I'm Brian Clough; I've come to sign Dave Mackay.

Nicholson was cool but polite...

Dave's out training. You can wait if you want to, but you're wasting your time...he signs for Hearts tomorrow. The deal's been done.

A couple of hours later: muddied, wet and weary Mackay trundled by:

Hey you! Young man...I want to sign you.
No chance, I'm away to Hearts tomorrow.
That's appropriate, but how much would it take to...away to Derby?
£14,000.

They shook hands and Brian rebuilt County around the barrel-chested Mackay; only Matthews and the trojan, Kevin Hector (Mars Aries), survived the following season's cull. Cloughie was the instigator, the catalyst, the ramrod who didn't listen to advice – except from Taylor or Harry Storer, the former Derby County manager. Brian had great respect for the wisdom of Harry and applied one pearl throughout his managerial career:

Once you have counted your players onto the coach, count them again and if you don't have 5 with hearts, go home.

When Taylor's book came out with personal revelations their love / hate relationship took a final turn for the worse. Brian felt betrayed by his Cancerian former goalkeeping friend and assistant. They never spoke again, to Clough's great regret. Perhaps there was something about Cancerians that brought out the best and worst in Cloughie? (It should be mentioned that he didn't like Don Revie (Sun Cancer) and Revie reciprocated. Why? Consider the dynamics of the Don's Leeds 'family'- was it coincidence that the only Aries player in his first team squad was the only player to be excluded from his tight-knit group?).

Gareth Sprake (Sun Aries Mars Pisces) was born on the 3rd April 1945 in Swansea. He joined Leeds as an apprentice and helped Revie win promotion to the First Division in 1964. He established himself as the first choice goalkeeper throughout Leeds' rise to the top and kept over 200 'clean sheets' along the way. The Don had treated him as a son, nurtured his progress, forgiven him for his impulsive errors, even put an arm around him when the Liverpool Kop greeted him with a chorus of Des O'Connor's hit song 'Careless Hands', but when Gary commented on Revie's character to the national press, Don felt betrayed and shunned him. Ironically, if Revie had signed another Aries player, for sake of argument let's say Bobby Moore, Leeds would have conquered Europe (you will understand my reasoning when we consider 'Winning Teams').

In 1993 Clough was alone at Forest. Having impulsively sold his star striker, Teddy Sheringham (Sun Aries Mars Aries), they had slid into the relegation zone.

At the City Ground for the last match, the dark tunnel behind him, the cameras in front, the disappointed crowd all around, defeated, stabbed by the Blades, the end of the journey for him and back to the Second Division for them, just another world-weary manager of a ragged team, but no, this was different – this was Brian Howard Clough. Dignified. Straight-backed. Vulnerable. There was no blame in defeat. No humiliation. The crowd rose chanting, in respect, chanting in admiration....Brian....Brian....Brian....Brian – Howard – Clough. They spilled onto the pitch and gathered around the wounded warrior; the tannoy man got the message – Frank Sinatra crooned across the City....

I did itttttMyyyyyyyyyWWWhhaaayyyyyyyyyahhhregretssss

A little girl appeared beside him with a flower for her champion, a perfect blossom, *for you, Mr Clough*. Wearing his red face and Lincoln green jersey holding out a shaking hand, graciously accepting the hero's garland from Venus – *hey, Beauty, don't cry* – then he was gone.

Barry Fry

Not all Arietian managers spend as much as 10 per cent of their time on tactics. Fiery Barry Fry (Sun Aries Mars Pisces), the charismatic former manager of Peterborough, said, *I don't do tactics*. He does burning desire and leadership, and as a director of the Posh he enjoyed an exciting, successful, and all too brief, partnership with Darren Ferguson (Mars Aries): driving them to two promotions in successive seasons.

Helenio Herrera, Arrigo Sacchi, Marcello Lippi, Rafa Benitez

Not all Arietian managers win the European Cup in successive seasons either; Cloughie did and Helenio Herrera (Sun Aries Mars Gemini) did with Inter Milan, but Rafa Benitez (Sun Aries Mars Pisces) just missed out at Liverpool.

Herrera was unique. He was the highest paid manager in the world. The son of a rebel Spanish anarchist, he grew up in poverty in Casablanca, eventually moved to France, played a few games for the national side and then tried management. He won titles with Atletico

Madrid and Barcelona and worked in Portugal, but his quirky methods and arguments with directors meant he soon moved on, however, he settled in Milan. He adapted the local 'door-bolt' method of defensive play and invented 'catenacchio', pioneering the swift counter-attack. He also pioneered the pre-match retreat: taking his squad into the country to relax before a big game, and just like Old Big 'ead, paid no attention to the opposition:

The secret to victory is finding the hero in yourself.

He stuck psychological slogans on the dressing room walls and forbade idle talk. Certain words were banned completely, for instance a player would be fined a week's wages for saying – *playing*, instead of – *winning*. He was demanding, autocratic, charismatic, physical, and demonstrative. He slapped his players on the backs, kissed them, punched their chests and stabbed a finger into their hearts as they prepared for battle: just a little reminder that he wanted them to show their courage on the field. He was a single-minded battler, who some said was insensitive to the feelings of others. Some said that he lacked compassion: that he didn't understand his players, that he was a dictator and that they were, *cogs in a machine*. He was the biggest star at every club, bigger than the directors and bigger than the players, and he wanted courage from them, yes, but with Mars in Gemini he also wanted intelligence. At Roma his captain was Fabio Capello (Sun Gemini) – they won the Cup.

Cloughie and Herrera weren't the only Arietians to win the European Cup twice. A former shoe salesman, who had never played the game professionally, did too. Arrigo Sacchi (Sun Aries Mars Cancer) won the Cup in 1989 and 1990 with AC Milan. He became the manager of Italy and took them to the World Cup final in 1994. He was wild-eyed, outspoken, and wherever he went he seemed to be in a constant battle with directors. He was innovative, pioneering, had a utopian vision of football, and a method that was invincible. Really? Yeah, his success was based on following his idiosyncratic belief in a cohesive system he called, *the Multiplier Effect*. What? He believed that if a team could feel the flow of a game as one entity, say like a swirling shoal of fish or flocking starlings, something mysterious happens – 11 becomes 13: the team of 11 players play as if they have 2 extra. Practice was intense and relentless: as one player moved to the right the rest of the team moved to the right, as one player moved to the left they all moved to the left, as one player moved forward they all moved forward, always in unison: in harmony. To perfect *the Multiplier* they practised with an imaginary ball. They synchronised their movement with the movement of a mental sphere. Then smaller groups would be drilled to perfect a 'spontaneous' response to any given match scenario, for example, the back 4 and keeper were drilled to resist an all-out-attack from 10 strikers for 15 minutes. There were no rules, only one condition – the defenders had to do exactly as Sacchi directed to the last detail, to the last second. Even against Van Basten, Gullit, and Donadoni they were never breached. Sacchi was a big personality, always the biggest at any club, brighter than the brightest star, brighter even than chairman and future president, Silvio Berlusconi.

Marcello Lippi (Sun Aries Mars Leo) didn't win the European Cup twice, but he is, arguably, the most successful manager. He won 5 League titles, the European Cup with Juventus, and the World Cup with Italy. As a player he was a competent central defender with Sampdoria but never reached the international heights. He never worried about that and he never worried about the opposition: he never dabbled in tactics. He relied on his personality, his strength of character and courage. His approach was uncomplicated, direct and straight forward – pick the right players for the right positions and blend them into a team. He knew what the players wanted from him, and they knew what he wanted from them.

Some said Sacchi was a great tactician; some said that he never changed his tactics regardless of the opposition, or local conditions. Some say that Rafa Benitez is a great tactician and others say that he changes too much; rotation: wingers, no wingers: zonal marking, man-to-man marking, both: players in position, players out of position: a balanced system, a cohesive system: a diamond in midfield, a Christmas tree with a star up top. Sports psychologists point out that not everyone responds well to uncertainty: some characters cope better than others and those others have to be reconditioned or moved on. It can lead to a big squad and a high turn-over of players (67 in 5 years at Liverpool), *but it works for me!* It worked in Spain, where he won the UEFA Cup at Valencia, with a win ratio over 55% – enough to both win the Cup and be ahead of Real and Barcelona in the League.

Rafael Benitez was born on the 16th April 1960. Aged 12, he was a junior with Real Madrid but injury hampered his progress; he left Madrid and wandered the lower leagues; in 1986 he returned to coach the juniors. In 1995, he left to coach Real Valladolid and, after a poor start and following a hammering from Valencia, he was fired in January 1996. By the end of the year he was coaching Osasuna in the Second Division, but after 7 games he was sacked, anyway, fortunately, there was a silver lining – Pako Ayesteran – Rafa was impressed with the rapport that Pako enjoyed with the lads. After initial success at CF Extremadura, the following season he was fired, but this time he used his time-out for research: he went to Milan to study the methods of his hero, Arrigo Sacchi. When he returned to management, at Tenerife with his new assistant, they were an immediate success. So when Valencia needed a manager to replace Hector Cuper – the coach who had taken them to two European Cup finals playing negative football – they thought of Rafa. However, some speculated that the directors had put their faith in young Benitez because, in contrast to Cuper, he had an attacking strategy; others said that the real reason was because he had no tactics and the directors thought they could manipulate him.

Initially he chopped and changed his players. He employed Sacchi's zonal marking system and applied his synchronised moves; he married *the Multiplier* to sports science. Both Rafa and his assistant were University graduates with Physical Education degrees and national coaching badges; Paco was a master of High Performance Sport and had devised an innovative coaching regime of his own, *the Integral Coaching*

Method: a method where training drills anticipate real game scenarios. It required exhaustive rehearsals: the envisioned phases of play were choreographed around the opponent's team profile. Having analysed their qualities, considered their strengths and weaknesses, Rafa contemplated the opportunities and threats that may arise during the contest and coaching sessions were planned accordingly. Pre-match, Pako would re-imagine the game for the benefit of all, and Rafa would give a final rallying call. The approach demanded supreme physical, mental, and emotional fitness:

Every game is different and requires a unique plan; but we always start off by doing the same things and if we take control, we continue, if not, we change.

Not only did Benitez analyse his opposition, and his players, he analysed himself: he recognised where he needed assistance. Certain psychological duties were delegated; he didn't want emotions to cloud his judgment so the responsibilities for creating the sense of peace and well-being the players needed to feel before a game were handed to his assistants: coaching staff needed to be complementary characters.

Benitez is friendly, but we seem to be cogs in a machine.
Steven Gerrard

And most important, he needed the right captain to carry out his instructions on the pitch: at Valencia he was Roberto Ayalla (Sun Aries Mars Aquarius). In 2005, Benitez took Liverpool to the Champions League final, where he conjured a football miracle to beat AC Milan. Outplayed from the start, the Reds were 3-0 down and facing total humiliation; at half time he changed tactics...ATTACK. They scored an early goal, then another and another, and then, following a penalty shoot-out, won the Cup.

In 2007 Benitez was back in the Champions League final. Again the opponents were Ancelotti's AC Milan, but this time Rafa's game plan was perfect: Milan were outplayed but, strangely, once again the better team lost.

DENNIS
BERGKAMP ♉

TAURUS

I am a stubborn person.
David Beckham

I'm not a quitter.
Avram Grant

I'd say Cesc Fabregas has Dennis Bergkamp's brain.
Bob Wilson

Taurus is the first of the EARTH signs. It is ruled by the goddess of Love and Beauty, Venus. Curiously, the more loving Taureans become, and the more they appreciate beauty, the more successful they seem to be and the more money they attract. They have a natural appreciation of art and music, and enjoy a luxurious lifestyle.

The brightest star in the constellation Taurus is Aldebaran: in Arabic it means the *follower* of the Pleiades, which is one of the finest star clusters in the entire sky containing as it does the bright and peaceful Alcyone, the powerful Atlas, and the mysterious Maya.

The age-old symbol of Taurus is the bull, suggestive of the Taureans' physical prowess and capacity for hard work, not to mention their stubborn streak. Although they are usually peace loving, when they are riled – by the proverbial red rag – they can rage.

As players they make creative and reliable teammates, however, if they are to fulfil their potential they must feel valued, and the most tangible measure of that is a fat pay cheque – otherwise they wander off to greener pastures. Deep down they are good-hearted, kind and generous; they are practical 'down to earth' and loyal, and as they don't really like change, once they have found the right club they are usually happy to stay; although they have to be sure that others don't take advantage of that trait.

THE BULLS

OWNER
JOHN MADEJSKI Reading

COACHES
JACK CHARLTON Ireland
STEVE McLAREN England
DAVID MOYES Everton
AVRAM GRANT Portsmouth
GARY MEGSON Bolton Wanderers

GOALKEEPERS
PETR CECH Chelsea
SHAY GIVEN Manchester City
IKER CASILLAS Real Madrid
DAVID ICKE Coventry City

DEFENDERS
FRANCO BARESI AC Milan
ALESSANDRO COSTACURTA AC Milan
STUART PEARCE Nottingham Forest
RICARDO CARVALHO Chelsea
PATRICE EVRA Manchester United
DANI ALVES Barcelona
LUCIO Inter Milan

MIDFIELD
ANDRES INIESTA Barcelona
CESC FABREGAS Arsenal
DENNIS BERGKAMP Arsenal

JOHAN CRUYFF Ajax
ALAN BALL Everton
NOBBY STILES Manchester United
DAVID BECKHAM Manchester United
KAKA Real Madrid
GRAEME SOUNESS Liverpool
ANTONIO RATTIN Boca Juniors
DIEGO SIMEONE Inter Milan
JOHN OBI MIKEL Chelsea

FORWARDS
JACKIE MILBURN Newcastle United
JEFF ASTLE West Bromwich Albion
JACK LAMBERT Arsenal
ARTHUR ROWLEY Leicester City
ZOLTAN GERA Fulham
DIEGO FORLAN Atletico Madrid

INSPIRATIONS
JMW TURNER
FORD
FERRARI
CHARLES ATLAS
SITTING BULL

Jack Charlton, Nobby Stiles, Alan Ball

Alf Ramsey valued Taureans more than any other. When it came to building his World Cup winning side his solid foundation was no-nonsense centre half Jack Charlton (Sun Taurus Mars Libra), fierce tackling Nobby Stiles (Sun Taurus Mars Cancer), and the flame-haired Alan Ball (Sun Taurus Mars Aries).

Ball was determined to succeed in football. Having initially struggled to find a club, eventually, he joined Blackpool and was fortunate to find himself lacing the boots of the legendary Stanley Matthews. He was inspired by the wizard and resolved to get in the England team by the time he was 21. Over-ambitious? Maybe, but he listened to Stan, devised his own plan, and stubbornly stuck to it. In the World Cup final he was Alf's 'man of the match' – his market value skyrocketed and he went on to break the British transfer record twice.

Appearances can be deceptive and they were with Nobby: with his thin wispy hair, his thick horn-rimmed glasses and tweedy jackets, Stiles looked like a school teacher from 'Kes'. Whatever, when he bared his teeth and put on the red shirt of Manchester United or England – he was more fired-up in red – he transformed into a ruthless exponent of the destructive arts and, whether he was playing for England or United, his instructions were always the same, *get the ball Nobby, then pass to Bobby*. Often he would be detailed to mark the opposition's star player – especially if it was the great Portugal and Benfica striker, Eusebio (later you will see why the 'Black Pearl' always had problems against him). Stiles is one of only two Englishmen to have won the World Cup and the European Cup: the other is Charlton (Bobby).

Jack spent his entire playing career at Leeds United. Aged 38 he became the manager of Middlesbrough. When his former boss, Don Revie, controversially resigned from the England job, Jack unsuccessfully applied. After some success at Middlesbrough, at Sheffield Wednesday, again at Boro, and then at Newcastle he became the Republic of Ireland coach. The Republic had no history of qualifying for World Cup Finals when Jack joined, but using an uncomplicated style they reached the 1990 quarter-finals. Although widely criticised for his simplistic tactics – based on pressure, collective hard work, punting the ball up field and having the midfield charge forward – Ireland enjoyed great success. They qualified for the next Finals and progressed through the Group stage; in recognition, Jack was made an honorary Irishman and given the keys to the City of Dublin.

Stiles spent his entire playing career at Manchester United and then joined the coaching staff. His special responsibility was developing the youth team, and, with Mars in the caring sign of Cancer, he nurtured many a young hopeful through the daunting Old Trafford labyrinth to the brink of stardom. From 1988 he was guide and mentor to a 13-year-old cockney hopeful, David Beckham (Sun Taurus Mars Pisces). They understood each other; they got on well, so well in fact that Nobby made Becks captain of the Under 16's.

David Beckham, Steve McLaren, Stuart Pearce

Born in Leytonstone on the 2nd May 1975, with a United fan for a dad, David received his first Red Devils shirt on his 3rd birthday and dreamed of playing for United. Aged 12, all the top teams were interested, *by the time I'm 18 I could be driving a Porsche*. Whatever, when he got the chance he chose his local team, Spurs, but when he went training and the youth coach couldn't remember his name...

Maybe I'd be better off at United after all – at least they'd remember me.

Nobby did value him. Aged 17, David was sitting in seat 17 on a tiny 17 seater plane flying to the south coast with Manchester United. He came off the substitutes' bench – for the last 17 minutes – to make his senior debut at the Goldstone Ground. He was pleased that he hadn't made a mistake, but he had a long wait before his next appearance, v Galatasaray in the European Cup. He played well and scored. The first to congratulate him was his captain, and hero, Eric Cantona (Mars Taurus). Aged 19, making slow progress at United and then being told he was going to Preston North End on loan, he was upset. He thought he had no future at Old Trafford, *it's all over before I've got started,* and confided in his coach, Brian Kidd (Mars Taurus). Kiddo reassured him, *you are highly-rated Becks...the loan is just for personal development reasons.* Preston made him feel welcome and he struck up a good rapport with their captain, centre half and future Everton manager, David Moyes (Sun Taurus Mars Leo). He settled in quickly; it was a happy 4 weeks and he wanted to stay longer, but things were changing at Old Trafford – Andrei Kanchelskis was injured – and Alex Ferguson threw David into the lion's den, otherwise, United v Leeds. He played well, worked hard, and was pleased that he hadn't made any mistakes. Kanchelskis was fit for the next match and Becks looked forward to another long stretch on the bench, but no, Andrei fell out with the manager and David never looked back – Beckham was now first choice right winger, and with the words of TV pundit Alan Hansen, *you'll win nothing with kids,* ringing in his ears, he joined the youngest United team in 40 years and nervously started the 1995-96 season.

On the opening day they were hammered by Aston Villa – Hansen seemed vindicated. David was disappointed but the manager reassured him, and Cantona inspired him. David was in awe of the charismatic Frenchman and stayed behind after the scheduled training sessions to watch the genius at work, and was surprised to find that Eric's routine was exactly the same as his own – the one his dad and granddad had taught him in Larkswood park:

Kick the ball as high as you can, son, control it, kick it as high as you can, control it...do it again. Kick it against the wall with your right foot...kick it against the wall with your left foot...right foot...left foot. Now take a free kick, son, bend it around the wall...bend it around the wall...bend it again...and again. Do it until your foot can do it without you.

United won the League and FA Cup double.

He could afford his Porsche now and was well on his way to becoming the richest player in the world; on that journey, in Russia as a matter of fact, he fell in love. She was a singer on television and it was love at first sight, *I didn't know her name or anything about her, where she lived or if she liked football or anything, only that she was in a band called 'the Spice Girls'.* He was determined to find her. When he got back to England he discovered that she was Victoria 'Posh' Adams (with Venus in Pisces it was a match made in heaven), and, as if Cupid had been scheming, she lived just around the corner from his parents, and then, curiously, he bumped into her at Crystal Palace – soon after, they married. He was on cloud 9, and when Glenn Hoddle called him up to join the England squad he was, *over the moon.* He was delighted with his first training session and Glenn was impressed; he was selected for the 1998 World Cup squad and picked for the crunch match, v Argentina. During the game he was closely marked by the destructive tackler, Diego Simeone (Sun Taurus Mars Gemini), he just couldn't shake the Argentine hard-man off: ankle tapped, niggled, now clattered from behind and lying face down, his emotions running high...*red rag*...kicked out...caught Diego a glancing blow...*red card*. England fought back, hung on, but were eliminated. *It was Beckham's fault!* Effigies were burnt in the streets. Dark days lay ahead. Anyhow, he concentrated on his practice, on his delivery of crosses and free kicks, and stuck close to Posh, to his family, and friends. Gradually the furore died down and didn't seem to have done any permanent damage. The following season he helped United win the 'Treble' and then when Peter Taylor took over, as caretaker manager, he was elevated to the captaincy, but when Sven-Goran Eriksson (Venus Pisces) arrived, David was apprehensive – he needn't have worried, they liked each other. It seemed things couldn't get any better when his former United coach, Steve McLaren, joined the England coaching staff. Becks' career, fame, and fortune were going from strength to strength; he led England to a 5-1 victory against Germany in Munich: he scored the crucial goal against Greece that qualified England for the 2002 World Cup Finals. He recovered from a crunching tackle by Aldo Duscher (Mars Pisces), and a badly broken toe, just in time for the Finals. In the first game, against Sweden, he delivered a perfect corner for Sol Campbell to nod in the goal that gave England a draw, then old rivalries resumed: Argentina...

Michael (Owen) is galloping into the box. Pochettino brings him down...penalty, Ref...penalty! I'm placing it. Simeone is standing in front of me saying something, trying to put me off...the lads push him away. I'm looking down...every nerve on edge...I can't breathe...I take a deep breath...deeper. I'm running up...I'm hitting it. I've dreamt this moment – I know it goes in. I'm running to the corner flag...the crowd is roaring in my ears...the effigy in me `ead stops burning. Wouldn't it be just great if it's the winner? All the right omens – the No 7 shirt...the No 7 seat on the plane – it's meant to be.

England went on to reach the quarter-finals and were unlucky to lose. Back at Old Trafford, still disappointed about losing to Brazil, and now in a disappointing *stand-off* with the manager,

We were winding each other up, then ignoring each other and with no Kiddo to confide in, it was upsetting my game. It was all going wrong. I confronted him; he said I had changed but I hadn't, and when that flying boot cut my eye (allegedly, kicked by the manager), and then when he dropped me for the biggest game of the season (Real Madrid), I could see – it was time to leave.

Aged 28 Beckham became the 4th Galactico at Madrid. He liked the history of the club and the atmosphere, but on the pitch the team didn't gel: there were no trophies.

    The first season was a disappointment and the manager lost his job.

A new manager arrived and another Galactico was signed, and another disappointing season followed. Then another manager, another Galactico, and another disappointing season followed; then Fabio Capello arrived:

He said, 'the players don't fit together – there will have to be changes.'

Ronaldo was sold and Beckham was dropped. Following a disappointing 2006 World Cup campaign he was also, surprisingly, dropped by the former Middlesbrough manager, former Manchester United assistant manager, former England assistant manager, and now England manager, Steve McLaren (Sun Taurus Mars Cancer). Steve was curiously quick to distance himself from his former England captain: David was bitterly disappointed. McLaren brought in Terry Venables (Mars Sagittarius) as his right-hand-man, made John Terry (Sun Sagittarius) captain, and drafted in Middlesbro' protégé, Stewart Downing (Sun Cancer). Dignified, and bemused, David wished them all well and departed. The England fans were just as bemused; some thought McLaren was justified in making a clean sweep and a fresh start: others thought that he was wrong. A record equalling run of England internationals without a win, confirmed the latter. And the problem? *The players just didn't fit together.*

It seemed that Steve's managerial problems would increase when Peter Taylor resigned as part-time Under 21 coach, but he got on well with Stuart Pearce (Sun Taurus Mars Aries) and the transition was seamless, although back at Manchester City, Pearce had his Boardroom critics and was sacked at the end of the season. When Fabio Capello arrived, Stuart became the full-time U21 coach.

As a player Pearce was a dependable full back with a ferocious tackle. He was a courageous, inspirational leader and was highly valued by Brian Clough. Cloughie made him Forest captain, despite having mixed feelings about his ability to negotiate top wages.

So dropped by the England manager, and dropped by the future England manager, *it was all over,* for Becks. He didn't want to but he had no alternative, he had to leave and struck the most lucrative deal in football history: £125M with the Los Angeles Galaxy. Back in England, McLaren's changes weren't working and back in Spain, neither were Capello's. He was recalled by Fabio, but it was too late to help McLaren. Capello moved the players around to accommodate David and astutely changed the system; it worked, they started winning and winning and won la Liga. The Madridistas protested, they wanted Becks to stay. They pleaded with him to cancel his Galaxy contract and the finance director joined in – David had cost the club £25M and generated £300M in revenues – but he went to LA as planned.

However, as Jimmy Greaves says, *football is a funny old game,* and, *who would bet against Becks breaking Bobby's record.* Becks was recalled, but there was a problem – all the travelling backwards and forwards to America was tiresome and the quality of football was below the required standard. Capello explained that if Beckham wanted to continue his international career and have a chance of playing in the 2010 World Cup Finals, he needed to find a solution. David devised a plan – he would honour his contract with the Galaxy and also play for AC Milan – but would it be too much for a 34-year-old? Even when his Achilles snapped, under the strain, he was determined to make a full recovery and help England qualify for the 2012 Euro Championships.

Kaka

Beckham fitted in at Milan and gelled with their star player, Kaka (Sun Taurus Mars Libra), who, having just turned down a £106M transfer bid from Manchester City, had almost become the most valuable player in the world. He had tormented Manchester United in the Champions League semi-finals and helped AC Milan win the Cup. He was voted Earth's best player in 2007, but it was a medical miracle that he could play at all. Really? Aged 8, he joined Sao Paulo and showed great promise, but at 18 he broke his spine in a swimming pool accident and the prognosis was grim; the doctors said that he would never play football again and, probably, never walk. Kaka didn't accept their bulloney and instead prayed, and – every day and every night – prayed. He made a full recovery, *I believe prayer is decisive.* He dedicated his life to God; every year he donates vast sums to charity, he is a leading 'athlete for Christ', he has 'God is faithful' stitched on the tongues of his boots and he has 'I belong to Jesus' printed on his T shirts. He lives a life of glamour and luxury, but remains humble and close to the people. When it seemed he was going to sign for City, there were protests in the streets of Milan. He explained to the fans that he wasn't motivated by money and pledged himself to the end of the season. He is the youngest person to hold the post of 'United Nations Ambassador against Hunger'. Aged 21 he was signed by Berlusconi for £4M; in 2009, aged 27, he joined Real Madrid for £56M.

John Madejski

In 2006, John Madejski (Sun Taurus Mars Aquarius) was made a Freeman of the Royal Borough of Reading for his transformation of Reading FC. As chairman, he steered them into the Premiership for the first time in their history and, making good use of his fortune, rebuilt the stadium. He shares his time between football, education, and art – he is not only generous to football, he gives freely to museums and has financed a flagship garden at the Victoria and Albert, adorning it with exotic plants tastefully illuminated by the Rolling Stones' lighting experts. It seems love and money do go hand in hand: his love of football has cost him a small fortune, however, he keeps some of his more valuable signings in glass boxes – Rolls-Royces, Ferraris, Bentleys, and Jaguars.

Johan Cruyff, Dennis Bergkamp

Johan Cruyff (Sun Taurus Mars Aries) is a hero in Holland. He was a dynamic centre forward with Ajax before moving to Barcelona. He captained the national side through their golden era and he went on to become a successful manager at Barca. Dennis Bergkamp (Sun Taurus Mars Sagittarius) was his protégé and successor at Ajax and for Holland. He played as a 'shadow' centre forward and when he retired, aged 37, he was the richest footballer in Holland. Curiously, it wouldn't have happened without Cruyff: as a slightly built 16-year-old with a delicate touch, and an eye for goal, the Ajax coach put him on notice, *I am sorry, Dennis, but you aren't robust or aggressive enough for Ajax.*

He started to think of a career outside football, possibly in physiotherapy, but before he could find something the coach was sacked and in came Cruyff. Johan liked Dennis and encouraged him to develop his strengths: he played him in the reserves and then in the following season put him in the first team. In 6 seasons Bergkamp scored 103 goals in 187 league games. He won the Dutch Championship, the Cup, the Cup Winners Cup and the UEFA Cup and became an established international. In 1992 he transferred to Inter Milan, but didn't settle. Even though he was admired and signed by Massimo Moratti (Sun Taurus Mars Aries), the oil-tycoon owner and president who was spending lavishly, and even though he had been bought to partner fellow Taurean, Ruben Sosa (Sun Taurus Mars Taurus), there was a problem: Ajax had schooled Bergkamp in *Total Football*, but Inter were not there yet. Dennis struggled and to make matters worse Sosa stubbornly refused to pass: the season before Ruben had top-scored playing as a lone striker and the Uruguayan saw no reason to change just to accommodate the non-flying Dutchman. As his form dipped and his stock fell, Arsenal signed him for a bargain price and in 1995 Dennis was glad to get away and become a Gunner. When Arsene Wenger took charge at Highbury, Bergkamp was one of the players to benefit most from the new regime. By 1998, he had regained his confidence and restored his reputation. His elegant style, his effortless movement, vision, and mastery of the 4 directions made him a favourite of Wenger and the fans; he could visualise a whole pitch as it was and how it would be and do the right thing without thinking. He was the ultimate playmaker, a player without a weakness in his game – a perfect 10 – but...

What about his lack of aggression?

Asked Ajax and those who hadn't seen him at Newcastle United, Sunderland, or Bolton, where he was red-carded for violent play (was there something in the northern *air?*), and...

What about his poor heading and fear of flying?

Hhhmmmm...*air*...anyway, to Arsene Wenger and the Arsenal finance director, Dennis was priceless.

Nominally a centre forward, Cruyff played where his muse took him: sometimes on the wing, sometimes in midfield or up front. He was 'European Footballer of the Year' 3 times. Johan joined Ajax Amsterdam aged 10 and by 17 he was in their first team. The following season they won the League title, the following year they won the League and Cup. He was the embodiment of *Total Football*. Yet in his first international, surprisingly, he was sent off, becoming the first Dutch player to be shown the red card. In 1973 he joined Barcelona; in 1974 he led Holland to the World Cup final. Aged 32, he was offered a lucrative contract with the Washington Diplomats. He returned to manage Ajax and then made his name again at Barcelona: in 1992 he coached them to victory in the European Cup. The world of football wanted to know, *how?*

I believe a winning team has a natural balance between binding players and inventive players. The binding players hold the team together; the inventive players create opportunities and are allowed to take risks. A winning team has a central axis with a telepathic link between the centre forward, the playmaker, and the central defender. The playmaker must be intuitive, if he has to think then he is too slow. The binders are asked to sacrifice themselves for the team, so they must be modest, unassuming, and humble. My wingers have chalk on their boots, and I always have an invisible man.

Invisible?

Yes, he must remain unseen and unmarked and be able to score goals out of nothing. But more important, I have the right assistant and the right captain: Tonnie Bruins Slot likes doing the things I don't like doing, and el Toro Alexanco (Sun Taurus Mars Aquarius) leads the team on the pitch. But most important of all – I have the courage of my convictions.

In his early career Cruyff dreamed of being rich and was a shrewd negotiator; in 1967 he signed a 4 year contract with Ajax and never needed to negotiate again.

In mythology, Ajax was a hero and king of Salamis. He was strong, fast, and had great skill-at-arms becoming the most valued warrior in Agamemnon's army. Ajax the Lesser, was a hero and legendary king of Locris; he was slightly smaller in stature, swifter, and had a deadly accurate shot. Perhaps Ajax really was in Dennis' and Johan's blood.

Petr Cech

Kaka was the best outfield player in 2007 and Petr Cech (Sun Taurus Mars Libra), of Chelsea, was the best goalkeeper. As a boy Petr played in midfield, but following a serious leg injury he returned to the game in goal and showed a natural aptitude. At 20, he was first choice keeper for

Sparta Prague and in his debut season made a record-breaking run of 'clean sheets' – 855 minutes without conceding a goal. He joined Chelsea in 2004 and proceeded to set a new Premiership record by not conceding for 1,025 minutes – at the end of the season he was awarded the 'Golden Gloves' for keeping a record 21 'clean sheets'. Sadly, at the Madejski stadium in October 2006, Petr fractured his skull diving at the feet of Hunt; unconscious, he was rushed to intensive care and there were fears that his career was finished, yet by January he had made a full recovery and, with the help of a padded helmet, returned to the first team. He proceeded to go a further 800 minutes without conceding; at the end of the season Jose Mourinho inducted him into the 'Untouchables'.

Arthur Rowley, Jack Lambert Jeff Astle, Jackie Milburn

The days when centre forwards barged goalkeepers into the back of the net with the ball in hand are in the distant past. But it is worth recalling them here, because most of the best exponents of the shoulder charging runs on goal were Taureans. Respected, admired, and feared wherever they roamed, the likes of Leicester's Arthur Rowley (Sun Taurus Mars Aquarius), Arsenal's Jack Lambert (Sun Taurus Mars Taurus), West Brom's Jeff Astle (Sun Taurus Mars Cancer), and Jackie Milburn (Sun Taurus Mars Aquarius), are fondly remembered.

Astle was born on the 13th May 1942 in the East Midlands pit village of Eastwood, home of 'Lady Chatterley's Lover' DH Lawrence. Strong, dominant, with a powerful header, Jeff scored 174 goals in 361 games for the Baggies; sadly, the heavy leather balls of the 1950s and 60s gave his head a merciless pounding. At the post-mortem, following his untimely demise, the coroner recorded 'industrial injury' as the cause of death.

Jack Lambert was bought by Herbert Chapman to spearhead a skilful Arsenal forward line. The bullish Lambert had built a reputation for striking dread into opposing defences when he was on the charge. He was scoring freely with his no-nonsense style for Doncaster Rovers when Chapman signed him, but he didn't fit into the Arsenal team and after a barren run was dropped. He languished in the reserves for the rest of the season and then all of the next: the forgotten man? Not by Chapman. Herbert continued his search to find the right partner for Lambert: Alex James, the tricky Scot – the inside right man – transformed him. James, the technically perfect precision passer put the ball just where Jack wanted it; Alex split defences, Lambert finished them off. In 1930-31, Jack scored 38 in 31 matches and helped Chapman found a dynasty.

Perhaps the best Taurean centre forward of all though was the warm-hearted 'man of the people', uncle to Bobby and Jack Charlton, Jackie Milburn. The legendary Newcastle United centre forward, Powderhall sprinter, and beloved of the north-east until his dying day was at his peak in 1951: he scored in every round of the FA Cup. In the final the Magpies faced the bookies' favourites, Blackpool; the Seasiders had magical strikers of their own – Matthews and Mortensen. The first half ebbed and flowed but, in spite of all the stars on show, there was no score at half time. In the second half Newcastle's Milburn and Robledo (Mars Aquarius) stepped up the tempo. The Seasiders hit back, only great saves from the Magpies goalie, Jack Fairbrother (the most expensive keeper in the world), kept them at bay. In the 50th minute, Matthews went on another mazy run: skinned the full back...got to the bye-line...crossed for Morty...Robledo anticipated...intercepted and in a flash released Milburn...Jackie took it in his stride...charged 50 yards...grunt...thump...goal. 4 minutes later, tightly marked 30 yards out...Ernie Taylor cow-heeled it...Jackie spun...struck it clean and true...2-0. So brilliant was the execution that, even in their disappointment, the Blackpool players gathered around to congratulate him. However, a wave of Geordie sympathy swept the old stadium as the 36-year-old Matthews collected his loser's medal, and vowed, *I'm not finished yet: I shall be back.* Milburn followed captain Joe Harvey (still holding his lucky 1901 penny) up to the 'Royal Box' to receive the Cup, and the crowd's acclaim to the strains of the 'Blaydon Races'. The following year Harvey (still holding his lucky penny) and Milburn repeated the climb to the 'Royal Box', but this time George Robledo was the hero after scoring the goal that defeated, unlucky, Arsenal.

However, it was unsung hero Arthur Rowley who broke the Football League's goal scoring record with 433 in 619 games: in the 1956-57 season Arthur scored 44 goals in 42 games to help Leicester City gain promotion to the First Division.

FABIO CAPELLO

GEMINI

If they are good enough, they are old enough.
Matt Busby

I would give all the champagne I ever drank to have played alongside him (Eric Cantona).
George Best

I look upon myself as two people.
Paul Gascoigne

Gemini is an AIR sign ruled by Mercury. Mercury travels around the Sun at an average of 30 miles per second, twice as fast as Earth, taking 88 days to complete its orbital journey. To the naked eye it is only visible above the horizon at dawn or dusk, either heralding the day and the appearance of the Sun, or following him into the night. Similarly, in myth, Mercury is the celestial go-between traversing the realms of light and dark; he conducts the souls of the deceased to Hades, and also inspires wisdom, fertility, and healing in the living. The image passed down to us from the ancients shows Mercury tall and lean, with wings on his feet and hat, suggestive of his fleet-footed athletic prowess and, quick wits. He has a reputation for versatility: he is a marathon runner, a cunning and eloquent negotiator, a messenger for the gods and, with his snake-entwined wand, has magical powers.

If you could join the starry dots in the constellation Gemini you would draw two tall figures standing, shoulder-to-shoulder, just above the Milky Way. The constellation contains the two bright stars Castor and Pollux, known to the Assyrians as the 'Twins'; in myth, they were courageous warriors who dressed for battle in bright armour, wielded silver spears, and rode white chargers. According to Homer they were both hardy of heart: Castor was a tamer of wild horses and Pollux, *a man nimble and agile in hand and foot,* was a champion boxer. The Spartans carried their symbol into battle for luck.

MERCURIAL GEMINIS

CHAIRMAN
RAMON CALDERON Real Madrid

COACHES
MATT BUSBY Manchester United
FABIO CAPELLO England
CARLO ANCELOTTI Chelsea
ROBERTO DI MATTEO WBA

GOALKEEPERS
PAT JENNINGS Spurs
OLIVER KAHN Bayern Munich

DEFENDERS
CAFU AC Milan
DANIEL PASSARELLA River Plate
ALAN HANSEN Liverpool
MARK LAWRENSON Liverpool
ANDONI GOIKOETXEA Athletic Bilbao

MIDFIELD
STEVEN GERRARD Liverpool
FRANK LAMPARD Chelsea
JAVIER MASCHERANO Liverpool
MICHEL PLATINI Juventus
MICHAEL LAUDRUP Juventus
PAUL GASCOIGNE Spurs
ANDREI ARSHAVIN Arsenal

DAVID PLATT Arsenal
WESLEY SNEIJDER Inter Milan
ALAN HUDSON Stoke City
PETER REID Everton

FORWARDS
GEORGE BEST Manchester United
BRIAN KIDD Manchester United
ERIC CANTONA Manchester United
LEE SHARPE Manchester United
ALAN BRAZIL Ipswich Town
PAUL MARINER Ipswich Town
MIROSLAV KLOSE Werder Bremen
STAN MORTENSEN Blackpool
IAN St JOHN Liverpool
BILLY WHITEHURST Sheffield United

INSPIRATIONS
JF KENNEDY
MARILYN MONROE
JONNY WILKINSON
WB YEATS
JAMES CORDEN
CHE GUEVARA

Geminis are thoughtful with enquiring minds; they have a way with words, are good communicators, make spellbinding orators and when their playing days are over, if they are not in demand as pundits or commentators, they are highly sought after as coaches. As players they are versatile, which means they often find themselves in midfield where they can quickly turn defence into attack or attack into defence. Off the field they often combine two occupations, live in two homes, drive two cars, and seem to be in two places at once. They are young at heart; they like practical jokes and trickery, and they – as you will see when we consider George Best (Sun Gemini Mars Leo), Michel Platini (Sun Gemini Mars Cancer), Eric Cantona (Sun Gemini Mars Taurus), Paul Gascoigne (Sun Gemini Mars Libra), Matt Busby (Sun Gemini Mars Pisces), and Fabio Capello (Sun Gemini Mars Leo) – have a touch of genius.

George Best, Matt Busby

George Best started to cast his spell on the world from the moment a Manchester United scout, Bob Bishop, spotted him playing football in Belfast and telegrammed Matt Busby:

I have found a genius.

And yet his local club, Glentoran, had previously turned him down saying he was, *too lightweight*; he was slightly built and certainly light on his feet but he was also strong and able to ride a challenge. With Mars in Leo he was brave and delighted in performing on the big stage; indeed, the bigger the stage the better he played which made the 'Theatre of Dreams' ideal.

Busby recognised Best's genius and gave him his debut aged 17. His mesmerising skills, intricate dribbling, sharp shooting, and general brilliance saw him score 136 goals, and create many more, in his 361 appearances for United; he won the First Division title twice and the European Cup. He top-scored for United in 4 successive seasons and by the time he was 18, he was celebrated around Europe for scoring twice in a fabulous performance against Benfica. In 1968 he scored against them again – and was voted 'Footballer of the Year' – as he helped United become the first English side to win the European Cup. At that moment, according to Pele, he was the best player in the world. Matt understood the complexities in George's character: he was on his wavelength and looked after him, turned an occasional blind eye, and turned him into a model professional. He also found him the right partner: although George was friendly with Denis Law, Law often complained, *I never get a pass from Besty,* and neither did Bobby Charlton, but the young Brian Kidd (Sun Gemini Mars Taurus) did, and in the European Cup final, Best, alongside his 19-year-old twin-striker, was devastating.

When Matt Busby retired, in 1969, it not only had an immense impact on Manchester United it rocked George. Matt was Manchester United. He had built a winning team in the 1940s and then built a great side in the 1950s only to have it sadly decimated in the Munich air crash; he then built another great side in the 1960s – with George a key figure. However, Best the good trainer started to miss training: he went out more at night than during the day and, aged 26, drifted out of Old Trafford for good. He went to London, took 'Miss World' with him, put on weight, slowed down and played for Fulham for fun. Slower still he joined Hibernian, then signed for Los Angeles and gave an exhibition of ball skills not seen by the Aztecs for 500 years, unfortunately, by the time he hung his boots up, at Bournemouth, he was battling against the *demon drink.* Away from football his wit, charm, and humour meant that he was in demand for after-dinner speaking engagements and television interviews. He earned a reputation as a mischievous football pundit: on one occasion he was asked about David Beckham – a successor to his No 7 shirt:

He can't kick with his left foot; he can't head the ball or tackle, and he doesn't score many goals, apart from that he is OK.

There was also another side to George Best. Whilst he gloried in playing and public speaking away from the limelight he was a quietly generous man. He never advertised his philanthropy nor drew attention to the people he helped.

Eric Cantona

Perhaps, understandably, Beckham's inspiration wasn't George but that other No 7 shirt-wearer, Eric Cantona. The French philosopher, film star, and mercurial genius had just helped Leeds United win the League title; he was adored by the Elland Road faithful and even though Manchester had made a derisory offer, even though the Red Devils were Leeds arch-rivals, he left. Howard Wilkinson, the Leeds manager, was reputedly eager to sell because he found the complex Cantona, *difficult to understand.* Indeed, there were two sides to Eric – the extrovert showman / temperamental star, and the introvert poet / esoteric philosopher. He drifted into Old Trafford aged 26. Alex Ferguson made him captain and built a side around him. He was an inspiration to United's young stars: Beckham, Giggs, Scholes, the Neville brothers, and Butt. He trained hard, led by example, and, ironically, helped United pip Leeds to the League title. He was the model professional, nonetheless, with Mars in Taurus he could occasionally rage and unfortunately the bull did get loose in Crystal Palace. At the time Eric was playing the best football of his career, he was the focus of United's play and the leading light in Jacquet's France, but all that was about to end: furious at seeing the red card, he marched towards the tunnel – and a taunting crowd – lost his rag, charged at a spectator and received a lengthy ban. After the court-case he faced the media to explain himself...

When the seagulls follow the trawler it is because they think sardines will be thrown into the sea.

What did you mean, Eric?

Philosophers wrote learned papers and psychologists analysed the meaning, but I had to say something and wanted to say nothing to the media so I say something that means nothing.

Nevertheless, Aime Jacquet had to make changes: he made Didier Deschamps captain, gave a chance to Zinedine Zidane, and when Cantona eventually returned from suspension he couldn't get back in the team – *c'est la vie*. He buckled down in training at United and, with renewed purpose, rebuilt his career:

I play with passion and fire. Sometimes this fire does harm. I know it does harm: I harm myself, I harm others, but I cannot be what I am without this other side of my character.

His speciality when putting the ball in the 'onion bag' was using his eyes to send the keeper the wrong way: of the 17 penalties he took at United, 16 times the keeper went the other way. In 1996 he captained United to the Premiership title and the FA Cup, and went on to be voted 'Footballer of the Year'. Aged 31 he walked out of Old Trafford, out of football, into films. The following year, Deschamps walked up the steps at the Stade de France to lift the World Cup.

Michel Platini, Michael Laudrup

In the 1980s the France captain was the magical playmaker, Michel Platini. Born on Midsummer's day 1955, with fairy dust on his boots,

Michel grew up to lead a vibrant team to the European Championship title in 1984. They were a side of flair and adventure and with his ability to read the game and pick out the telling pass, for a time, they were irresistible. At his peak he was their best player, but it would have been very different without the support and persistence of his dad. As a slightly built teenager Michel had repeatedly tried, and failed, to join Metz football club: he couldn't pass the medical. In the end the doctors at Metz declared him unfit on account of respiratory concerns and worries that his heart wasn't strong enough for the rigours of the profession. Anyway, his dad disregarded their opinions and managed to get him a chance at Nancy, aged 17 he made his first-team debut. Although, overall, his first season was a disappointment; his second season was worse – he broke his leg. The following season was much better – 17 goals in 32 games; the following season was better still – 22 goals in 38 – and to cap it off he was called up to the national squad. In 1978, he was a hero for putting 2 past the legendary Italian keeper, Dino Zoff. His fame and fortune grew; he transferred to St Etienne and then to Juventus – he told the Italians that he felt at home in Turin:

I embody two cultures: my grandfather was an Italian who travelled to France and settled – I feel half Italian.

He felt that playing for Juventus had opened his mind, before, when he was wholly French, he believed wine and cheese were the most important, now he thought football was. He won the European Cup with Juve, but what should have been a cause for celebration turned into a human tragedy as part of the Heysel stadium collapsed. In the 1985-86 season, Platini was enjoying a good understanding, and a remarkable run of form, with his midfield partner Michael Laudrup (Sun Gemini Mars Taurus). Laudrup dribbled at speed, had an accurate pass and a powerful shot; his trademark move was to look one way and send his marker, or the keeper, the other. He was the master of the assist and created many opportunities for his partner. Michael went on to star for Barcelona and was voted 'European Footballer of the Year'. Whilst

Platini was appointed head of the organising committee for the 1992 World Cup; he thought deeply about his purpose and set out his goals in a 'Mission Statement':

I don't want the event to be elitist or only for those who are crazy about football, I want it to unite the country and appeal to the wider world.

The tournament was a big success, made more joyful for the French by France winning the Jules Rimet trophy. Platini was a winner, but not at any cost: a teammate recalled Platini's reaction to France going a goal behind to Argentina in the 1978 World Cup in Buenos Aires....

It is almost worth going a goal behind just to enjoy the spectacle of 72,000 Argentinians celebrating.

In 2006 he was appointed UEFA president. Early on he took the opportunity to express his concerns for the future of the game and set out his main aim:

I aim to protect the spirit of football from profiteers. I would be worried if I were English because of all the foreign ownership. They could be rich people coming to help English football and develop it, but they may just want to make money. I fear your clubs will lose identity. If it was in France, I would fight it. (Prophetic? In January 2010 the collective debt of the 20 Premier League clubs was £5,000,000,000).

In 2008 he shared his wisdom with business leaders and politicians:

The values championed by football are a powerful force for social integration and civic education. Her values include: openness, opportunity and financial solidarity. The naked operation of the free market cannot guarantee to preserve the variety, unpredictability and excitement of the sport.

He wanted to protect fair play, fair competition, and promote respect for referees and opponents. He believes that money does not buy success and hopes that the fascination of the people with football prevails over their fascination with money. As coincidence would have it, at the same time Michel was pleading for a level playing field, the Dalai Lama was calling for ethics in sport:

Freedom, fairness, openness and equality are not only the principles enshrined in the Olympic Games but among the highest human values.

Fabio Capello

A few years after Platini left Juventus one of the biggest and most successful coaches in the game arrived. Fabio Capello is consistently successful, winning 4 successive Italian League titles and the European Cup with AC Milan, winning la Liga with Real Madrid, and then another Scudetto – this time with Roma.

When he returned to the Black and Whites of Turin, and took them to 2 successive League titles, his place as the best coach in the world seemed to be secure, but the Italian match-fixing scandal implicated Juventus and cast a shadow on the celebrations. 10 years after his title-winning season in Spain, he returned to Real Madrid and did it again, but rather than confirming his genius he got the sack – the rousing finish to the campaign couldn't mask a season of discontent. The president and the crowd were unhappy that Ronaldo had been transferred, that Beckham had been dropped (but then reinstated), and that Capello had adopted defensive tactics. Even though he had brought success, Madrid wanted more.

Capello is complex. He has successfully separated his public and private lives; he is a student of the game, a master tactician, an avid art collector, and has interests in psychology, ancient history, and archaeology.

Born in north-east Italy on the 18th June 1946, Fabio Capello started out as a thoughtful forward with a shrewd eye for a goalscoring opportunity. The more crucial the match, the more decisive the moment, the more focused the young man. His career blossomed when he was signed by Juventus. He starred for his country and one of his most memorable moments came at Wembley, when he scored the winner against England. The relaxed, humorous, and charming conversationalist showed no indication, at that stage of his career, of the strict disciplinarian he would be as a manager. His loyal assistant, Italo Galbiati, at AC Milan, Roma, Real Madrid, and then for England, had this to say about his boss:

He has two characters: he is serious at work and fun away from it. And do you know why every player wants to play for him? Because he makes them champions.

In 2007 Capello offered some of the secrets of his success:

My idea of football has never changed. Even so, I recognise that the world has changed dramatically since I started out on the football path. I have learned that one method, one system, doesn't work – such a path doesn't lead to trophies.

To be successful requires great humility and, therefore, I have tried to dispense with egotistical principles: one must not let the ego get in the way of doing the right thing. I respect every player: every player is an individual. I respect every club: every place is different and so every club is also different – the fans, customs, traditions, values, environments, finances, politics – everything is different. For example; Milan is a family club and they must play like a family if they are going to be successful: Roma was not used to winning, so I had to make the Romans believe that it was their right to conquer again: the Black and Whites of Juve receive their spirit and power from the 'Old Lady' and the president's car factory, the club is a delicate, well-maintained, precision engineered organisation and the players must be refined, finely tuned athletes: Real Madrid have a long and celebrated history, their legend is pure, their strip is pure white, and their fans expect pure football. I understand the strength of the imagination and – once I understand the genius loci – if necessary, I will create a vision for a player, or a club, to believe in.

I am light-hearted and serious. I am hot and cold. I am compassionate or ruthless depending on the circumstances. I select intelligent players who can read the game. I select players who can stay cool in the heat of battle. Size and power are not important: ability, skill and intelligence are. I then design my team according to the opposition; the system, the formation, the tactics, all must be of the moment and remember – psychology takes precedence.

There were reports that you were interviewed for the England job?

Yes, I would have liked the job very much: the Twin Towers of Wembley were made for me, but who knows the future?

What are you doing whilst you are out of work, Mr Capello?

I am researching. I'm visiting ancient sites, discovering works of Art: Chagalls, Twomblies, but my favourite is still AC Milan.

6 months later in a London press conference....

Congratulations, Mr Capella.*

Thank you all. I am very happy, a little sad for Steve McLaren, but I must say that he used the wrong tactics against Croatia and defended too deep against Russia....

So, what changes will you make?

I come to help England play without fear.

---

*Capello or Capella? Capello is one of Gemini's brightest stars – Capella is one of the brightest stars overlooking Gemini. As we know from the Bible – Job 9 / 38 and Corinthians 1 – the ancients had a profound knowledge of the stars and their influences. They not only named the planets and the zodiac, they also knew many other constellations including: Orion, the Pleiades and Auriga. Curiously, they named the brightest star in Auriga – Capella. The glories (characteristics) they ascribed to those born under its influence include: wealth, honour, a position of public trust, a love of knowledge, wisdom and clarity of mind.

Paul Gascoigne

According to Alex Ferguson, Paul Gascoigne was the best player of his era. As a schoolboy in Newcastle he was exceptionally bright, intelligent, versatile, excelling at mathematics, chess, tennis, fighting, fishing, but above all he dreamt of being a famous footballer. He was thoughtful, nervous, anxious, hyperactive, shy with strangers, obsessed with the number 5 and death. He hated being 13. He was superstitious, reckless, a practical joker, spontaneous, and highly strung with a low boredom threshold. As a teenager he went for trials at Ipswich, Southampton, and Middlesbrough, but failed to perform. It was different with the Magpies: he felt at home there. He did well in the trials and became the captain of a successful youth team. Jack Charlton gave him a chance and then Willie McFaul helped him develop into a creative midfield playmaker. In 1990, he made the England World Cup squad and was in inspired form as he helped Bobby Robson's side to the semi-finals. The following year he helped Terry Venables' Spurs side to glory in the FA Cup final, but there was personal pain and disappointment too: in the earlier rounds Paul had been in scintillating form scoring 6 on the way to Wembley, but in what should have been the highlight of his career there were tears of pain and suffering as he ruptured knee ligaments in a reckless challenge and ended up not knowing whether to laugh or cry as he watched his teammates collect the Cup – from his hospital bed. Nobody knows why he made such wild tackles on Notts Forest's Garry Parker and Gary Charles. Some said that it was because he hadn't got the hang of rhyming slang. Wot? In the bar the night before, he supposedly over-heard a bunch of Snotts...*Old Big `ead has a new signing, duck, and he'll surprise Spurs. Oh aye? Yeah, the enchanter from Bordeaux. Oh aye? Yeah, Christophe Dugarry!* The two Garrys were marked men.

12 months later he transferred to Lazio of Rome, a city split with football rivalry, and fitted in. He was idolised and after a couple of seasons of injury-interrupted success, he moved to Glasgow Rangers,

another city split with football rivalry, and fitted straight in. Even though he inflamed the religious tensions between Rangers and Celtic, and even though he received death threats from the IRA, it was the happiest, and most productive, time of his career. Perhaps his most memorable moment came against Scotland in Euro 96: receiving the ball between two defenders and with former teammate Colin Hendry closing in...Gazza feinted one way...flicked the ball up and over Hendry with his left foot...as the defender was falling...right foot...volley...goal. As the 1998 World Cup drew near, Paul was beset with personal problems. He was also apprehensive when Hoddle was appointed England manager, but seemed happier when Glenn suggested that they visit a local brewery. Gazza was keen, but when he arrived he was disappointed to find that they were visiting Eileen Drewery, the faith healer. Happily, Gazza was selected for the World Cup 'warm-up' squad and joined the other 27 players at La Manga, although, when he didn't make the final 22 he reacted as if stung by a scorpion: screaming, jumping, rampaging around the hotel room flinging pots, kicking doors in and, just about to smash the windows, Ince and Seaman restrained him. He was, *down for a year,* and admitted himself into hospital.

Maybe the flair and beauty of his genius didn't find full expression, maybe he would have been better off at Manchester United after all. Anyway, he is still idolised on Tyneside, and did represent his country 57 times and scored 10. In 2005, he was interviewed by Alan Hansen and told of his ambition to become a coach. On the 5th December, he got his chance at non-league Kettering, but the following month, was sacked.

In 2008 he was sectioned at the Malmaison hotel, Newcastle. His family and friends rallied around; he made a comeback and featured in charity events, the media, and mused...

There are two Gascoignes: Paul and Gazza.

Paul is sensible, reasonable, intelligent, responsible, mature, kind, caring, and shy; he thinks about the past and worries about the future of his family and friends, about the plight of poor people, about people who are homeless, about people who can't afford to put the electric fire on in winter. He gives generously to charity, but he does it discretely. He keeps out of the limelight. He likes to spend his holidays on Loch Lomond with his family: fishing and golfing.

Gazza is fearless, reckless, a boxer, a practical joker, witty, paranoid, superstitious, spontaneous. He drinks to be sociable; he talks just to break the silence. He finds pain in joy and joy in pain; he sees meaning in everything and takes the sweetness out of sorrow.

Among his most valued awards is a medal from, supporter and former goalkeeper, Pope John Paul II.

Carlo Ancelotti, Steven Gerrard, Frank Lampard

Having starred for AC Milan in 2 European Cup winning sides, in 2001 Carlo Ancelotti (Sun Gemini Mars Leo) became their manager. Nevertheless, his reign started with some difficulty: he was criticised for being too defensive by his president, Silvio Berlusconi. But Carlo won over the critics with the European Cup (2003), 2 years later he took Milan to the final again – even though they were the better team they lost to a Steven Gerrard (Sun Gemini Mars Virgo) inspired Liverpool. 2 years later, Ancelotti was in the final again and, although outplayed by a Gerrard inspired Liverpool, justice was done. Before the game Carlo was heavily criticised by the press for picking the aging Maldini and the 'past it' Inzaghi, but Maldini was calm and assured, whilst Inzaghi scored the winning goals. In the summer of 2009 Carlo joined Chelsea. In a pre-season interview he said that he admired the technical ability of Frank Lampard (Sun Gemini Mars Virgo) and was looking forward to working with him. After a couple of weeks training, he said how impressed he was with Frank's character.

Alan Hansen, Mark Lawrenson

The symbol for Gemini is sometimes depicted as a pair of Corinthian columns, one in sunlight and the other in shadow, at the entrance to the Halls of Wisdom. Liverpool's European Cup winning side of the 1980s featured a pair of centre backs with a passing resemblance to those twin columns. Alan Hansen (Sun Gemini Mars Cancer) and Mark Lawrenson (Sun Gemini Mars Cancer) formed a watertight defensive unit; they had good positional sense, good anticipation, and a good understanding. Some said that they were the ideal combination; others said, they were too similar. Hansen would have agreed with the others, as he preferred to play alongside Phil Thompson (Sun Aquarius). Bob Paisley (Sun Aquarius: the most successful English manager), having seen him play alongside Alex McLeish (Sun Aquarius) for Scotland, agreed. Hansen was lucky to play for a manager with the right philosophy, for him:

In my mind I was a forward but – even though I wasn't a good tackler, was only average in the air and didn't relish marking strikers like Billy Whitehurst (Sun Gemini Mars Leo) – instinctively, I was a defender. (Billy was a combative centre forward with Sheffield United and reputed to be the bare-knuckle boxing champion of the Football League).

There are two sides to Alan Hansen; the cool, calm and collected self-confident Liverpool captain Alan: and the self-conscious, avoidance of the spotlight Partick Thistle Hansen.

In the 1978-79 season, he was key in one of the finest sides in Europe: a defensive lynchpin in a team that conceded a miserly 16 goals in 42 games and won the First Division title comfortably. He is detached and unemotional and yet when he visited the bereaved following the Hillsborough disaster, to offer his support, he broke down in floods of tears and the victims comforted him. As a player he was dependable and made very few mistakes; as a pundit he makes less, possibly only two: ironically (for a young at heart Gemini) he said that Manchester United wouldn't win anything with a team of youngsters – as we know they went on to dominate English football – and then within days of Andres Escobar, the Columbian defender, being tragically shot for scoring an own-goal, Alan said that an Argentine player should be shot for making a defensive blunder. Or three? Following their disappointing partnership in England's Euro 2008 qualifying campaign, he claimed,

Lampard and Gerrard cannot play together. They duplicate each other's runs and get in each other's way.

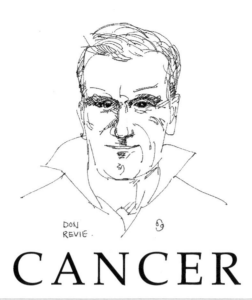

DON
REVIE.

CANCER

Sir Harold Thompson, the chairman of the FA, treated me like an employee,
these Arab Sheiks treat me like one of them.
Don Revie

Sometimes the manager just doesn't fancy you:
I did all I was asked to do.
Robbie Keane

Cancer is a WATER sign ruled by the Moon. When it is above the horizon the Full Moon dominates the night sky. The silvery queen of the dark is 2,000 times brighter than the planet Venus and 24,000 times brighter than the brightest star, Sirius. It is about 384,000 kilometres away from us, takes around 24 hours and 50 minutes to complete a circuit of Earth and about 29½ days to wax and wane; it is the predominant force controlling the tides.

The constellation Cancer is composed of relatively few stars and some of them are almost submerged in the vast watery mists of time and space. When Cancer rises in the sky it appears to do so backwards, as if keeping a cautious eye on a potential adversary. Its age-old symbol is the crab; in the Greek myths it was a crab who battled heroically against Hercules, and although defeated, his courage and tenacity won him eternal respect from the gods and they named a constellation in his honour.

Cancerians are family orientated. They are compassionate, caring, and protective of their relatives, friends, and especially their nippers. They are emotional and sensitive and to perform at their best they need to feel that they are an intimate part of the club: when they feel at home their commitment to the cause is total. The crab is adaptable: it can live on the land as well as in the sea and likewise the Cancerian can settle anywhere. He is loyal and reliable and doesn't want to drift from club to club. As managers, coaches, or captains they try to build a family atmosphere wherever they go; they are supportive and will always help out in a crisis, if needs be they will get involved in fundraising initiatives and community projects. They are ever faithful to their home town team.

A FAMILY CLUB

CHAIRMAN
JIMMY HILL Fulham

COACHES
DON REVIE Leeds United
STEVE COPPELL Reading
CRAIG BROWN Scotland
DARIO GRADI Crewe Alexandra
GIANFRANCO ZOLA West Ham United
OWEN COYLE Bolton Wanderers

GOALKEEPER
FABIEN BARTHEZ Manchester United
MARK CROSSLEY Nottingham Forest

DEFENDERS
CARLOS ALBERTO TORRES Santos
TERRY COOPER Leeds United
GIACINTO FACCHETTI Inter Milan
PAULO MALDINI AC Milan
GARY PALLISTER Manchester United
MICAH RICHARDS Manchester City
ERIC ABIDAL Barcelona

MIDFIELD
JAMIE REDKNAPP Spurs
KEVIN NOLAN Newcastle United
ZINEDINE ZIDANE Real Madrid
RAUL Real Madrid

ALFREDO DI STEFANO Real Madrid
PATRICK VIEIRA Manchester City
SAMIR NASRI Arsenal

FORWARDS
RUUD VAN NISTELROOY Real Madrid
EMILIO BUTRAGUENO Real Madrid
STUART DOWNING Aston Villa
LIONEL MESSI Barcelona
DIRK KUYT Liverpool
ROGER HUNT Liverpool
CRAIG BELLAMY Manchester City
ROBBIE KEANE Spurs
PAULO DI CANIO West Ham United

ADMINISTRATOR
ROBERT GUERIN France

INSPIRATIONS
DALAI LAMA
SUE RYDER
HELEN KELLER
EMMELINE PANKHURST
GEORGE ORWELL
JACK RUSSELL

Don Revie

Don Revie (Sun Cancer Mars Leo) was Leeds United. When he finished his playing career at Elland Road he stayed on as manager, and virtually built the club from nothing into one of the leading sides in Europe.

Don was born in Middlesbrough in the 1930s. There was no work and no money in his neighbourhood; his dad was one of the long-term unemployed, his mum took in washing and Don helped: he estimated it was a 4 mile walk to collect the dirty clothes and return the clean linen to the rich folk on the other side of town. Whatever, the daily trek helped keep him fit and gave him time to dream as he kicked his rag ball around. Aged 14, he was apprenticed to a bricklayer during the week and at weekends played for the local youth team and imagined he was a Boro star. Aged 17, Leicester City were sufficiently impressed with his cultured inside-forward play that they offered him a contract. Although his early days with the Foxes were difficult – he was homesick – with the support of his experienced teammate Septimus Smith, and a good rapport with his manager, Johnny Duncan, he settled in. He was also welcomed into Duncan's family home, clicked with Johnny's daughter, Elsie, and was soon enjoying a family life of his own. He was playing well, his career was flourishing, and he seemed to be content – but he wasn't. He was worried about the whispering in the dressing room, *what are they saying behind my back*? Did the players think that he was only in the first team because he was married to the boss's daughter? It was niggling him, it was affecting his game, so he asked for a transfer.

Arsenal were interested, but he chose Second Division Hull City because of his hero Raich Carter. Whilst his football education progressed playing alongside Carter, his career was floundering and then out of the blue Manchester City made a bid. The City manager, Les McDowall, wanted to emulate the Magical Magyars and play with a 'deep lying' centre forward. Les believed that Revie would be ideal at confusing the opposing defenders with the fluidity of his play and his tactical acumen. City rose up the League and, to the strains of 'Blue Moon', reached the 1955 FA Cup final. Whilst slight favourites to win the Cup, they were beaten by a Jackie Milburn inspired Newcastle United. Nevertheless, Revie was voted 'Footballer of the Year' and vowed that he would return to Wembley next year. At the end of a long, hard, and ultimately disappointing season, Don needed a break. He explained to the directors that he hadn't taken a family holiday for 6 years; they were sympathetic and gave permission for him to take extended leave and start pre-season training later than the others. On his return, however, McDowall was furious: apparently he hadn't been consulted. A series of disagreements followed – Revie was dropped, humiliated, and only played once on the way to the 1956 FA Cup final. Obviously, he wouldn't fulfil his vow now – or would he? 3 hours before kick-off, Bill Spurdle's face burst out in a painful attack of boils – he was out of the side – Revie was in. 3 minutes into the match, Don took control: slid the ball to Roy Clarke on the left wing...Clarke returned it...then Don drilled a precision pass into the path of Joe Hayes...1-0. With a combination of brave goalkeeping from Bert Trautmann and clever scheming from Revie, City went on to win 3-1. Don was voted 'man of the match', regardless, McDowall sold him to Sunderland when the acclaim died down.

Revie never really took to the Black Cats, and they didn't take to him. In 1958 Don made his Leeds debut. They adored him at Elland Road; they made him club captain, but after leading them to relegation, and believing he was jinxed, he resigned. Was he being too hard on himself? Nobody at Leeds blamed him, indeed his relationship with Harry Reynolds, the self-made millionaire soon to be chairman, was blossoming. They got on well, saw football the same way, and in 1961 Revie became player/coach. Although heavily in debt, Don managed to keep Leeds out of the relegation zone, and with the backing of the Board, and the help of a willing, able, and optimistic assistant, Maurice Lindley (Mars Leo), he devised a plan to take Leeds to the top of European football and emulate his hero's – Alfredo di Stefano's – Real Madrid. He changed the strip to all white, hired a Scarborough fair romany to lift a gypsy curse off the pitch, took the unlucky peacock off the club badge, brought in talented youngsters, created a family atmosphere, and signed an inspirational captain: Bobby Collins (Mars Leo). In 1964, they were promoted to the First Division and Revie gradually introduced his talented youngsters: Billy Bremner, Eddie Gray, Norman Hunter, Peter Lorimer and Gary Sprake. Anyhow, their apparent 'win at any cost' attitude (they had more players sent off than any other team in the Football League) was not only masking their natural ability, it was making enemies in high places. Personal attacks were made on Revie's integrity; his players were labelled 'dirty'; ex-professional players lined up to accuse him, and fellow managers were critical, none more so than his former near neighbour turned arch-enemy, Brian Clough. Old Big `ead called Revie, *the Godfather of football's most villainous family*. He joked about Don's superstitions: his 'lucky' blue suit, his peacockless badge, and the gypsy curse. He was ridiculed for playing bingo and carpet bowls; Don was hurt by all the sniping, but the emotional bond between players and coaching staff deepened as a result: it became Leeds, v the rest...*United we will never be defeated*.

By 1974 Leeds had almost conquered football, but Revie was worried that this was as far as they could go. They had won the League, the FA Cup, the League Cup, and the Fairs Cup and secured more runners-up prizes than was good for his health, but the players had grown old together. His dream of emulating Real Madrid wouldn't come to pass; though there had been glimpses, games of near perfection, games of technical excellence and beauty. He had done his best, but now he faced an agonising dilemma, with Alf Ramsey sacked and Joe Mercer a stop-gap, Revie was the best manager around and a logical choice for England. Leaving Leeds though would be heartbreaking, on the other hand it would be mortifying to tell his boys that their careers were over – he let the FA know that he was interested. Within hours an FA delegation, led by secretary Ted Croker, was formed and persuaded Revie to serve his country. Lord Harewood, Leeds president and former FA president, gave permission and the contract was signed. Unfortunately, Don was not a popular choice for the England job, even though by the end of his

Leeds reign he had partly redeemed himself in the public eye with his creative midfielders, tricky wingers, and his free-flowing football. Pundits assailed him – predicting that his 'close-knit family' style of management wouldn't work with England because he wouldn't have enough time with the players to build any meaningful relationships, plus, the lads from rival clubs wouldn't have the inclination. His first game in charge was a tough European Championship qualifier against a talented Czechoslovakian side which England won comfortably enough 3-0, although the press were less than complimentary, describing much of the England approach play as, *pedestrian,* and then explaining how the goals only came, *because the young Czechs were tired at the end.* The next game was a scoreless, *boring,* draw against Portugal, but then an exciting 2-0 win over West Germany was reported as, *unimpressive,* and a 5-0 win over Cyprus was, *unimaginative*: however he won it seemed that he couldn't please any of them. To make matters worse, some of the players were pouring scorn on the detailed dossiers he had painstakingly prepared, whilst others complained of being forced to play bingo. Ted Croker heard rumours of the dissent and began to wonder whether appointing Revie was a mistake. He wasn't happy either about team selections and grilled Revie over, *handing out caps like boiled sweets;* as if in confirmation that he was the wrong man, Ted nearly choked on his morning coffee and biscuit when his secretary informed him that Revie had no coaching qualifications – not that Don ever claimed to have any – and he saw the trap lying ahead: the FA's high-profile coaching initiative would be seen as irrelevant.

The increasingly isolated Revie cut a lonely figure around Lancaster Gate. Powerful enemies were gathering; he was humiliated at a black-tie dinner by Sir Harold Thompson, his relationship with Croker broke down, and stories appeared in the press claiming that Leeds had tried to bribe their way out of the Second Division. Don came to believe that there was a plot to oust him: was someone tipping him off or was it paranoia? Whatever, he felt that he had no alternative – he had to secure his family's future and struck a lucrative deal with the United Arab Emirates. Slighted, and furious, the FA laid charges on Revie of bringing the game into disrepute. At the hearing, overseen by Thompson – who both directed proceedings and gave evidence – Revie was found guilty and banned for 10 years: prompting defending QC, Gilbert Gray, to say that the hearing was against natural justice. Obtaining justice was long, hard, stressful, and expensive for Don. Nevertheless, he tenaciously pursued his appeal through the High Court, where the judge eventually found in his favour. His reputation outside of Leeds was in tatters, but the love and affection of his former players, and the Leeds fans, never died. Revie believed that he had been badly treated:

The FA treated me shabbily. I was judged unkindly by pompous asses; it was a tragic comedy, even the judge couldn't help putting the boot in: calling me selfish, greedy, notorious, disloyal, discourteous, brooding...oh yes...and innocent. But the real tragedy was what happened to Leeds. It was my tragedy too as we are one and the same, united, eternal...Elland Road became me.

The FA said I should have had coaching badges, but they didn't understand the secret of our success. It wasn't from a coaching manual; it wasn't a style of management, it was me. I treated the players as I treated my family. I looked after them, nurtured them, gave them everything; it was all about unity, about sticking together in adversity, making sacrifices for each other – building a fortress. These are not management styles, not transferable coaching manual skills – these are values, hard lessons in living.

They criticised the bingo and bowls. They called them childish parlour games but they didn't understand what I was doing – what the objective was. I had to get to know my players when they were relaxed, being themselves. Yes, it was about building a family atmosphere, but it was more than that, and I needed to know who was lucky. Bingo is a game of chance, there is no skill involved, only luck; play bingo and you find out who is lucky. Some people win now and then, some lose all the time and others always seem to win: for instance, I rated Mick Channon, he was a good player and lucky – now he is lucky with the horses, but unlucky with injuries.

Homespun and naive I may have seemed, but there was method in my madness. In my first 9 games we never lost: including 3-0 against the Czechs, 2-0 against the Germans, and 5-1 against the Scots. It was only when the FA undermined me that we faltered. They should think about that – how they damaged England.

They call me superstitious, but what is Superstition? Who can deny Revelations and say there are no revelations or deny the Prophets and say there are no prophecies or say there are no gifts from Spirit? I pray every day. I carry the cross of St John everywhere.

How do you see football now?

It has changed out of all recognition, but it is still a beautiful game and Leeds is still closest to my heart.

Have you any regrets?

I should have gone to Turin.

In recent years his sterling qualities have been re-evaluated by the wider world and though largely still unloved outside his native stronghold, he has gained some respect. Kevin Keegan, the former England star, spoke in remembrance...

It saddens me that the public has the wrong impression of Don. He was kind, generous and caring. When he left the England job he did the right thing for his family but the wrong thing for the country. He'd have been just as successful as Alf Ramsey if he had stayed and England had been good enough, but he didn't and we weren't.

Robbie Keane

He has played for Leeds United, he has played for Inter Milan, he played for Coventry and starred for Wolverhampton. He played for his childhood heroes, returned to Spurs and played for Celtic. Robbie Keane (Sun Cancer Mars Virgo) was born on the 8th July 1980 in Dublin, and brought up as a music lover and passionate Liverpool fan.

Robbie started playing football aged 9 months; aged 9 years he was playing in organised games. But he was a lot smaller than the other lads and it needed his uncle to become the club coach for him to get a *fair craik*. Nine years later, along with his close friend and fellow Dubliner, Richard Dunne (Mars Cancer), he was helping Ireland make history by winning the UEFA Under 18's Championship. However, that may never have been but for a stroke of luck: overlooked as a 15-year-old for being too small, and dropped from the Under 16's for the same reason, he thought he may never get a chance, but at the last minute one of the bigger lads was injured and Robbie was drafted in. He played well, scored a goal, and kept his place for the next match. The scouts were impressed: Nottingham Forest were interested and so were West Ham, Wolves, and his boyhood favourites – Liverpool. The Anfielders showed Robbie around: he met his heroes, admired their trophies, visited the famous boot room and got the feel of the place and then it was time to sign, but the place didn't feel right. He needed time to think. He discussed it with his mum and dad, and still it didn't feel right. Instead, he accepted Wolves' invitation to have a look around Molineux: watch a match, meet the players and get the feel of the place. It felt right. Wolves did everything they could to make him feel at home. They arranged 'digs' with Josie Edwards and she made sure he was well looked after, so much so that he became part of Josie's extended family. He was also fortunate that he was on the same wavelength as his manager, Mark McGhee (Mars Cancer). McGhee boldly gave 17-year-old Robbie his opportunity in the first team – playing just behind legendary Steve Bull (Mars Virgo). They struck up an immediate understanding and Robbie scored 2 goals on his debut:

Mark McGhee was great: when he told me I was in the first-team squad I was on my way – then me and Bully just clicked.

The following season McGhee told Robbie that he was going to rebuild Wolves around him. He was elated. The season started well, but then Bully pulled a hamstring and was out for 6 weeks, and worse was to follow: as Robbie stretched to reach the television remote, his knee twisted, and he was out for 6 weeks. With both strikers injured, results suffered and McGhee was sacked. At the end of the season Keane became the most expensive teenager in the Football League when he was transferred to Coventry for £6M. It was home-from-home: he commuted to Coventry and scored 2 on his debut. His confidence was sky high, he was playing well, his teammates laughed at his jokes, and he felt that he belonged. But Coventry were beset with financial troubles and had to sell their prize asset at the end of the season; Inter Milan made a £13M bid – the Sky Blues made a £7M profit and Robbie was on £35,000 a week – everyone was over the financial moon. He was excited at the prospect of working with the great Marcello Lippi and having the opportunity to play alongside world-class strikers: Ronaldo (Sun Virgo) and Christian Viera (Sun Cancer), and with Clarence Seedorf (Mars Cancer) in midfield, it all seemed too good to be true:

I owe Clarence big time – he made life a lot easier for me.

However, both Ronaldo and Viera were struck by injury, results suffered, Lippi was sacked, the new manager didn't fancy Keane, and it looked as though he would be loaned to Cagliari. Just as it seemed things couldn't get any worse, Harry Redknapp made a £10M bid to take him to West Ham, but Inter turned it down:

I'd have loved to have bought Robbie, he is a fantastic player, if the chance ever comes up again, I still would.

Inter wanted more money, and with 9 other clubs interested there was every chance they would get it; in stepped big spending Leeds United under manager David O'Leary and Robbie joined some familiar faces in the Elland Road dressing room, including Gary Kelly (Sun Cancer) and his nephew Ian Harte (Sun Virgo), but he was competing for a starting place with local hero Alan Smith: he was in one week, then dropped, then picked, then dropped. He seemed to be swimming against the tide, it was affecting his game and he went 14 months without scoring. He didn't fit in.

For the money we paid we didn't get good value. He was obviously a quality player but it's not his fault that he didn't click with the manager.
Peter Lorimer

However, in spite of the disappointments in Leeds, his Ireland career was on the up-and-up; he became a national hero when he scored the vital goal against Iran that helped them qualify for the 2002 World Cup Finals. After an explosive start to the World Cup campaign, following a tectonic confrontation between manager Mick McCarthy and captain Roy Keane, Robbie helped boost Irish morale with a couple of goals in their final pre-tournament game with Hiroshima, and then following a draw in the opening match against Cameroon he secured a place in Irish folklore: facing Group favourites Germany and losing 0-1 with seconds remaining...

I knew what was coming next; afterwards, I told Quinny that I knew he was going to come off the subs' bench and flick the ball to me. It was like a film, only it was in me `ead. To score at the World Cup is a dream come true and then in the next match, Gary Kelly sent over a looping cross, I made the sweetest contact and we were through to the next round. If you can't raise your game against Raul (Sun Cancer Mars Taurus) and Spain...who can you? When we got the penalty it was like another film in me `ead. To make history is just a dream come true.

In the Summer of 2002 Leeds sold Keane to Spurs for £7M:

Robbie feels as if he's come home now: playing alongside Jamie Redknapp will help him settle. He will do well here; he is similar to Zola (Sun Cancer Mars

Gemini) and di Canio (Sun Cancer Mars Cancer) and I think he can be as good as them.
Glenn Hoddle

In 2003-04, Keane was the club's top scorer and was voted 'Player of the Year'. Unfortunately, the following season Hoddle was sacked and the new manager, Santini, seemed to unsettle Robbie, then the new manager, Martin Jol, preferred Jermaine Defoe. In 2008, Jol was sacked and the new manager, Juande Ramos, sold Robbie to Liverpool for £20M. Robbie was delighted to join his boyhood favourites, but, was the funny feeling still there? Benitez's rotation policy seemed to unsettle Robbie: moreover, it soon became clear that he was competing with Dirk Kuyt (Sun Cancer Mars Libra) for a starting place, and it was also clear that Rafa preferred Dirk – Robbie's form dipped and his confidence suffered. However, back at White Hart Lane Spurs were struggling, Ramos was sacked, Harry Redknapp arrived and, as predicted, swooped for Robbie. But the new Spurs captain soon found that he was competing with Jermaine Defoe for a starting place – Jermaine had a good understanding with Peter Crouch – and Robbie was loaned to Celtic.

Zinedine Zidane

As Don Revie was packing his bags to fly to the Middle East, a young Algerian immigrant was juggling a homemade rag ball in the backstreets of Marseille. Zidane (Sun Cancer Mars Cancer) would go on to play for Don Revie's favourite continental club and emulate his hero. He established himself as the best playmaker Real Madrid have had since Don Alfredo, but his career would end in controversy: Marco Materazzi insulted his mother in the 2006 World Cup final and Zinedine let his emotions get the better of him – at 22:16 Berlin time, 9th July, his glorious career came to an undignified end. The red card not only spoilt what should have been a celebratory night for him, it also put paid to France's chances of winning the World Cup:

We wanted to forgive him. I forgive him, but at the same time I don't forgive him.
Claude Makelele

To do what he did is anarchy.
Lilian Thuram

However, back home there was no blame, only sympathy and support: he would always be a hero in Algeria. As a young boy Zinedine had immigrated to France and lived in a poor quarter of Marseille; it was a rough neighbourhood and although surrounded by crime and drugs, he was well looked after by a protective family. Most of his playtime was spent juggling a football or practising judo; frequently he would combine the two, juggling whilst spinning through a 360 degree turn, or leaping like a crane whilst keeping the ball under control, and then as he landed he would sweep the ball away with his other foot before zigzagging across the sandy, sun drenched square back home. Aged 13, Jean Varrand, a scout from Cannes, spotted him, *I have found a boy who has hands where his feet should be.* Zinedine was invited for trials to Cannes, stayed for three days and was rejected: he was too slow, had no stamina, no strength, and he seemed to meander through games without any sense of direction.

However, Varrand's belief in young Zinedine was unaffected and he eventually persuaded Cannes to give him a chance. Once his parents had been reassured about his schooling and general welfare, they allowed him to join the youth academy and live with the family of one of the club's directors. Zidane worked tirelessly to improve his game, whilst the club worked hard on building his strength and stamina. At long last he was given an opportunity in the first team, but it was a disappointing season, Cannes were relegated and he was sold to

Bordeaux. Happily, his old school pal, Christophe Dugarry, was there and helped him settle; he did well and, following the Cantona kung-fu incident, was called up by Aime Jacquet, made an immediate impact – scoring both goals in a 2-2 draw against a talented Czech side – and was proclaimed the new Platini...

Zidane could be as successful as Platini.
Marcello Lippi

In 1996 Lippi signed him for Juventus, however, he was slow to settle and the media were critical. He felt the need to explain himself:

Platini is unique. I am Zinedine Zidane not Platini. It's important that you understand that I can never be Platini on or off the pitch – it's not in my character.

Zidane had no intention of changing to please anyone, so Lippi changed the formation: picking 2 holding-midfielders – the little general Deschamps, and the ball-winner Conte – allowing Zidane to roam. Results improved, but Lippi was still not satisfied: Zidane would control a game for 70 minutes and then fade, still short of breath and lacking stamina. The Juve medical team prepared a special diet and supplemented it with vitamins and minerals, his performances improved: the trophies followed. In 1998 Zidane was the key to Aime Jacquet's World Cup winners:

In football, spontaneous creativity isn't enough; you also need hard work, determination and belief. Now Zidane has everything.

In 1998 Zidane was voted 'World Player of the Year'. He had all the skills, and something of the avenging knight; his sending off in the 2006 final was not an isolated incident: in the early rounds of the 1998 World Cup he had been sent off for stamping on the back of his marker, all in all he was sent off 14 times for retribution. In 2001 he was transferred to

Real Madrid for a world record £47M; his languid runs, his defence splitting passes, and cultured finishing reminded the Madridistas of the *blond arrow.*

Alfredo Di Stefano

Idolised by Don Revie, emulated by Zidane, and according to Herrera, the blond Argentinian Alfredo di Stefano (Sun Cancer Mars Aries) was the best player in the world. Before di Stefano joined, Real was a club of great potential: after, they were great.

Alfredo was born on the 4th July 1926 to Italian immigrant parents in Buenos Aires. His parents worked a small farm on the outskirts of the Argentine capital and Alfredo developed a powerful physique from helping. Aged 15, he signed for River Plate and made his first-team debut the following year. He won 2 Argentine championships and then moved to Colombia where he won 4 championships and became a South American superstar. However, he remained unknown in Europe until Millonarios played Real Madrid in a friendly and he met Santiago Bernabeu in the pre-match promotional radio broadcast; Bernabeu reportedly told a radio executive, *this guy smells of good football.* The next day Di Stefano took Madrid apart and Bernabeu moved swiftly to sign him, but it was not straightforward: Barcelona were moving just as fast, however, Real reputedly got their man with the help of fanatical Madridista, General Franco.

If Santiago thought his side was now complete, he had to think again: Alfredo needed a midfield partner on his wavelength – he wanted his elegant Argentine teammate, Hector Rial (Mars Cancer). Bernabeu obliged and the di Stefano / Rial partnership was immediately effective. Don Alfredo went on to win 8 Spanish League titles, 5 European Cups, and was voted 'European Player of the Year' twice. 5 times he was the Spanish League's top scorer, and he was the first player to score 4 goals in a European tie. In 1958 Bernabeu made a signing that both improved the team and extended the 31-year-old's career. Up to then Alfredo was finisher, midfield dynamo, playmaker, and sweeper, with Puskas (Sun Aries) in the side he could stroll through games dictating the tempo. Following the televised 1960 European Cup final he joined the immortals – scoring a hat-trick against a technically excellent Eintracht Frankfurt (Eintracht had beaten Glasgow Rangers 12–4 on aggregate in the semi-final). 42 years later the old Don was back at Hampden Park, as part of Madrid's centenary celebrations, to watch history replay: Real Madrid v the champions of Germany. Perhaps he was still brooding as he took his seat in the stands (Real never gave him the 'golden-handshake' he felt he deserved) to witness Real's best player since himself – Zidane – inspire the *White Storm* to another famous victory.

Paulo Maldini

Probably, the best players in the 2006 World Cup were Cancerians: Zidane and Paulo Maldini. A year later, aged 38, Maldini went on to lift the European Cup for AC Milan. The most complete central defender in the modern era was now a 5 times winner of the ultimate club competition. Curiously, Maldini was following in his father's footsteps – César had won the European Cup in 1963.

Paulo joined his dad's club as a 10-year-old and stayed his entire career. They are a family club; they nurture their players; they have back room staff to help with every aspect of football and specialists for everything: dieticians, chiropractors, physiotherapists, psychologists, and more:

It is impossible for me to think of my life without Milan, maybe I wouldn't have liked football at all.

They created the right environment for him, and he was loyal through the difficult times, through the match-fixing allegations, through the points deductions, through the traumas, and the many trophy-winning seasons.

Jamie Redknapp, Micah Richards, Lionel Messi

Without his family connections perhaps Paulo would not have made any impact in football. The same could also be true of Jamie – Sun Cancer Mars Aries – Redknapp, and Micah – Sun Cancer Mars Virgo – Richards. Jamie's dad played for West Ham and became a successful manager, whilst Micah's dad ran a football school in Leeds.

My size was beginning to haunt me; everyone was saying that I was too small to be a footballer. I think that too much emphasis is put on size in England. Just look at Lionel Messi (Sun Cancer Mars Cancer. Lionel was 4ft 11in when he went to Barcelona, yet he went on to become the youngest to play in La Liga: he scored 38 goals – helped Barca win the Treble in 2008-09 – and was voted World Player of the Year), who knows how many talented boys are lost to English football because bigger lads brush them away.
Kevin Keegan

Figures from The Association of Football Statisticians indicate that most of the smaller boys are Cancerians. Their study looked at every player registered with a Premier League side from the inception of the League up to the time of the survey in 2005. Cancer was the least represented sign: 4.5%. At the top were the Librans: 13.5%, followed by Scorpios and Virgoans, both on 13.1%. One of the main reasons suggested for the Cancerians' low representation is that they are disadvantaged by the

Academic year. Pardon? The school year starts around the end of August in England, so when the bigger clubs are scouting for young stars of the future, the Cancerians are almost a year younger, and smaller, than most of the other kids in their group, and, unfortunately, it seems that most teachers and coaches make no allowances.

Craig Brown

Born in Glasgow on the 1st July 1940, Craig Brown (Sun Cancer Mars Cancer) is the unofficial father of Scottish football. As a young lad, Craig supported his local side Hamilton Academical, but his first hero wasn't a player but his grandfather: young Craig dreamed of becoming a train driver just like him. However, granddad had other ideas and encouraged Craig's footballing talent. Aged 17, 5ft 7 in tall, and weighing 10 stones, Craig concluded that to compete with his bigger opponents he would have to body build. In addition to following a special diet, training every day and playing 3 matches a week, he took a job as a steel bender's assistant. When he made his debut for Rangers, he was heralded as the Scottish Pele. However, Brown's punishing regime went way beyond his physical capacity and he suffered with water-on-the-knee. He was on the brink of winning his first international cap, but the fluid swishing in his knee joint prevented him from playing. Anyhow, he took some comfort from the news that the Brazil manager had given Pele a dressing down for over-training, but Edson was that bit luckier. Craig was out of the Rangers side, left to his own devices, and eventually sold to Dundee where he became Bob Shankly's first signing. Bob had recognised Craig's condition and believed that, with proper treatment, he would make a full recovery. Not only did Bob help Craig get fit, he whetted his appetite for coaching. Craig was impressed with the family atmosphere that Bob had created and the loyalty it inspired in his players; he came to appreciate the value of team spirit; he noticed how

Shanks kept players involved when they were injured, how he made them feel wanted when they had lost form, and how he inspired confidence in the club when everything seemed lost. And in 1962 Dundee became Scottish champions for the first time. Unfortunately, the tide was coming back in – his knee swelled up again forcing him to pack football in.

However, as soon as the waters receded he joined Falkirk, then hobbled through a few games for Stranraer before the fluid swished back in, forcing him out of the game for good. Well, not quite, happily, his old pal Billy McNeill recommended him to the Clyde Board: he got the job, managed them to promotion, and was on his way to the top of Scottish football. In 1996 he led his country to the European Championship Finals and then to the World Cup Finals in 1998. He was awarded an Honorary Doctorate from Paisley University, conferred Commander of the British Empire, and continued to support Hamilton Academical.

Jimmy Hill

Jimmy Hill (Sun Cancer Mars Taurus) former TV celebrity, pundit, union leader, match official, chairman, director, abolisher of the maximum wage and unofficial father of the English game, played over 300 times for Fulham before going on to manage Coventry City, write the club song, turn the main stand 'all-seater', introduce a sky-blue strip and lead them from the Third Division to the First Division in 3 years. Nevertheless, that didn't stop him responding to the call from his first love: Fulham. In 1987, the historic club was on the brink of bankruptcy; they needed help and Jimmy did everything he could to retain their identity and independence. As President of Corinthian Casuals (the historic amateurs and inspiration for both Real Madrid and Brazil's Corinthians), he has pledged to uphold football's eternal values.

THIERRY
HENRY

6l

LEO

First is first, that's the way I was brought up,
second or third are nowhere.
Alan Shearer

Arsenal will always be in my blood as well
as in my heart.
Thierry Henry

*I believe in fate.**
Roy Keane

Leo is a FIRE sign ruled by the Sun. The Sun is the central body of the solar system, its gravitational force holds all the other planets in orbit; it is a ball of fire with temperatures hot enough to generate a wind that blasts off its flaming surface at 2 million mph carrying sub-atomic particles to Earth and way beyond. It is our main source of heat and light and science expects that it will be about 5 billion years before it burns to a cinder.

Leo, the constellation, shines brightly in the night sky close to the Big Dipper. At its centre is its brightest star, Regulus (the Little King).

Just as the lion is king of the jungle, so Leos are kings of football. They make dignified managers and courageous captains and ever since England adopted the lion as a national symbol – when Richard the Lionheart added a third lion to the 'Arms of Anjou' – her football fortunes have become strangely entwined with Leo: every year a Leonid meteor shower provides a bright spectacle over Wembley. Usually there are about 10 or so meteors visible per hour, occasionally there are a few hundred, and on very rare occasions there are thousands. When that happens, folklore says that a special occasion is being celebrated or a rare event is being signalled; curiously, the highest number of Leonids ever recorded was over 100,000 per hour in 1966 – England won the World Cup.

---

*fate or Fate, Roy? The dictionary definition of fate is, the power beyond human control; destiny. Whereas, to the Greek philosophers Fate has 3 levels:

1) Pre-determined – that which has been allotted, such as: when and where you were born, your parents and what you inherit from them.

2) Necessity – events and experiences in life arise as a consequence of natural laws: cause and effect, what you sow is what you reap, what you think is what you create, etc. It is a pseudo-fate because, with knowledge, it can be changed.

3) Providence – the divine intention for you. Fate that you can change, but shouldn't be tempted to try – 'to be or not to be' who you are.

THE LIONS

CHAIRMAN
BERT MILLICHIP FA

COACHES
MARIO ZAGALLO Brazil
JOE MERCER Manchester City
LOUIS VAN GAAL Ajax
ROY KEANE Ipswich Town
ROY HODGSON Fulham
LAWRIE McMENEMY Southampton

GOALKEEPERS
DAVID JAMES Portsmouth
RAY CLEMENCE Liverpool

DEFENDERS
WAYNE BRIDGE Manchester City
MARTIN KEOWN Arsenal
WILLIAM GALLAS Arsenal
MARCO MATERAZZI Inter Milan
PHIL JAGIELKA Everton
JOLEON LESCOTT Manchester City

MIDFIELD
MICHAEL CARRICK Manchester United
OSSIE ARDILES Spurs
WILSON PALACIOS Spurs
GIOVANNI RIVERA AC Milan
GEOFF THOMAS Wolves
ESTEBAN CAMBIASSO Inter Milan

FORWARDS

ALAN SHEARER Newcastle United

THIERRY HENRY Barcelona

LOUIS SAHA Everton

ROBIN VAN PERSIE Arsenal

GARRY BIRTLES Nottingham Forest

JUST FONTAINE Real Madrid

DJIBRIL CISSE Sunderland

KEVIN PHILLIPS Sunderland

DAVID HEALY Sunderland

JOSE ALTAFINI AC Milan

FILIPPO INZAGHI AC Milan

KLAAS JAN HUNTELAAR AC Milan

JURGEN KLINSMANN Spurs

INSPIRATIONS

PHIL TAYLOR

BOUDICCA

ROGER FEDERER

ALDOUS HUXLEY

GEORGE SOROS

CG JUNG

PAUL BARRY-WALSH

Whether Leos are royals, captains of industry or figureheads in football, with their dignified bearing, and natural authority, they readily assume command. They aspire to greatness and are a constant source of energy and inspiration to their teammates. Leos are dramatic and thrive on the big stage, the bigger the game, the better they perform; they like to be the centre of attention and when appreciated they really are at their formidable, and predatory, best. Mister Leo is loyal, honest, warm hearted, brave, generous, and proud. However, he has to be careful not to burn himself out, and he should also remember that old saying, *pride comes before a fall.*

Mario Zagallo

It was Mario Zagallo (Sun Leo Mars Libra) who created what some regard as the best team ever: Brazil (1970). An adventurous, goalscoring winger himself he had already won the World Cup twice as a player in Brazil's sunflower yellow shirts (1958 and 1962). As the national coach he managed to combine the nation's appreciation of flair and beauty with a hard-working team ethic. It was difficult. The players complained: they didn't like their roles, were unhappy with his tactics, and they objected to having their natural flair restrained. Nonetheless, Zagallo stuck to his principles – but not for long – he had a potential mutiny on his hands and compromised. With a squad including Rivellino, Carlos Alberto, Pele, and Jairzinho, he managed to find the right blend.

Thierry Henry, William Gallas, Robin Van Persie, Louis Saha, Djibril Cisse

Whilst Zagallo preferred Librans to captain his sides the Libran, Arsene Wenger (Mars Leo), preferred Leos as he sought to establish his own style at Arsenal. In his early days at Highbury, Wenger appointed Tony Adams (Mars Leo) captain, when Adams retired he appointed Patrick Vieira (Mars Leo), when Vieira left he appointed Thierry Henry (Sun Leo Mars Gemini), and when Henry went to Barcelona he gave the armband to William Gallas (Sun Leo Mars Gemini). When Gallas openly criticised his teammates for not having pride in the shirt, Wenger gave the captaincy, briefly, to Robin van Persie (Sun Leo Mars Cancer) before settling on Taurean Fabregas.

Arsenal became the most attractive team in the Football League and one of the most successful, but in 2005 they faltered: there were injuries, key players lost form and self-confidence seaped out of the squad. Strangely, the Leos seemed to be the ones most affected – was it just at Arsenal? What about Roy – Leo – Keane, the rampaging captain of arch-rivals Manchester United; what about his teammate, deadly striker, Louis – Sun Leo Mars Libra – Saha; what about Newcastle's talismanic captain Alan – Leo – Shearer; and Liverpool ace, Djibril – Sun Leo Mars Cancer – Cisse, how was he doing? Worse than the others: for almost 3 years Cisse had one serious injury after another. Nevertheless, that didn't stop the flamboyant France international performing – on a different stage. In addition to his eye-catching hair styles, Cisse acquired the titled lifestyle of an English gentleman and exercised his Lordly prerogative to ban the local fox hunt. In 2008 he was fully recovered and scoring freely again. In the meantime, van Persie had shaken off a series of niggling injuries and was back on form at Arsenal, and also enjoying a good partnership with fellow-Dutchman Huntelaar (Sun Leo Mars Cancer) that was helping propel Holland into the 2010 World Cup

Finals. Saha had also recovered and was hitting the back of the net regularly for Everton, whilst Shearer had had to hang his boots up but was hoping to stay in the game as a manager. Keane did go into management, and Henry recovered to enjoy a new lease of life as France captain and Barcelona spearhead, however, could it be as good as it was at Arsenal? Henry and Wenger had a special bond:

Arsene Wenger is a man I trusted instantly. When he spoke to me I felt an immediate connection and I'm sure he felt it too.

As a teenager Thierry went for trials at Clairefontaine, the successful equivalent of the failed England academy at Lilleshall. In those days Clairefontaine had a reputation for being the toughest youth trial in the world: designed on the lines of the French Foreign Legion's idea of a football boot camp. Henry was one of 800 trialists selected from the best young players in France to compete for 24 places in the academy. After 3 months intensive tests Henry emerged as one of the elite survivors, along with Gallas and Saha. His coaches were impressed with his intelligent feet, his quick acceleration and his high scoring ratio, but they also had their concerns: he was proud, he wouldn't pass, and he wouldn't work for the team. He believed scoring was his sole purpose. His youth coach explained to him that football is a team game and he needed to play his part: Thierry nodded, while thinking....

No way, I am the one who scores, not the one who chases back.

But they persisted with him and hoped that as he grew up his attitude would change. After 3 years boarding he graduated and signed professional with Arsene Wenger's AC Monaco. It was with the professorial Alsatian, the man Thierry came to regard as his second father, that his career began in earnest. Aged 17 Henry was given his opportunity in the first team. He wasn't an instant success but Wenger had faith, and encouraged him to play to his strengths, however, the team were struggling and Arsene got the sack. To make matters worse the new manager, Jean Tigana, was on a different wavelength; Henry was dropped and sat out the rest of the season on the substitutes' bench. Nevertheless, he continued to be selected for the national side and captained the Under 18's to European Cup glory. Aged 20 he made an impressive full international debut as a left winger and – even Tigana couldn't ignore him now – was recalled to the Monaco side. Henry helped them reach the semi-finals of the Champions League and broke the goalscoring record of the France legend, Raymond Kopa. His peformances were drawing the attention of leading European clubs: Manchester United sent scouts to watch him and Claudio Ranieri, at Fiorentina, pleaded with his chairman...

Henry is the Muhammad Ali of football. He has elegance and speed. He does everything with style, please – PLEASE – buy him.

Juventus offered £12M, Monaco accepted, but Thierry struggled to settle into their set up and despaired in the reserves. In the meantime, Wenger had been appointed manager of Arsenal and swooped for the out-of-favour left winger. Thierry was grateful but confessed to having some misgivings when Arsene suggested that he switch to centre forward:

I owe everything to Arsene. He suggested that I play through the middle and believed in me even though, at the beginning, it was hard for me to change.

In his first season he was Arsenal's top scorer with 17 goals, the following season he top scored with 32 as Arsenal did the League and FA Cup double. In 2003 he was voted 'Footballer of the Year' and won it again the following year. He scored more goals in the Premier League – between 1999 and 2009 – than anyone.

Giovanni Rivera

Child prodigy Giovanni Rivera (Sun Leo Mars Taurus) was born on the 18th August 1943 in Italy. Aged 17, he made his debut for AC Milan wearing the playmaker's shirt. The slightly built, thoughtful inside-forward became the heart beat of the *Rossoneri*. He played with style and grace; he was composed and never hurried; he belied his years with the maturity of his positioning and his natural authority. His movement was fluid, his touch and timing, immaculate. He strolled through games in regal splendour – untouchable. They built a team around him; alongside was Maldini, ahead were the goal-machines: Jose Altafini (Sun Leo Mars Leo), and, briefly, Jimmy Greaves (Mars Taurus) – Altafini wouldn't pass to Greavesie, so he left. Anyhow, Rivera went on to score 10 goals in his first season and helped Milan qualify for the European Cup; aged 19 he took control of the final – setting up both goals for Altafini in a 2-1 victory. Over 40 years later Maldini's son, Paulo, lifted the Cup following Milan's victory over Liverpool with both their goals, curiously, scored by another Leonine goal-machine: Inzaghi.

If there has been a better goalscorer in the last 20 years, I haven't seen him.
Stan Collymore

Filippo Inzaghi

Filippo Inzaghi (Sun Leo Mars Aries) was born on the 9th August 1973 in northern Italy. He was the star on Ancelotti's famous formation: the 'christmas tree'. He was the top scorer in the Champions League and joint-topscorer in all European competitions – 65 in 102; his strike rate for Italy – 25 in 57 – is only bettered by Christian Vieri and Roberto Baggio. The bigger the game, the better he plays. Not only did he break the hearts of Liverpool, he broke the hearts of the Portsmouth fans in the 2008 UEFA Cup: after an impeccable display from England international goalkeeper David James (Sun Leo Mars Leo) that had denied him, and despite hitting the post 3 times, and the crossbar, and with time running out, he persisted...eventually the ball surfaced through a sea of legs...Pippo dipped his toe...the ball bobbled beyond the diving James for the winner. Regardless of his achievements, he is not considered a good footballer by Johan Cruyff. Pardon?

He is ungainly, he doesn't work for the team, he doesn't head the ball very well, and he isn't skilful.

Even his friend and former teammate, Del Piero, never received a pass from him. Filippo confessed – *I am a selfish player, so what* – his goals are his justification.

Joe Mercer

Whilst Zagallo was building, possibly, the best team in the world, genial Joe Mercer (Sun Leo Mars Virgo) was building, probably, the best team in England – Manchester City. As a player with Everton, then as the captain of Arsenal, he had been an adventurous midfielder with natural authority and a relaxed, confident style. He captained the England national side and was voted 'Footballer of the Year' in 1950. He was a quiet, joyful, and commanding leader who encouraged teamwork and adventurous football. At City he built an exciting and fluid outfit; he enthused his players, encouraged his staff, and delegated well. His second-in-command Malcolm Allison (Sun Virgo) took charge of coaching and his captain, Tony 'chip off the block' Book (Sun Virgo Mars Leo), took responsibility on the field. As well as being courageous leaders, Leos are loyal to their subjects and expect loyalty back, so when Allison challenged Mercer's authority it signalled the end of Joe's reign at Maine Road. So having won promotion from the Second Division, won the First Division title, the FA Cup, the 1970 League Cup, and the European Cup Winners Cup, their successful partnership came to an abrupt end. When Alf Ramsey was sacked, Joe took charge for 7 matches, made Emlyn Hughes (Sun Virgo) captain and had some fun – England won 3 and drew 3.

Roy Keane

Whilst Manchester City's most successful manager was contemplating life away from Maine Road, the most successful captain of Manchester United was being born. Roy Keane (Sun Leo Mars Aquarius) arrived on the 10th August 1971 in Mayfield, County Cork. Leos are born for the stage and one of the biggest stages is the 'Theatre of Dreams'. As a teenager Roy dreamed of being a professional footballer and wrote to several English clubs for trials, only to receive letters of rejection in return. Anyway, he remained hopeful and his heart skipped a beat when he was invited to the Ireland Under 15 trials; he played well but it ended in disappointment. The door to a career in football slammed shut in his face – or so it seemed. Having neglected his school work in pursuit of his dream, he had failed to prepare for a 'normal' job and left with no prospects. He slipped into semi-skilled work and then into vocational training and then back into semi-skilled work. He reset his sights on football and resolved to try harder. He made the Ireland Under 18 trials but the scouts showed no interest. *Why?* Why couldn't they see his talent, his passion, his determination, his willpower, his selfless 'box to box' running, fierce tackling, bravery, goals or his inspirational leadership? He concluded that the scouts had no talent, joined Second Division Cobh Ramblers and drew up a new plan: he persuaded the management to nominate him for a Government sponsored football training programme. He hoped that it would lead to the top, but they ignored him. Back at Cobh his hopes were raised as the Ramblers reached the National Under 18 Cup final; it was a huge game with all the big clubs talent-spotting.

Damn! Cobh were taking a beating: 4-0 down with 20 minutes remaining and Roy struggling to make an impression. His teammates were there in body, but had gone and surely all the scouts had gone too. There was nothing to play for, except, *pride*. Demented with frustration Roy blazed – the Ramblers responded. He urged them forward, he drove them on and on, through the emotional barrier, through the mental barrier that insinuates:

You've lost, you're tired, save your energy – give in.

He did not and not all the scouts had gone, one had stayed to the bitter end: Brian Clough's man was impressed. Keane thrived under Cloughie's guidance. Roy found Old Big `ead generous and supportive, and would forever be grateful,

Who would give a 19-year-old Irishman – with no experience – his debut at Anfield? A genius!

Even when Cloughie landed a right hook on his chin, Roy's admiration and respect never wavered; he put it in perspective and understood that making a sloppy back pass in the FA Cup was unacceptable. Keane didn't resent him, neither did he get upset when Cloughie criticised him for not signing a new contract. Roy owed him everything for giving him his chance in football, but when his chance came to play for the Reds that was different. Roy signed for Alex Ferguson's Manchester United and became the most expensive player in English football. However, there was a burden of expectation that came with the price tag, but in his first serious game he rose to the challenge, scored, and then scored another in a 3-0 victory. He went on to win 7 Premiership titles, 4 FA Cups, and the Champions League; for most of the time he was club captain. In contrast to his club career, his international career was a disappointment. He was frustrated with the amateurish set up, the poor preparation, and he had little respect for manager Jack Charlton's methods and tactics. He was happier when Mick McCarthy (Sun Aquarius) took over; McCarthy believed in the passing game and Roy hoped things would improve. They agreed on what needed to change. Mick made Roy his captain and they qualified for the 2002 World Cup Finals. McCarthy chose the beautiful island of Saipan as the training base. Roy was optimistic, however, it soon became clear that there would be no 5 star hotels, no first class travel, no top quality training facilities, and no royal treatment for Roy or his teammates. He complained in private to Mick. Perhaps he should go home rather than accept second best and the failure that would inevitably follow, but he thought better of it and tried to keep his disappointment to himself. Nevertheless, Mick called a meeting to clear the air:

Is everyone happy with the arrangements on the island? Are you happy, Roy? Why is he asking me, he already knows.

He needs unity. He needs his captain to be on-side.

I know, but I'm not going to pretend that second best is good enough.

Did you have to go home?

It was a beautiful island, but it wasn't Utopia. When we visited 'suicide cliff' I saw what was coming: we were supposed to be there to prepare to win the World Cup but we were heading for a fall. Things happen for a reason, you have to try to understand what that reason is. When Mick called the meeting, I knew what he was going to say, he already knew my feelings. Sometimes you have to take a stand for what you believe in. Sometimes you have to be prepared to give up the biggest prize to have something more important.

Why did you go into management, Roy?

Football is in my blood so I agreed to meet the Sunderland owners in County Kildare: there were some issues to work out first with Niall, then in the August, ironically, I followed McCarthy into the hot seat. We won promotion; the owners were delighted and came up with money to strengthen the team: I re-built the side around my captain Dean Whitehead (Sun Aquarius), bought Liam Miller (Sun Aquarius), brought in Anton Ferdinand (Sun Aquarius), Pascal Chimbonda (Mars Aquarius), and El Hadj Diouf (Mars Aquarius). I also needed a striker – there was speculation that I would bring back former black cat, Kevin – Leo – Phillips, but I signed Djibril – Leo – Cisse instead; he had scored the winner on his Liverpool debut against Spurs with 17 minutes to go, his Sunderland debut was also against Spurs and, with 17 minutes to go, he scored the winner. David – Leo – Healy also scored on his debut for us – in his case, and as Fate would have it – against Forest, at the Brian Clough Stand end!

In April 2009, Keane followed in the footsteps of England's two most successful managers – Alf Ramsey (Sun Aquarius) and Bobby Robson (Sun Aquarius) – at Ipswich Town.

Alan Shearer

In April 2006, Sunderland suffered their heaviest defeat in 50 years against their fiercest rivals, Newcastle United. Not since the days of Jackie Milburn had they been so humiliated on their home patch. It was a turning point for north-east football; it was a low point for Sunderland but it was also a low point for Newcastle. After 71 minutes the 'Lion of Gosforth' was injured and limped off for the last time. Alan Shearer (Sun Leo Mars Leo) had finished his Newcastle career as he had started it, with a goal. In the intervening decade he had broken the goalscoring record of Milburn, but this injury was one that he knew he wouldn't be able to shake off. As if in confirmation that this really was the end, the sky darkened, a sheet of lightning flashed around St James Park, the heavens opened and a curtain of rain came down.

Born in Newcastle on the 13th August 1970, the son of a sheet-metal worker from the Tyne, Alan's childhood ambition was to wear the black and white No 9 shirt. However, it wasn't on Tyneside but on the south coast where he blasted to fame. In 1984 he signed for the Saints – managed by the charismatic Geordie, Lawrie McMenemy (Sun Leo Mars Cancer) – and, on the 9th April 1988, he made an impressive debut against the Arsenal: scoring a hat-trick.

In 1992 Jack Walker (Mars Leo), the steel magnate and self-made multi-millionaire chairman of Blackburn Rovers, was investing in success. He wanted the best for Rovers and broke the British transfer record to sign the best centre forward in the country. Alex Ferguson was also prepared to break the record to sign Shearer, anyway, when Alan met Jack they formed an immediate bond. His goals did help Blackburn become Champions but they had to wait until 1995 for the honour – a season after Roy Keane did it.

In 1996 Kevin Keegan was the manager of Newcastle and was prepared to break the world transfer record (£15M) to bring the Geordie home. Fergie also tried again, but the lure of fulfilling his childhood dream was too much – Jack Walker understood that and didn't stand in Shearer's way:

He's been a second father to me; this is the way I want to leave, no animosity – just friendship.

In 1997, Keegan suddenly resigned and his old Blackburn manager, Kenny Dalglish, arrived. In 1998 they reached the FA Cup final, but, in spite of Shearer being at his peak, the omens were not good: the club coach had a flat battery and failed to start, Tony Adams was in commanding form, and the Newcastle midfield failed to ignite. 18 months later Dalglish was sacked and the new manager turned out to be Shearer's biggest critic: Ruud Gullit. They were clearly on different wavelengths and the unhappiest period of Alan's career followed. His form dipped, the goals dried up, his confidence drained away, he was angry, frustrated and sent-off for the first time in his career. He had the captaincy stripped away; he was dropped for the biggest game in the Newcastle calendar, v Sunderland, and humiliated on the bench. The fans revolted, Gullit resigned, and in came Bobby Robson to restore Alan's wounded pride.

Shearer's international career had started well with a goalscoring debut for the Under 17's against the Republic of Ireland and it started well for the Under 21's under McMenemy. Shearer repaid Lawrie's faith in him with a brace of goals on his Cork debut. His full international debut started just as well against France; Les Bleus were enjoying a 19 game unbeaten run, but were undone by big Al. He went on to become England captain and score 30 goals in 63 matches. Aged 29, he retired from international football following crowd abuse; the fact that the England fans had booed him off the Wembley pitch was too much for a proud Leo. Would it have been different under another manager, someone with a different opinion about Shearer's best strike partner? Curiously, Brian Clough always maintained that the ideal partner for Shearer was Kevin Phillips (Cloughie was usually right: when we consider Partnerships, in Part 2, you may agree with him).

In 2008 Kevin Keegan was appointed manager of Newcastle, again. On a wave of public emotion he was hailed as their saviour and the fans petitioned for Shearer to be Keegan's assistant – *the dream partnership* – and then one day, just maybe, Kev would hand over to Al. After all it was his ambition:

Hi, Al: how would you like to come home? Come back to Newcastle and be my assistant, pal. What do you say?

I've contracts to honour, Kev, business commitments, an endurance bike ride for charity to train for: 335 miles for Sports Relief. Perhaps the timing isn't right, mate....let's review it when I come back off holiday. You know I'll help in any way I can. (Hmmmm...assistant...no one's asked me to do that before).

In September Keegan surprisingly resigned.

On 1st April 2009 Newcastle were in the bottom 3, manager Joe Kinnear was recovering from triple-bypass heart surgery and Shearer was appointed for the last 8 games:

It's a club I love and like many thousands of people, I desperately do not want the club to go down. I will do everything I can to prevent that.

Newcastle were relegated.

Marco Materazzi

In 2006 Europe dominated the biggest stage: France and Italy reached the World Cup final – Cannavaro and Inzaghi duelled with Gallas and Henry, but someone else stole the show: *behind you…behind you…*screamed the excited crowd…*behind you, Zizou…*they shrieked as the pantomime provocateur insulted his mother. Zidane turned on Marco – the Matrix – Materazzi (Sun Leo Mars Taurus). The complex Marco combined courage and a bullish tackle with the need to be centre stage. He had reached the pinnacle of football but his early career didn't show any signs of what was to come: he flopped at Everton and struggled back home. In 2000 he was playing for Perugia, but he wasn't shining there either – until he threw caution to the wind, drove himself and the team forward, blasted a few goals against big-time clubs and caught the eye of Inter Milan. Whilst his raw-boned performances continued to lack refinement, his leadership qualities won over the *Nerazzuri* and he became a cult figure. He compared himself with the best England defender:

I am like Tony Adams.

David Healy

In the European Championship qualifying rounds for the 2008 competition, an unsung Leo striker was making the headlines. A man for the big occasion, who couldn't get a regular game for his club side, was making a big impact on the international scene. Pardon? David Healy (Sun Leo Mars Gemini) scored 13 goals to break the 12-year-old record of Davor Suker, whatever, in March 2008 Michel Platini (Sun Gemini) announced:

He deserves to be recognised. This is why I will be presenting him with a special award to celebrate his fantastic achievement.

Geoff Thomas

Even in retirement Leos are beacons of leadership. As Shearer was inspiring the north-east, Geoff Thomas (Sun Leo Mars Cancer) was inspiring the south. The former captain of Crystal Palace and Wolves was fighting back from serious illness; an inspiration to other cancer sufferers, he was intent on completing a gruelling charity bike ride: The Tour de France. To put his effort in context – when Shearer was training for his ride, he underwent medical tests to determine how efficient his body was at transporting oxygen (VO2 rating), a fit and healthy 30 something would expect to score around 45, champion bike rider Greg le Mond scored 92.5, Shearer scored 42. Thomas didn't do the test; who knows how low his score would have been, but no matter, he wasn't pedalling on oxygen but raw courage, willpower, and encouragement from his fans and well-wishers. As he wheeled along the pollarded byways of Bordeaux he was cheered on by a thin line of black and old gold – 3 lion – flag wavers.

RuuD GuLLIT

mD

VIRGO

Someone said to me, 'football is more important to you than life and death',
look, I said, it is more important than that.
Bill Shankly

Malcolm Allison is the best coach that has ever been.
Colin Bell

It's all about teamwork.
Ruud Gullit

Virgo is an EARTH sign. It is a symbol of nature; it signifies the beauty of the countryside, the abundance of agriculture and represents fertility and our staple foods: wheat and corn, peas and carrots, turnips and swedes. Virgo is also the young woman working hard to bring home the harvest to feed her extended family. She does not discriminate between species or races, everyone is welcome at her table. She is in tune with the seasons and the rhythm of life and instinctively knows when to sow and when to reap, when to pass and when to move. She is modest, virtuous, just, practical, and elegant: adorned with sparkling diamonds.

The constellation Virgo has some of the brightest stars in the sky, including Spica and Vindemiatrix, however, there is something deep, dark, and mysterious about this cluster of stars. Some astronomers think that at its magnetic centre there is a giant black hole of swirling, radio-wave emitting matter and anti-matter. Virgo and Gemini are both ruled by the great communicator, Mercury, and some speculate that Virgo is a channel to other dimensions.

Virgoans are efficient, hard working, versatile, and they believe that teamwork is the key to success. They take good care of their health, they exercise regularly, eat organic food, take their vitamin supplements, and avoid over-indulgence. They are alert, witty, and take an interest in arts and crafts, but they are anxious: many of them are worried that nature is being destroyed by chemicals and radiation. They are recycling, reading environmental books, studying Confucius, Schumacher, and listening to Satish Kumar.

TEAM VIRGO

CHAIRMAN
BILL KENWRIGHT Everton

COACHES
BILL SHANKLY Liverpool
TOMMY DOCHERTY Chelsea
GRAHAM TAYLOR England
MALCOLM ALLISON Manchester City
HELMUT SCHOEN West Germany
FRANZ BECKENBAUER West Germany

GOALKEEPERS
PETER SHILTON Nottingham Forest
DAVID SEAMAN Arsenal
PEPE REINA Liverpool

DEFENDERS
TONY BOOK Manchester City
RICHARD DUNNE Aston Villa
PAUL BREITNER Bayern Munich
FABIO CANNAVARO Real Madrid
SOL CAMPBELL Arsenal
PAUL MADELEY Leeds United

MIDFIELD
EMLYN HUGHES Liverpool
RUUD GULLIT AC Milan
GUNTER NETZER Borussia Monchengladbach
DIETMAR HAMANN Liverpool
EMMANUEL PETIT Arsenal

GARY SPEED Newcastle United
DAVID BENTLEY Spurs
EIDUR GUDJOHNSEN Spurs
RAY WILKINS Chelsea
DECO Chelsea

FORWARDS
BOBBY TAMBLING Chelsea
RONALDO AC Milan
HENRIK LARSSON Barcelona
NAT LOFTHOUSE Bolton Wanderers
JOHN CAREW Aston Villa
DENNIS VIOLLET Manchester United
ALEX JAMES Arsenal

INSPIRATIONS
NELSON MANDELA
ARNOLD PALMER
JETHRO TULL
MICHAEL JOHNSON
HARRY POTTER

2,500 years ago Chinese unemployment was rising, habitats were being destroyed, millions were rioting and Confucius was worried. The old sage advised his people to plant a tree every 5 years. He explained that trees provide a habitat for birds and insects, they aerate the soil and promote fertility and that meant they would be self-sufficient: having enough food and enough timber for home-building, fuel, and trade. In the second half of the 20th century the German economist philosopher, EF Schumacher, called the free-market institutionalised non-responsibility and said that man had stopped caring about how goods were being made and the damage that was being done to the planet, and people, in the process. Now, Kumar and Prince Charles are reminding everybody that the root of the economy is still ecology; that nature is our capital, not income, and that if capitalism is to survive then capitalists must be unselfish, and wise, enough to recognise when they have enough.

Bill Shankly

They would have struck a chord with Bill Shankly (Sun Virgo Mars Gemini): modest, down-to-earth Bill was a practical 'man of the people' and in spite of his great achievements, and acclaim, he lived a simple life. He was born in Glenbuck, Ayrshire, on the 2nd September 1913 to hard-working parents. His father was a community spirited, teetotal, middle distance runner who made a living as a postman and tailor. His mother was from a sporting family with brothers who were professional footballers: uncle Bob played for Glasgow Rangers and uncle Willie played for Preston North End and Portsmouth, before becoming chairman of Carlisle United. Aged 14, young Bill started work at the local pit; aged 16, he was made redundant and experienced the grinding poverty of a mining community being broken up by the Conservatives and betrayed by Labour – he grew to deeply distrust politicians.

When his opportunity came to play for Carlisle he jumped at it. He trained harder than anyone else at the club and soon established himself as a regular in the Brunton Park engine room. He developed into a teetotal, hard running, strong tackling, technically excellent wing half. His value to the side was widely recognised and in 1933 Preston made a bid, but Bill was worried – he was anxious that he couldn't trust the hard-nosed businessmen with their big city, sharp practices. After all he was liked and looked-after, he fitted in with the other lads and was happy. He decided that they were not to be trusted and said, *no*, but big brother Alec found out, went mad, and made Bill change his mind. He was glad that he had been made to see sense when he arrived at Deepdale: the players were honest and the fans, welcoming. He trained hard, played hard, got on well with the coach and liked the quick, accurate passing. Results were going well and, gradually, his anxieties faded away. He was the first at training and the last to leave – he was the fittest man at the club. He was polite, well-mannered, ate the right food, avoided the wrong drink, and was neat and tidy both on and off the pitch. He was the model professional and was beginning to attract the attention of bigger clubs, including the mighty Arsenal, but he was loyal to the Lilywhites and decided to stay. Both he and the club prospered and in 1938 they won the FA Cup. However, after 16 war-interrupted years the directors decided, much to Bill's disappointment, that his career was over. His original worries, about heartless businessmen, now seemed well-founded as the directors proceeded to diddle him out of his severance pay. The fans, knowing that he had been swindled, showed their solidarity and raised the princely sum of £169 pounds for Bill and his family. The kind gesture from the ordinary working folk on the terraces touched him deeply and he never forgot: at every opportunity he repaid them. However, for now, he had to find a job to feed his family. He thought he might become a physiotherapist and completed a correspondence course, but when he was offered the chance to manage Carlisle he jumped at it. Good wishes, congratulations, and telegrams poured into the Shankly home – including one from his long time opponent, Arsenal captain and midfield adversary, Joe Mercer (Mars Virgo):

In my humble opinion, no player ever gave as much to football as you.

In May, Shankly believed that justice was done when Preston were relegated, but he had no time for gloating and threw himself into repairing Brunton Park. The ground was more dilapidated now than it was when he joined as a teenager; he fixed the roof, mended the gates, painted the fence, and polished the brass. His enthusiasm was infectious and an army of volunteers mustered to help. He devised new training regimes, specified what meals the players would have and when: every detail of running the club was addressed, even buying a washing machine – under Bill everything had to be shiny bright, and with Mars in Gemini (the sign of wit and communication) it was only natural that he would commandeer the loudspeaker on match days. He chatted with the crowd, joked, told them what had happened since the last home game, read the team sheet, reminded them that it was their club and invited their comments. Results improved, his reputation spread and in 1951 he was shortlisted for the Liverpool manager's job. He believed he didn't get it because the other interviewee was a Freemason. He moved to Grimsby and soon had the Mariners playing as a unit. He cajoled the players, engaged with the crowd and got the place ship-shape. He needed money for the team, but the directors' ambitions didn't match his own so he joined Workington and got the town to believe; the fans loved him and flocked in.

He joined Huddersfield Town as reserve-team coach and they responded to his ideas and enthusiasm: they flew up the League whilst the first team went down. Following a poor start to the new season the manager resigned and Shankly was promoted. Nonetheless, starved of funds for team building and doubting the ambition of the directors, he was soon ready to move on. Liverpool were now bottom of the Second Division, Anfield was falling down and, with no Freemason on the shortlist, Bill was appointed. He was promised money to improve the club and threw himself into renovating the dilapidated ground. He repaired the roof, mended the gates, painted the fence, cut the grass and, inspired by his enthusiasm, plenty of fans volunteered. He assessed his squad and took the time to explain to those who had no future at Liverpool, why they had to leave. He was sensitive to their feelings and worried how they would cope financially; he used his contacts to find them other clubs or jobs in the community. He knew that a man needs time: time to adjust, time to come to terms with himself, time to review what he has done, where he is from and where he is going. Bill intended to make new signings and build his own team, but the Board went back on its word and he felt let down. He talked to his friend, Matt Busby (Sun Gemini), and was persuaded to stay for one more season and see what turned up – it was the unexpected. The sympathetic Everton chairman, John Moores, recognising the plight of his near neighbours decided to help and offered the expertise of his finance director, Eric Sawyer. Sawyer and Shankly formed a good partnership. Sawyer was impressed with Shankly's plans for the club and persuaded the Board to back him. Bill's first priority was to get more goals and find the ideal strike partner for Roger Hunt; in his opinion that was Ian St John (Sun Gemini) of Motherwell. Luckily, St John wanted to sign, and Motherwell were prepared to sell – for the small fortune of £35,000. The Hunt / St John combination was a huge success. Liverpool scored over 100 goals in their first season together and to mark the dawn of a new era, Bill changed the strip to, *socialism in action,* all red...

Every player in my team has to play for the team, not himself. Here we do things collectively.

The Reds won promotion and then in 1964 were crowned First Division champions. In 1965 they won the FA Cup and in 1966 they won the League; now there was some rebuilding to be done and it wouldn't be until 1973 before they did it again. The following season they won the FA Cup; as Bill swaggered onto the balcony at St George's to address the fans and share the victory, the craggy Scot was on top of the world looking like a cross between his screen idol, James Cagney (Mars Virgo), and 'Red Leader' Mao...*I have fought every step of the way for you...he* lifted the trophy, waved it above his head, passed it to Em, and took a deep breath...*it's your Cup...it belongs to the best supporters in the world*....they were hanging onto his every power-packed, heart-felt word. If he had asked them to walk with him to Birmingham to join the peace marchers, they would have; if he had asked them to walk with him to Albert dock to abolish slavery, they would have. He was Liverpool's past, present, and future.

I've drummed it into our players that they are privileged to play for you, and if they didn't believe me then, they believe me now.

They burst into song...

Youuullllllnneeeverrrrwwwalkaaaalone....SHANKLYSHANKLYSHANKLY

Bill said,

Above all I would like to be remembered as a man who was selfless, who built up a family of people who could hold their heads up high and say – we are Liverpool.

When he passed away the city came to a standstill. A little part of every Liverpudlian died on the 29th September 1981. Thousands gathered on the streets to pay silent tribute to a very extraordinary ordinary man, a working man's man, a man who dribbled his hard-boiled egg to his egg cup every morning. A man who did everything he could to make the people happy. In remembrance, Emlyn Hughes (Sun Virgo Mars Cancer) said,

It was my privilege to know Shanks for 16 years and I can honestly say that I loved him. For Mrs Shankly to say that I was closer to him than anyone is the best trophy I ever won.

And his pal, Tommy Docherty....

He was a complex character who came across as uncomplicated. At various times he was outrageous, ironic, uncompromising and ruthless but he was also kind, compassionate and had a wicked sense of humour.

Was Tom talking about Bill or himself?

Tommy Docherty

Preston missed Shankly, although it took relegation for them to realise how much. Bill had been their driving force on the pitch, their heart-beat in training, part of their bedrock. If Bill Scott, the Preston manager, could have cloned Shankly he would have, instead he did the next best thing – signed his double. In November 1949, Thomas Henderson Docherty (Sun Virgo Mars Gemini), the workaholic, fitness fanatic, hard-tackling wing half from Glasgow Celtic arrived at Deepdale, fitted straight in, and helped Preston to promotion at the first attempt. In 1954 Docherty drove them to the FA Cup final. With the Marston 'rock' at centre half, the Doc commanding midfield, and captain Tommy Finney in attack, Preston were the bookies' favourites to beat WBA, but from the first whistle the Throstles were on song and after 21 minutes they went ahead. 2 minutes later the Doc burst forward and deftly lobbed the Albion defence for Wayman to equalise. Early in the second half he was at it again, splitting the Baggies back line with a precision pass for the 2nd, then defusing attacks in his own area, gathering clearances from Joe Marston and bombing forward, unfortunately, a crunching last ditch tackle gave away a penalty...2-2...and with Finney failing to find his best form WBA ran out 3-2 winners.

When he hung his boots up Docherty went into management and made his name at Chelsea. He took charge when they were a mediocre Second Division side, made wholesale changes, introduced a youth policy and controversially made 21-year-old Bobby Tambling (Sun Virgo

Mars Aries) club captain. He thought deeply about tactics and made detailed plans for each game. Nevertheless, one of the last games of their promotion season was a home defeat to league leaders Stoke, it made a lasting impression:

When we ended runners-up to Stoke City we both set a record: Stoke had the oldest team to win a League title and we had the youngest team to win promotion. I know those facts tell me something important about football, but I still don't know what.

Stoke won 1-0 that day – despite his meticulous planning to stop their 48-year-old winger Stanley Matthews; to stop their 33-year-old, 5ft 6in, centre forward Jackie Mudie; and to stop their 31-year-old midfield general Jimmy McIllroy. It wasn't because of any lack of quality in his Chelsea side: he had young England stars like Terry Venables, Barry Bridges, and Bobby Tambling. Neither was it for lack of fitness, Chelsea were the fittest team in the Football League, nor was it because they were ill-prepared, or lacked motivation. So what was wrong?

In 1972, he was appointed Manchester United manager and took them into the Second Division. He thought he would be sacked; he thought about resigning, but he battled through and the club were supportive. He bounced back – winning the FA Cup in 1977 – but, ironically, a few weeks later he was sacked: the media had rounded on him for having an affair with the physio's wife. The newspapers found plenty of people willing to criticise his character and conduct. They asked Shanks for a quote:

Of course Tommy has his faults: for a start he can't sew....

They tracked down his former Commanding Officer:

Tommy was my sarge. He was as bright as a button and dependable – I could always rely on him to do the right thing.

And the Doc was happy to share his wisdom...

When I was out of work a friend advised me to, 'take a holiday, Tom, take some time-out to find yourself.' I told him, life is not about finding your self, it's about finding your heart, and then having the courage to follow it.

Malcolm Allison

In the Spring of 1972 United were sliding down the League whilst their rivals, Manchester City, were 4 points clear at the top. Guided by Joe Mercer and Malcolm Allison (Sun Virgo Mars Virgo) City were cruising to the title – or so the players thought.

Allison was the coach, tactician, trainer, researcher, health food and vitamin supplement experimenter, and cigar smoking media manipulator. He imported energy drinks from America. He studied the training methods of world record holder, Jim Ryan, and brought Russian ballet dancers to Maine Road to help improve the players' balance and agility. He studied the explosive sprinting technique of Olympic gold medal winner Valeri Borzov. His attention to detail was legendary and it had helped City overcome the likes of Spurs, Leeds, Liverpool, Arsenal, Chelsea, and United, but the perfectionist in him wanted more. There was one more detail, one more piece of the jigsaw required, *we need Rodney Marsh*. He persuaded Mercer that the international playmaker was the key to City's success. Marsh arrived with 9 games remaining – City won 3 and slipped to 4th place. That summer there was a disagreement: Allison wanted more control but was refused, instead Joe left and Malcolm was promoted. The new season started badly for City, after 2 months they were lying bottom of the League and had been knocked out of the UEFA Cup. There was no cohesion, team spirit had evaporated and when the Sky Blues of Coventry beat them – with their new manager, Joe Mercer – it was the final straw. Bell blamed Marsh: he believed that it was Rodney who had unbalanced the side – *Rodney cost us £200,000, and the title.*

Ruud Gullit

30 years after the Doc's Chelsea were beaten in the FA Cup final they returned to set the record straight: this time under a young Virgoan in his first season of management. However, Ruud Gullit (Sun Virgo Mars Cancer) had an uneasy relationship with his chairman and, although lying in 2nd place in the League the following season, was sacked. In 1998 Gullit became the manager of Newcastle United and in his first season led them to the FA Cup final. Nevertheless, he had an uneasy relationship with the local hero – Alan Shearer – and, after handing the captaincy to Gary Speed (Sun Virgo Mars Sagittarius), had an uneasy relationship with Rob Lee, and then following a humiliating defeat to Sunderland his relationship with the fans broke down.

As a player Ruud was a technically perfect exponent of the Dutch style of *Total Football*. In 1988 he helped Holland win the European Championship; he was named 'European Footballer of the Year' and was voted 'World Footballer of the Year' twice; he was a star at Ajax, Sampdoria, and Chelsea, but it was at AC Milan where, perhaps, he really felt at home,

It was the family atmosphere, emotional ties and team spirit that made Milan special.

Gullit was a clever, politically-aware player with a critical eye for detail. He grew up sharing a one-room flat with his mother on the poorer side of Amsterdam. His mum had to set off early for work leaving young Ruud to make his own breakfast and get ready for school. He was bright enough to know that having talent was no guarantee of success. He knew that there was more to it than ability – he needed to be noticed – so he wore the brightest strips. When he received the 'European Footballer of the Year' award, he dedicated it to the, then imprisoned, freedom-fighter Nelson Mandela as a gesture of solidarity:

Now I have many friends, but when I was in prison Ruud was one of the few.

In 1993 there was discontent in the Dutch dressing room, they were already without the injured Van Basten for the crucial World Cup qualifier with England, and now manager Dick Advocaat's dreadlocked star was threatening that he wouldn't play: there was a principle at stake and that was more important to Ruud.

Graham Taylor

Advantage England – or so Graham Taylor (Sun Virgo Mars Libra) thought. Taylor had taken over from Bobby Robson following England's successful 1990 World Cup campaign and had inherited a strong squad, including Gary Lineker, Chris Waddle, and Paul Gascoigne. As a young manager at Watford, Graham had come under the spell of wing commander Charles Reep – a pragmatic statistician with a scientific approach to the game. Reep had proven from analysing well over 500 matches that direct football / 'Route 1' (otherwise known as the long-ball game) was the best way to score goals and win matches. With a few technical modifications, Taylor put the long-ball theory into practice at Watford and reaped the rewards: taking the Hornets from the Fourth Division to 2nd place in the top Division in 6 years. Whilst it brought success to Vicarage Road, it annoyed the purists, and the free spirits weren't keen on it either. When he was appointed England coach they were horrified, *would he be tempted to go 'Route 1'?* Sensitive to their feelings, Taylor reassuringly varied his tactical plans – after all he did have some of the best players in the world and they had only just lost in a penalty shoot-out, so why would he want to change much, if anything?

I hear what you say, but a successful team must try different tactics and systems if it is to stay ahead; if it is to improve it must be progressive. Germany played with a sweeper, 3 centre halves, 5 across the middle; surely we should experiment, at least in the friendlies.

As a player Taylor had been a hard working, defensive half back in the lower leagues. He was articulate and persuasive, so much so that his Grimsby chairman had him down by the fish docks selling bottles of fresh air to raise a few quid for the depleted club coffers. As England manager he needed all his charming, counter-intuitive salesmanship to sell the long-ball game. He dropped the in-form wing wizard Waddle and then did the unthinkable – substituted Lineker in the crucial match against Sweden with England desperate to score and with Gary desperate for a goal to equal Bobby Charlton's record. As it was England finished bottom of the pool and then the post-mortem began: did Graham not like Sagittarians?

For the crucial World Cup qualifier against Holland would Taylor keep the same side that beat Poland 3-0 the month before or would he bring back Shearer, Merson, Parker, Dorigo, and Carlton Palmer? He would, so, even without van Basten and Gullit, Holland went on to win. After such a disappointing campaign, perhaps Graham was left wishing he could have called on the technical excellence of Beckenbauer, the craftsmanship of Netzer, or the selfless running of Hughes.

Franz Beckenbauer, Gunter Netzer, Helmut Schoen, Paul Breitner

Franz Beckenbauer (Sun Virgo Mars Cancer) was born on the 11th

September 1945 into a working-class family in a bombed-out part of Munich. Aged 18 he was selected for the national squad, but when his girlfriend fell pregnant and he wouldn't marry her – a national scandal at the time – he was dropped and then banned. However, eventually, the ban was lifted and Franz went on to represent his country in 3 World Cup Finals, captain West Germany to victory in the 1972 European Championships and the 1974 World Cup Finals, and then manage Germany to victory in the 1990 World Cup final. He was also voted 'European Footballer of the Year' twice.

Gunter Netzer was born into a middle-class family on the 14th September 1944 during an Allied bombing raid on Monchengladbach. He was a versatile playmaker who strolled through games seemingly disinterested, only to surprise the opposition with a 50 metre precision pass to Der Bomber Muller, with a floated diagonal to Grabowski, or by blasting one into the back of the net. For most of their time playing in Germany they were rivals: Beckenbauer was the soul of Bayern Munich and Netzer was the heartbeat of Borussia Monchengladbach. As their careers developed, so the fortunes of their clubs multiplied. They were both lucky to get their international chances early, but Franz was that bit luckier to have more in common with the most successful World Cup manager ever, Helmut Schoen (Sun Virgo Mars Cancer). Schoen was a crafty tactician who liked to experiment: in friendlies his teams played with flair and his creative players were allowed to express themselves, but when the chips were down he took no chances. Sometimes he surprised his opponents – as he did against England in the 1972 European Championship quarter-final at Wembley – on that rare occasion Ramsey was outwitted by the 'silver fox'. Shoen deployed Netzer in the playmaker role and protected him with the hard-tackling Uli Hoeness; Beckenbauer led the side from the centre of defence, alongside the politically minded, fan of Chairman Mao, Paul Breitner (Sun Virgo Mars Leo). Breitner was being groomed for the future and the technically gifted, hard-running defender did emerge as a devastating partner for the free-scoring Karl-Heinz Rummenigge (Mars Virgo), but, for now, he was covering the forward runs of Der Kaiser.

England had no answer. Netzer delivered an inspirational display of flair and craftsmanship not seen since Hidegkuti dismantled England two decades before. Whatever, the pragmatic Schoen could find no place for Netzer in his 1974 World Cup winning side.

Outside of football Gunter was a lover of music and art. He was a socialite and successful businessman with interests in leisure and recreation. As a manager he had success at Hamburg, taking them to the European Cup final only to be beaten by Nottingham Forest, and a world-class goalkeeping display by Peter Shilton. Netzer's star player was 'European Footballer of the Year' Kevin Keegan. Keegan had this to say about his boss:

I am fortunate to have met a lot of principled people in the game, but I can honestly say, there were none more honourable than Gunter Netzer.

Peter Shilton, David Seaman

Peter Shilton (Sun Virgo Mars Leo) was born on the 18th September 1949. He trained with his local club Leicester City as a 13-year-old and, on the recommendation of Gordon Banks, was signed. Peter was a precocious talent and by the time he was 18, ironically, he had displaced Banks from the Leicester side. In 1972 he was England's understudy to Gordon, however, following Gordon's disabling car crash, Shilton was expected to make the jersey his for years to come. But there were surprises ahead, starting with the World Cup qualifier against Poland. Commentators claimed that it was Shilton's blunder, rather than Hunter's stumble, that was to blame for England's failure to qualify. Although in his defence, Shilts was partly unsighted by Emlyn, nevertheless, he did have plenty of time to assume the text-book starting position, plenty of time for the cameraman to get the right angle, time to throw his cap on it, but time ran out – the ball trickled in. There were more setbacks for Shilton: when Don Revie took over he preferred Ray Clemence, and then Ron Greenwood preferred rotation. It wasn't until Bobby Robson (Mars Virgo) took over that Shilton regained the No 1 position, but by then he was 32. Anyway, the fitness-fanatic keeper still went on to play a record 125 times for England, played in 3 World Cups, won 2 European Cup winner's medals, and only made two mistakes, and one of them wasn't even his fault – the 'Hand of God'. As Peter was entering a keeper's twilight years, Robson was grooming his successor: the technically excellent QPR goalie, David Seaman (Sun Virgo Mars Scorpio). David was lucky to be highly regarded by Robson and then find that he was also on the same wavelength as Taylor. The hard working, neat and tidy Seaman was expert at goalmouth geometry and went on to be a key player in an exceptional Arsenal defence: he won 2 Premier League and FA Cup doubles with the Gunners.

If it is possible to compare players with cars then Beckenbauer and Netzer would be Mercedes. Franz: black, sleek, diplomatic and reliable. Gunter: silver, soft topped and sporty with his blond hair flowing in the Black Forest breeze. Whilst Shilton and Seaman would be Bentleys. Peter: gold and spotless glinting past Royal Ascot, David: open topped, pony tail bobbing as he looked for somewhere to park outside Barbara Hepworth's secret garden.

LIBRA

We did it by playing football: pure, beautiful, inventive football.
Jock Stein

What looks logical in football is the wrong logic.
Arsene Wenger

It's a beautiful game.
Pele

Libra is an AIR sign ruled by Venus, the goddess of Love and Beauty. Libra in the sky is a fairly pale constellation of complex, variable, double and binary stars. It is visualised as the Scales, as its position in the zodiac holds the symbolic balance in the heavens. In the calendar the autumn equinox – when day and night are equal – also falls in Libra, and whereas in Taurus, Venus loves nature and ecological balance, in Libra she loves peace and harmony. In the Greek myths Venus has a powerful ally in her pursuit of justice: the wise, warrior goddess, Athene. Athene has an enviable record of success in battle, having

117

never been beaten – even Mars was defeated by her ingenious strategies. However, unlike Mars who fights for fun, Athene fights for peace.

Librans are sociable and enjoy being with family, friends, and loved ones. They are thoughtful, artistic, and diplomatic; they can see both sides of any argument and often find themselves in the middle of disputes playing peacemaker. In football the arguments may be about flair, fair play and upholding the Corinthian spirit – versus – doing what's necessary to get a result, even if it means playing ugly. As if to help Librans find the middle ground, events seem to conspire to swing them from one extreme to the other.

As players, they are at their best when they get on well with their teammates and are in a system that allows them to express their natural flair and creativity; they excel as ball-playing schemers; they are entertaining match-winners who prefer to play alongside a partner who complements their style. As coaches they have the knack of nurturing skill and developing latent talent.

THE DIPLOMATS

CHAIRMAN
SIMON JORDAN Crystal Palace

DIRECTOR OF FOOTBALL
TREVOR BROOKING FA

COACHES
ARSENE WENGER Arsenal
JOCK STEIN Celtic
JIMMY HOGAN MTK Budapest
SAM ALLARDYCE Blackburn Rovers

GOALKEEPERS
LEV YASHIN Dynamo Moscow
BERT TRAUTMANN Manchester City
JIM MONTGOMERY Sunderland
PAUL ROBINSON Blackburn Rovers
RONNIE SIMPSON Celtic

DEFENDERS
GEORGE COHEN Fulham
TOMMY GEMMEL Celtic
TONY ADAMS Arsenal
NEMANJA VIDIC Manchester United

MIDFIELD / FORWARDS
DUNCAN EDWARDS Manchester United
JOHNNY HAYNES Fulham
BOBBY CHARLTON Manchester United

PELE Santos
DIDI Botafogo
MICHAEL BALLACK Chelsea
TOTTI AS Roma
GEORGE WEAH AS Monaco
IAN RUSH Liverpool
JERMAINE DEFOE Spurs
NILS LIEDHOLM AC Milan
ANDREI SHEVCHENKO AC Milan
GUNNAR NORDAHL AC Milan
MATT LE TISSIER Southampton
JIMMY JOHNSTONE Celtic
RODNEY MARSH QPR
WOLFGANG OVERATH FC Koln
DIDIER DESCHAMPS Juventus

INSPIRATIONS
LORD NELSON
MAHATMA GANDHI
JOHN LENNON
HARRY HILL
MERLYN

Alfred North Whitehead, the British philosopher, discovered that...
The purpose of the Universe is to produce Beauty.

Pele, Didi

A philosophy shared by, perhaps, the greatest footballer of all, Edson Arantes do Nascimento (Sun Libra Mars Libra): Pele. His dad, Dondinho, was a well-respected part-time footballer for Brazilian side, Bauru. However, being paid by Bauru was dependent on Dondinho's performances; scoring goals wasn't the problem – he was prolific – making appearances was. A series of niggling injuries eroded his earning capacity and prematurely ended his career, plunging young Pele and the rest of the family into penury. The relatives rallied around, managed to put food on the table and keep a roof over their heads. The silver lining, however, was that Dondinho could spend almost all of his time coaching Edson. He taught him the goalscoring arts: how to shoot with either foot, with his back to goal, with his eyes closed, with his head, chest, knee, backside, instep, laces, and sole. And just when there was no more to be learnt from dad, a former Brazil international, Waldemar de Brito, turned up. Brito, now a coach with Santos, spotted Pele and rushed to telegram his manager...

I have found a boy who will be the greatest player in the world.

Pele's education continued under Waldemar: how to feel the flow of the game, how to develop awareness of the 4 directions, how to be in the right place at the right time, and how to do the right thing without thinking. Aged 15 he was ready to sign:

It was Waldemar's faith that made me believe I could be a star.

On the long train journey to Santos, Brito continued coaching...

He told me not to smoke, not to drink alcohol, eat right and don't take any notice of the media; finally, he told me to relax and play football as if I was back in Bauru having a kick-about with my mates.

Well-prepared physically, mentally, and emotionally he was ready to get into the first team. Fortunately,

You need Lady Luck on your side to get anywhere in football and at Santos – She was.

Just as Pele arrived the No 10, Vasconcellos, broke his leg. Pele was given his chance and took it. The following season he was called up by Brazil: it was World Cup year and he was selected. He made a huge impact. However, Pele wasn't the brightest star in Sweden, he was outshone by his teammate, midfield general and inventor of the 'falling leaf' pass – the pass that defies aerodynamics as it lobs aimlessly, hovers, and then gathers pace and direction – Didi (Sun Libra Mars Scorpio). Didi and Pele were on the same wavelength, they understood each other, linked seamlessly and, along with the stylish winger Mario Zagallo (Mars Libra), were unstoppable.

Brazil progressed smoothly to the semi-finals, as did the hosts, as did France and West Germany. Many felt that it would have been England in the semis but for the Munich air disaster and the loss of star players, including Duncan Edwards. Edwards had enjoyed a telepathic partnership with fellow Libran midfield general, Johnny Haynes: in the run up to the Finals they had helped England beat Denmark 4-1, the Republic of Ireland 5-1, and the mighty France 4-0. Anyhow, the Swedes with their own devastating Libran pair – Nils Liedholm and Gunnar Nordahl – swept Germany aside. Whilst France, with their soon-to-be-crowned 'European Footballer of the Year' Raymond Kopa (Sun Libra Mars Scorpio) linking seamlessly with legendary Just Fontaine (Mars Libra), were giving Brazil a fright – until Didi took control and Pele hit a breath-taking hat-trick.

Sweden started the World Cup final surprisingly quickly: in the fourth minute captain Liedholm surged forward to hit a well-placed shot, low and hard...1-0. Sweden were comfortable in possession and continued to look dangerous on the counter-attack, but the assertive Didi gradually wore them down with his sublime passing and by the end, Vava had scored 2, Pele 2, and Zagallo 1. Pele would go on to help them win the World Cup again in 1962, and then captain Zagallo's 1970 World Cup winners. In 1966 he won the hearts of the English with his sportsmanship, style and grace; at the end of his last match, in New York, he won the heart of America as he addressed the crowd from the centre circle – *love...love...LOVE.*

Pele became minister of sport, worked for the United Nations, and became football's unofficial global ambassador.

Nils Liedholm, Gunnar Nordahl, Andrei Shevchenko

Nils Liedholm (Sun Libra Mars Capricorn) was born on the 8th October 1922 in Valdemarsvik. Aged 16, he was the rising star of Swedish football, but it wasn't until his move to IFK Norrkoping, aged 24, that he fulfilled his potential. The key was teaming up with like-minded Gunnar Nordahl (Sun Libra Mars Virgo), together they transformed IFK and led Sweden to the gold medal at the 1948 London Olympics. Shortly afterwards he signed for AC Milan, but in those days Milan were not the club they are now – they had just gone 50 years without a single Scudetto. All that was about to change: in the next 8 years they won the championship 4 times. Nordahl still holds the goalscoring record for a season in Italy with 35, and remains AC Milan's top scorer with 210.

When Andrei Shevchenko (Sun Libra Mars Libra) scored his 100th goal the *Rossoneri* celebrated with him, and then burst into a rapturous chant: Gre-No-Li...Gre-No-Li...Gre-No-Li. Pardon? In remembrance of Gunnar Gren, Nordahl and Liedholm, and then they chanted: *Il Canoniere...Il Canoniere...Il Canoniere.* Pardon? For Nordahl's cannon-ball shots.

Liedholm was a tall, fair, straight-backed schemer, with clever distribution and the capability to make powerful dribbling runs and finish them with a fierce shot. He set the tempo for Sweden and Milan. He led his country in the 1958 World Cup final, but age was against them; Liedholm was 35 years old: Gren, 36: and Nordahl, 37. In the final, Didi stretched their defensive lines, whilst the zippy 17-year-old Pele proved too much for the old guard. Liedholm retired in 1961 and coached Milan twice – during his second spell he gave a 16-year-old, Paulo Maldini, his opportunity.

Sweden were the best European team in 1958: thanks to the irascible, English outcast George Raynor. When Raynor brought Sweden to Wembley, in 1959, he inflicted only the second defeat by continental opposition: few remember the occasion and fewer, the architect. Unlike 1953 when Gusztav Sebes' Magyars were universally acclaimed. However, at the celebratory cocktail party, Sebes was humble and generous in his praise for a football genius – a prophet – unknown in his homeland:

No other match in English football ever had as much impact as this one. When the soccer history of Hungary is told Hogan's name should be written in gold letters – he taught us how to play.

Jimmy Hogan

Jimmy Hogan (Sun Libra Mars Scorpio) was born on the 16th October 1882, in the soot-laden Lancashire mill town at the heart of the industrial revolution, Nelson. Curiously, Hogan's hometown was named in honour of England's heroic naval commander: the courageous hero of Trafalgar, Admiral Lord Horatio Nelson (Sun Libra Mars Scorpio). In addition to Hogan's strange geographical connection with Nelson, and the similarities in their astrological profiles, physically and experientially there were uncanny parallels. They were both slightly built with refined features that belied inner strength. According to contemporary reports, when anybody met the naval warrior in the flesh – this captain with the most feared reputation of any sailor on the Seven Seas – they were unimpressed. He didn't look like a hero. He was a charming God-fearing gentleman, but the more discerning reader of character noticed a steely glint in his one good eye that told the real story. Nelson and Hogan were both tactical geniuses. They were also torn between the loves of their lives; Horatio between his first love, Fanny, and the society beauty, Lady Hamilton: Jimmy, by the Church of Rome and Burnley Football Club. Aged 18, Jim was playing in the local leagues, either as an inside forward or as a left winger, weaving his magic around Pendle Hill to the rattle of 'spinning jennies'. He admired the Scottish quick pass-and-move approach and played the game with style and grace, which put him at odds with the rest of English football and its emphasis on power and aggression. As he was not prepared to compromise, his career went nowhere. His tactical beliefs – based on swift interplay, crisp passing, intuitive partnerships, and technical excellence – were considered eccentric and he was unable to find a coaching job. Believing that there was a witch hunt, he gathered his notes, had some business cards printed, and set sail for Holland. He did find a job there, enjoyed a little success, and then moved to Dresden Football Club. The Germans were more receptive to his philosophy; they liked his ideas about technical expertise, tactical preparation, mastery of the football and were keen to apply them. He encouraged his players to keep the ball on the 'carpet', inter-change positions, kick with both feet, be comfortable in possession of the ball and play without fear. Away from the pitch he continued to delve into the secrets of the game: seeking out the source of the invisible thread running through successful sides, and pondering that other great mystery – balance. In the next 3 years, Dresden won the league title 3 times. Then Jimmy moved to Austria for a new challenge, whilst back in Germany his protégé, Helmut Schoen, picked up where he left off. Following success in Vienna, he was invited to Hungary to make MTK Budapest invincible; the Hungarian Football Authorities were so impressed with Jimmy that they asked him to share his secrets with the national coach.

When Hungary came to Wembley in 1953, Hogan was semi-retired coaching the Aston Villa Youth team. He took some of his Villains to watch: sitting attentively beside him was Villa's future captain, Peter McParland (less than 4 years later Peter scored twice to help defeat Manchester United in the FA Cup final), what McParland saw that day made a lasting impression:

People sing the praises of Brazil (1970), but this was the best team I have ever seen play football.

Hogan was at odds throughout his life with the cynical way football was coached in England, whilst he felt that his homeland produced the most naturally talented players in the world, he believed that the players were badly led. Coaching had stagnated in his opinion, and he despaired at the level of instruction, which amounted to:

Give it some altitude, lads...come on get stuck in...work harder...make `em `ave it.

Physical intimidation, powerful heading, and shoulder barging was the norm, whereas Hogan believed in pure football. When he chose players for his squad, he demanded natural talent and intelligence. He studied the opposition and planned how to exploit their weaknesses; he analysed the grounds and took advantage of the elements. He had great respect for Herbert Chapman, but of all the coaches he ever met or worked with...

the best was Hugo Meisl (Sun Scorpio).

Johnny Haynes

Hogan may have been the best coach, Didi may have been the most creative player, Edwards may have been the most inspirational, but Pele said that the best passer of a football was Fulham's Johnny Haynes (Sun Libra Mars Leo). Johnny played a pass like a Zen Master. He was captain of Fulham and England; he was a stylish playmaker dictating the tempo of a game and commanding the ball. His teammate, and World Cup winning full back George Cohen (Sun Libra Mars Aquarius), remembered a Haynes work of art:

It was in a charity match on a wet and windy day, on a bumpy pitch in a long forgotten place: the ball zipped across the slippery surface and, with the slightest movement of his feet and adjustment of his weight, Johnny made a sublime pass inside the full back and into the stride of the on-rushing winger. A pure footballer – Johnny could give you goose bumps in any game, anytime, anywhere.

When the maximum wage was abolished, in 1962, Haynes became the first £100 a week player.

Bobby Charlton, Lev Yashin, Bert Trautmann

Such a vast sum didn't go unnoticed at Manchester United. Matt Busby was worried – what would his star players want? Bobby Charlton (Sun Libra Mars Capricorn) was earning £18 a week, but what was he worth now? Not as much as Johnny, yet. Bobby was still spending long stretches freezing on the left wing, whilst Johnny Giles (Mars Libra) was freezing on the other wing. Neither was happy about his position, nor his wages, but it was Giles who tackled Busby, not Bobby. Quite soon, Giles was making his name at Leeds United, whilst Busby was building a new side around Charlton.

Bobby was born on the 11th October 1937 in Ashington, into a family steeped in coal mining and football. As a boy, and when he was not dreaming of having a square meal, he would dream of being a professional footballer. He excelled at school, represented his county and aged 15, with just about every leading club in the country after his signature, joined Manchester United. He gelled with his teammates and immediately fell in love with Old Trafford. He also got on well with his coach, Jimmy Murphy (Sun Scorpio Mars Libra), they liked each other and Jimmy took the time to systematically turn Bobby into a professional. One by one Murphy stripped away Bob's amateurish beliefs about the game and replaced them with harsh realities. But a year of intensive tuition later, young Bob still believed that the team with the best players wins:

They don't, Bob, not until they understand the other side of football.

He taught Bobby how to elude the players who had been schooled in the destructive arts: how to take up the right position, how to receive the ball and the most important – how to shoot:

Keep your balance and let the power flow through your body: let it shoot.
And avoid the eyes of the keeper....especially if they are Bert's.

Bert Trautmann (Sun Libra Mars Libra) played for United's arch-rivals, City. He was born on the 22nd October 1923 and arrived in England as a German prisoner-of-war and settled in Manchester. Although heavily barracked at the start, he won the hearts of the Maine Road faithful with his courageous performances. None more memorable than the 1956 FA

Cup final: for the last 15 minutes he struggled on with a broken neck. In 2004 he was awarded the 'Order of the British Empire' for promoting German – British understanding. He may have been the best keeper in the Football League, but the best keeper in the world was the Russian 'black cat' Lev Yashin (Sun Libra Mars Scorpio), also born on the 22nd October.

On the 6th October 1956, Bobby fulfilled his boyhood dream when he made his first team debut against Charlton. Charlton Athletic were a mediocre team at the time, but for Bobby they were transformational. Just before kick-off his whole life flashed before him – all the people who had helped his dream come true were present: Uncle George, Jackie Milburn, and the Welsh wizard Murphy:

With all their support I knew the game would go well.

United won and Bobby scored twice. Everything Jimmy Murphy had drummed into him came out. Charlton went on to play 759 games for Manchester United, scoring 249 goals, winning the League Championship 3 times, the European Cup, the FA Cup and the World Cup. He would also break the England all-time goal scoring record, be voted 'European Footballer of the Year', and be welcomed in every football-loving country. He was knighted, appointed director of Manchester United, and was a staunch supporter of Sir Alex Ferguson (Sun Capricorn), when Alex was struggling.

Duncan Edwards

For all his successes though, Charlton never really got over the Munich disaster and the loss of colleagues, teammates, and especially his friend, and favourite player, Duncan Edwards (Sun Libra Mars Virgo):

Duncan didn't have a weakness in his game.

And in Murphy's judgement:
He is the best player I've ever seen.

Born in Dudley in 1936, Edwards was physically strong with a boxer's physique; he had stamina, a ferocious tackle, a powerful shot in both feet, and when he attacked the ball in the air, the opposition bounced off. He was skilful, artistic, and with Mars in Virgo, had perfect technique, and he never stopped running. He was combative and fair, and combined grace with explosive power. In his posthumously published book 'Tackle Soccer this Way' he advised his grieving fans:

A player should be able to defend and attack: a wing half should be perpetual motion.

The theme of his book was: respect your opponent and the fans, uphold the Corinthian spirit and play hard but fair; winning was important, of course, but it was more important to keep your integrity and have good manners. He disproved the old adage that there is no such thing as a one-man-team: he was the exception who proved the rule, he was the hero who could single-handed turn a game. He was the inspirational captain who could grasp victory from the jaws of defeat – Roy of the Rovers come to life. Duncan reminded his fellow professionals of their duties:

You are role models; youngsters look up to you and copy your every action – do your duty by them.

Jock Stein

Matt Busby built one great team around Edwards and another around

Charlton. In 1968 United were the first English club to win the European Cup, but Matt was the second Scot to do so. The season before, the European trail had been blazed by Jock Stein's (Sun Libra Mars Capricorn) Glasgow Celtic. Stein became immortal in May 1967 – according to Bill Shankly. His great achievement was made more remarkable by the origins of his team: every one of them was born within 30 miles of Glasgow. For a spell they swept all aside, *this team will never be beat,* he declared in Lisbon after beating the unbeatable Inter Milan.

Born on the 5th October 1922 into a tough, hard drinking, staunchly Protestant, Lanarkshire coal-mining community, Jock grew to be a sociable youth who joined his mates on a Friday night, after a gruelling week down the pit, drinking, larking, and fighting around town. But no one ever saw him take strong drink or join in the fighting. Neither was he a slave to tradition. He was a raw boned, tower-of-strength in defence of Albion Rovers – with a professional career going nowhere. Before and after games he co-analysed strategies and outcomes with the manager; he studied the strengths and weaknesses of the opposition and knew more about the players' temperaments, and tactics, than the coach. He managed his pit-deputy into giving him shift patterns that didn't interfere with training; he did everything he could to get on, but still got nowhere. Then one day he disappeared: non-league Llanelli had big ambitions to get into the Football League and offered Jock a full-time contract. It seemed too good to turn down, although, when the FA turned down the Welsh club's application, and when they were knocked out of the FA Cup in the early rounds, and then when the miners went on strike and the players were in dispute with management about money, and when his Glasgow home was burgled and his wife was homesick – he had had enough. He told the manager he was going back to Scotland – there were no hard feelings – packed his kit bag, sunk to his lowest point, and then...

It was laughable: Celtic wanted to sign me.

They wanted cover for their injury-prone centre half and Stein would be a stop-gap signing. As it turned out the unlucky centre half had sustained a serious injury and would be out for a long time, long enough for Stein to establish himself in the first team. He fitted in well, played well, Celtic were winning and they made him captain. When his long and successful playing career ended, he was appointed reserve-team coach; he was doing well, but realising that there would be no promotion – because of his religion – he moved on. He became manager of Dunfermline Athletic and, ironically, his first match was against Celtic and against all the odds, won. He guided them to the Scottish Cup final and, against all the odds, won. Overnight he was a cult hero – Merlyn – a magician from the Valleys.

Jock was warm and kindly; he was also a cool headed, strategic thinker who kept his players in a state of creative, nervous tension: when Ronnie Simpson (Sun Libra Mars Cancer) asked for a pay rise, he was shown the door and told that he would never play for Dunfermline again:

When I talk to supporters about the old days, they say how shrewd Jock was to transfer me to Celtic before he got there: as if it had all been a cunning plan.

In 1965 Celtic won their first trophy under Jock and 2 years later they were in the European Cup final: at half time they were 0-1 down to a dubious penalty. In the dressing room Stein was calm and calculating: he asked the players if they knew who they were, and just in case they had forgotten...they were wee Jimmy – Jinky – Johnstone (Sun Libra Mars Libra) the trickiest winger in Europe: they were Tommy – educated left foot – Gemmel (Sun Libra Mars Gemini): they were Ronnie – stalwart – Simpson: and they were Billy – Caesar – McNeill of Glasgow Celtic, and sent them out to keep playing pure football. As the referee headed down the tunnel, Stein lambasted him for his bad decision; as Herrera walked past, Jock spat bile and threw volcanic gestures of contempt. The green and white hoops were quickly into their stride...*square it...square it...square it*...screamed Gemmel. Tommy controlled it...the defender closed in...time stood still...*let fly*...1-1. With

20 minutes left, Inter were tiring, with 5 minutes to go they had all but gone...2-1. Jock ran onto the pitch, hugged Ronnie and hailed Billy. He was generous in victory, praised the high standard of refereeing, complimented Inter, and reflected:

There is not a prouder man on God's Earth than me at this moment. Winning was important, aye, but it was the way that we won that has filled me with satisfaction.

Arsene Wenger

In contrast, Arsene Wenger (Sun Libra Mars Leo) the professorial strategist, neglected the local talent and famously fielded an Arsenal team of 11 continentals, yet strangely,

It's a great regret to me that we have not played to our potential in Europe.

He was the first Frenchman to manage an English club. He joined in September 1996, *I want to give confidence to the players first*. But no one had heard of him in England: it was left to George Weah (Sun Libra Mars Leo) – 'World Footballer of the Year' – to sing his praises,

Arsene is the best coach I have ever played for. He brought the best out of me as a footballer and I would love to play for him again.

He inherited a successful side but they were boring. He studied his players, built up dossiers, considered their strengths, and laid down the law. He made changes, but the players were resistant so he compromised and gradually signed players on his wavelength. Within 3 years he had changed everything, now they were playing, *pretty football:*

Every manager can only be successful if he gets his team to play the way that he holds deeply within himself. I have an ideal of how football should be: there should be stability in the overall shape of the team – in the balance of the side, in the players who play well together – and I only change those things that give us a better chance of winning.

He won the Premiership title and the FA Cup double. He made inspirational Tony Adams (Sun Libra Mars Leo) captain and encouraged him to bring the ball forward: he evolved a style within a style. He introduced a new diet, vitamin injections, warm-downs, warm-ups, responsibility, less long runs, more individual freedom, osteopaths, minerals, pure water, and Arsenal were never outplayed – until the 25th February 2001. Then the Gunners were hit for 6 by Manchester United – their worst defeat in 50 years – a goal down after 5 minutes, they fell apart. There was much analysing to be done...

What went wrong? Was it being forced by injury to make a change in the back 4? Was it Wiltord and Henry? Every time they play together we seem to lose – maybe Bergkamp really is the key.

The following season he won the Double, again.

Arsene Wenger was born on the 22nd October 1949 in Strasbourg, a city that was once German but was now French. As a child he thought the most important thing in the world was football; his early idols were Pele and the German playmaker, Wolfgang Overath (Sun Libra Mars Gemini). On leaving school he turned professional with RC Strasbourg and, although falling short of international class, helped them win the French title in 1979. For a short spell he combined the coaching, playing, and captaincy duties at the club. After an inauspicious start in management at Nancy, he moved on to AS Monaco and won the League title in his first season. The key was signing the ball-playing Spurs midfielder Glenn Hoddle (Mars Libra), and successfully linking him with Weah – supplied by Hoddle's defence-splitting passes George became the deadliest finisher in the world.

In 1991 Wenger won the French Cup and job offers rolled in: Bayern Munich were interested, and so were France, but as a principled man he wouldn't break his contract, nevertheless, the following season he was sacked. He enjoyed some success in Japan before joining Arsenal. He asked fellow 'J League' manager Stuart Baxter to assist him, but Baxter is a Leo...*hmmmm*...and had ambitions of his own. As the manager of one of Europe's leading football clubs and business empires – every home game in 2008 grossed over £3M in revenues, whilst the cost of the new stadium was £350,000,000 – Arsene is in demand for both his football wisdom and business acumen. He is happy to share his thoughts at international conferences...

People perform well when they are happy, when they feel needed and when they feel useful. It is always difficult to find the right balance between making players happy and demanding that they always perform at their highest level. Therefore I am not a friend to them; I am objective and logical and, of course, I must also balance the books. (By January 2010 the Arsenal debt had been reduced to £200,000,000).

A few weeks later Wenger was put to the test: following a disappointing defeat, captain Gallas was openly critical of his teammates for, *lacking pride*. Wenger stripped him of the captaincy. Objective? When his former captain, and France captain, Thierry Henry, cheated against Ireland in a crucial 2010 World Cup 'qualifier', Wenger was asked for his views, *I support Thierry, but I do not condone what he did. He should have confessed to the referee*. Logical?

When Arsene talks of the, *wrong logic*, in football is he suggesting that the right logic is astro-logical? Whether he is or not, if he hadn't been a success in football he wouldn't have become a business astrologer – he would have fought for world peace.

GLENN
HODDLE   ♏.

SCORPIO

I was waiting for my teammates to embrace me,
but no one came.
Diego Maradona

Glenn (Hoddle) was Maradona without pace.
Ossie Ardiles

I firmly believe in astrology.
Luis Felipe Scolari

Scorpio is a WATER sign ruled by both Mars and Pluto. It is, perhaps, the most complex and powerful of all the signs. As we mentioned earlier, Mars is the god of war, however, in Aries he is an impulsive warrior who rushes headlong at the enemy, whereas in Scorpio, he is more calculating and waits for the right time to strike. Pluto's characteristics are more difficult to grasp because he lives in the shadowy underworld for half the year and wears a helmet of invisibility, nevertheless, an idea can be obtained from the words – plutonium: used in making atomic weapons, and – plutocrat: someone with enormous power and wealth.

In the sky, Scorpio is one of the bigger constellations, but it isn't easy to get a clear view; wherever you are on Earth it always seems to be difficult to see. However, it does contain some of the biggest and most distinctive celestial bodies, including the massive red star, Antares – in ancient Egypt and Greece temples were aligned to it. Scorpio holds some of the deepest mysteries of life and death, of heaven and hell, of change and transformation, of contrasts and extremes: it embraces the loftiest and deepest of human feelings. Of the 12 tribes of Israel – symbolic of the 12 character types – the tribe of Gad represents Scorpio. When Gad's mother was giving birth she cried out in her labour, *an army cometh*.

Scorpio's best known symbol is the scorpion, but there are others: the snake, the eagle, and the phoenix. The snake grows by shedding its skin, the eagle soars to heaven, and the phoenix rises from the ashes of defeat.

In Libra the days were filled with love and beauty, with the elegance and artistry of Pele and the sportsmanship of Bobby Charlton. In Scorpio there is intensity, passion, and explosive energy.

THE EAGLES

OWNER
ROMAN ABRAMOVIC Chelsea

COACHES
CARLOS MENOTTI Argentina
GLENN HODDLE England
RON GREENWOOD England
GUUS HIDDINK Russia
LUIS FELIPE SCOLARI Brazil
DUNGA Brazil
MARK HUGHES Wales

GOALKEEPERS
PETER SCHMEICHEL Manchester United
EDWIN VAN DER SAR Manchester United
HARRY GREGG Manchester United

DEFENDERS
RON HARRIS Chelsea
NORMAN HUNTER Leeds United
DAVE MACKAY Spurs
RON YEATS Liverpool
CHRIS MORGAN Sheffield United
RIO FERDINAND Manchester United
THOMAS VERMAELEN Arsenal

MIDFIELD
MARTIN PETERS West Ham United
ENZO FRANCESCOLI Marseille
JOE COLE Chelsea
PAUL SCHOLES Manchester United

DARRON GIBSON Manchester United
NANI Manchester United
ALAN SMITH Newcastle United
JOHNNY GILES Leeds United
JEAN-MARC BOSMAN Standard Liege

FORWARDS
WAYNE ROONEY Manchester United
GERD MULLER Bayern Munich
JEAN-PIERRE PAPIN Marseille
GARRINCHA Botafogo
MARADONA Boca Juniors
MARCO VAN BASTEN Ajax
JOHN BARNES Watford
IAN WRIGHT Arsenal
MARK HATELEY AS Monaco

INSPIRATIONS
PICASSO
ALBERT CAMUS
LESTER PIGGOTT
PRINCE CHARLES
HIAWATHA

As players, Scorpios are at their best when they are emotionally fired-up and believe in what they are doing. They are determined and fearless; they are more powerful than they look and can change the course of a game with a clinical pass, a deadly strike or a hurtful tackle, but they need to take care not to *go over the top*. Djwal Khul, a Tibetan holy man, said there are 2 great powers in the universe: Love and Change, and the more powerful is Change. Librans love the game – Scorpios change it.

Maradona

On the 30th October 1960, in the Evita Peron hospital in the shanty town suburbs of Buenos Aires, a plutonian baby with super-human powers was delivered: Diego Armando Maradona (Sun Scorpio Mars Cancer). Living on the wrong side of the economic and political tracks in Argentina – with no television, no car, no computer – there were no distractions for young Diego:

The Great White Beard knew what He was doing when He gave me La Tota and Don Diego for parents and that long walk to fetch water every day.

Diego's journey began at Los Cebollitas: wearing the No 10 shirt he inspired his side to 136 wins in a row. Aged 13, in the final of the Evita junior Cup, he was living in his future:

I was trying to read the flight of the ball when my hand scored.

And....

They said I beat seven players to score my second, but I only beat five.

Aged 15 he made his debut for Argentinos, and after only 11 games, was called up by the Argentine head coach, El Flaco – the thin man – Menotti (Sun Scorpio Mars Libra). Carlos Menotti had been appointed, by the military Junta, to win the World Cup that Argentina was about to host. He was a great admirer of Maradona and at their first training camp, told Diego that he would be a substitute in the next match and, if all went well, would make his international debut. The game did go well and, aged 16, Diego's dream came true,

*I loved that thin man and I'll never forget that he gave me my big chance, and I will never forget that he left me out of the 1978 World Cup squad – I swore I would get **revenge**.*

He trained 3 *times harder* than anybody else, fuelled by anger he joined Argentina's youth squad and willed them to victory in the World Youth Cup final:

Being captain made me responsible, but even so I was fixated on revenge. I was obsessed with proving him wrong; he had made a big mistake and I wanted Argentina to know it. I went into the showers before the game to pray. I got down on my knees and asked the Great White Beard for help; even when we went 0-1 down, I never lost faith – we scored three in quick succession – I lifted the Cup, thanked God, and savoured my revenge.

Maradona's first international goal was scored at a special place: Hampden Park, Glasgow. The ground where his hero, Alfredo di Stefano (Sun Cancer), had scored a hat-trick in the 1960 European Cup final, *in celebration of La Tota conceiving.* As he continued to establish his reputation, offers came in from leading clubs: he chose Boca Juniors...

It was mad – they were broke and the coach didn't like me – so what, it was my dream to play at the Bombonera.

However, the fans loved him...

I was freezing up front – it was sleeting as if the South Pole had shifted – in my first derby, v River Plate, the ball was swung into the danger zone...I swooped...left foot...right foot...wham...bang...goal...and then I felt the love of the Bomboneros. Then I was warm.

He became so popular that he had to stay home for fear of being mobbed. He couldn't go to the beach, he couldn't go shopping: he was unhappy. He stayed in his apartment and dreamed of joining Barcelona, but when his dream came true – it was a nightmare. Barcelona played a system that he didn't like and that didn't suit him...

They wouldn't pass; no one understood me, except Berndt Schuster (Mars Scorpio) and he was persecuted too.

He got injured and then fell seriously ill. He was at his lowest point when the president intervened:

He sacked the manager and brought in El Flaco – now 3 people understood me.

Barcelona won everything with Maradona, but Menotti couldn't change everything: it was still Barcelona, still the wrong city for Diego, *the place was ill-fated.* He was dogged by injuries and they were about to get worse...

Andoni – the Butcher of Bilbao – came up on my blind side and snapped my ankle. I prayed to the Great White Beard and a miracle happened: in 106 days I was healed.

Whilst off the field all his investments were going down the drain. He decided he needed to make a new start, and chose Naples,

to be the idol of the poor. Napoli were bottom of the League and, if I was going to help them be champions, I needed a new body: I prayed to the Great White Beard and in 40 days He rebuilt me.

He went on to a special diet, trained harder than ever and, the following season, Napoli won the Scudetto for the first time in 60 years and, on the way, Maradona broke the goal scoring record of the legendary Luigi Riva (Sun Scorpio Mars Scorpio). Surely things couldn't get any better: they didn't. He was so popular he couldn't go to the shops, he couldn't go to a restaurant, he couldn't go out. He was unhappy, then he was linked with drugs and banned:

*The club didn't stick by me, so I returned to Buenos Aires with all the **branca** (anger) in the universe. They called me a delinquent, drug addict but I kept quiet. I thanked Him for my family, for my fitness, for my skill, for my branca and asked Him to help me get revenge.*

Back in Naples: at the final whistle...

*I shouted from my soul: Scudetto championi. The nightmare season was over – well not quite – I was called for a drugs test, but I know myself and know that I am not a delinquent drug addict and this was my proof – I was clean – and I savoured my **revenge**.*

In 1986 another dream came true when he was made captain of Argentina for their World Cup campaign, however, in the lead up to the Finals nothing was going right:

We were persecuted by the media, nobody liked us – not even our own fans – but we had something special, something indestructible – solidarity.

Nevertheless, results were rubbish: they lost to France in the build up, then were crushed by Norway. The media called for the head of the manager – Maradona stuck by him. With 30 days to go to the Finals the training camp was thrown into disarray by the walk-out of former captain, Daniel Passarella. Just when it seemed that things couldn't get any worse, they didn't: the team gelled,

*There was spirit, intensity, unity, and then the final came early. They had invaded our islands in 1833, refused to give them back, and then when we tried to force them out they shot a lot of our boys – for what? We blamed the England players for everything. This was more than a football match, it was for justice – for **revenge**.*

It was a game that would be remembered for the best goal and the worst. Steve Hodge (Sun Scorpio Mars Leo) had the ball to the right of the England penalty area, he tried to clear it but it sliced off his boot:

Hodge sliced the 'banana': it looped up and into the zone...I challenged the giant...God dazzled the officials – even the great Shilton couldn't see at the moment of Truth – and raised my left arm in triumph, shouting at the BBC: go weeping to church, England.

The second was voted the most beautiful goal of the 20th century:

*I received the ball on half way and darted between Reid and Beardsley, raced away from Hodge and Hoddle, swerved past Butcher, Fenwick was tracking back, holding off...dancing beside. I was ready to pass to Jorge, Valdano was signalling, I dummied Fenwick, he bought it...I carried on. Fenwick followed...still holding off...Butcher was hacking back...I darted inside – darted outside...Fenwick alongside....now I'm closing in...now I'm facing Shilton...I can't see the goal – he is a giant. Now I'm on the exact spot I was in `81 when I shot and missed: it goes through my mind, the words of my little brother echoing around the Azteca and inside my head 'Go around him dummy – slide it in, slide it in.' I dummy Shilton, he buys it. GooooaaaaLLLLLLEllll ...crunchhh...aaaghhh – butchered – a little cut, a lot of **revenge**.*

I read in the papers that I had beaten seven players on the way to goal, but that was an illusion, I only beat five.

He supported President Menem's election campaign. He worked for UNICEF; organised charity football events; was dubbed 'Master Inspirer of Dreams' by the Oxford University Union, and shared his secrets with the students: *love – keep loving the football, keep loving the game, keep loving each other.* He fell out with the Pope; had a bitter disagreement with the head of the Argentine FA (Grondona – Mars Scorpio); had audiences with Fidel Castro, and had his hero tattooed on his right arm:

The greatest Argentinian, some call him terrorist, some say butcher, but I call him Che – Freedom Fighter – Guevara.

And then his dream ended...

The drugs test was positive; I said goodbye to all those who had loved me, to all those who hated me, to those who had butchered me....addios to the vendettas. Some say I hate them when we have a bitter dispute, but I say – no – I hate no-one. I am on good terms with everybody: even with Andoni, even Pele, even the mad dogs. I love everyone. The only people I hate are those who abuse children and, steal. And so it was finished, the game – the life I loved – finito.

Or so he thought – God had other plans. When Argentina needed a new manager he phoned his old adversary, Grondona – *we were on the same wavelength: we were both hot heads* – and told him why Argentina needed Maradona:

The Great White Beard knew what he was doing when He gave me the opportunity; and just to let me know He was still by my side, I had a perfect start....1-0....at Hampden Park.

Nonetheless, in the lead up to the 2010 World Cup Finals nothing was going right: the Argentine media persecuted him, former stars were critical of his tactics and team selections, only Grondona and his captain, Mascherano (Mars Scorpio), stuck by him.

Glenn Hoddle, Ron Greenwood

There were many leading European coaches talent spotting at the 1978 World Cup Finals. Among them was the newly installed manager of Tottenham Hotspur, Keith Burkinshaw. Burkinshaw came away from the tournament impressed with the Agentine midfielders, Ossie Ardiles (Mars Scorpio) and Ricky Villa (Mars Scorpio). So when he was advised that they wanted to play in Europe, he was happy to oblige:

Looking back some people say that signing the Argentines to blend with Glenn Hoddle (Sun Scorpio Mars Libra) was a master-stroke, but it was serendipity. It just happened, they just clicked. What a trio that was though; we went on to win the FA Cup twice and the UEFA Cup; Ossie and Ricky brought the best out of Glenn.

There is no doubt in my mind that Hoddle was the most skilful player in English football. I recall going to Forest – the European Cup holders – and Glenn destroyed them. I recall going to Feyenoord – when Johan Cruyff was their star – beforehand, Cruyff was dismissive of Glenn, he said that Hoddle was nothing special, that he didn't know what all the fuss was about. As Cruyff was speaking, I could see the hairs on the back of Glenn's neck bristling and steely determination in his eyes. I didn't say anything, I didn't need to, I could tell that he had accepted the challenge – it was personal – it was Hoddle v Cruyff. By half time we were winning 4-0, Glenn had destroyed them.

When people ask if I've any regrets about my career, I say, yes – if I'd trusted in Hoddle more, we would have won more; talent like his comes along once in a month of Sundays – he was magnificent.

In 1986 David Pleat arrived at Spurs and Hoddle found himself marginalised. In November, whilst sitting on the subs' bench he realised he had to leave: Pleat's style didn't suit him, but it wasn't getting the desired results either, so David changed tack. He decided to recall Hoddle and play Ardiles and Hodge alongside. It worked. The midfield clicked, results improved, the season was saved, but the damage was done. His teammates noticed that he was disillusioned – not just with Spurs – with English football: Glenn would come back from international duty disappointed and frustrated. He was widely believed to be the most gifted playmaker in Europe, if not the world, but couldn't get a regular place for club or country:

Although I resented it at the time, now I can see that being dropped by Spurs was the best thing that could have happened. The manager wanted me to do things I didn't like in a system that didn't suit me. It made me think about what I really wanted; I decided to concentrate on my own game, not try to please him.

Paris St Germain were interested but slow to conclude a deal. Napoli were also interested, but it was Monaco's Arsene Wenger, after being urged by his centre forward Mark Hateley (Sun Scorpio Mars Scorpio), who signed him.

I had watched tapes of Glenn and could see that he was a very skilful player; it was always Hoddle who provided the best passes for the forwards.
Arsene Wenger

If Hoddle had been born in France he would have had 150 caps and been a hero.
Michel Platini

If Hoddle had been born in Holland he would have been as big a star as Cruyff, Van Basten, and me.
Ruud Gullit

Burkinshaw didn't trust his talent and Ron Greenwood (Sun Scorpio Mars Libra), the coach who gave Hoddle his first international cap, never really trusted him either. On his England debut Glenn scored a spectacular goal from 20 yards in a 2-0 win over Bulgaria. He was on cloud 9. The media built him up, he was an overnight sensation and they predicted great things: a long and glittering career and at least 150 caps – in fact he was dropped for the next game. That became the pattern for the next decade: in total he won 53 caps. Years later Greenwood explained,

Glenn didn't have enough arrogance.

The former Bradford Park Avenue and Chelsea player had made his name establishing the West Ham football academy – renowned for its emphasis on skill, artistry and entertainment. To Ron's eternal credit he also developed world-class talents: Martin Peters (Sun Scorpio Mars Gemini), Trevor Brooking (Sun Libra Mars Scorpio), Bobby Moore, and then transformed a mediocre wing half into a hat-trick scoring World Cup hero.

Curiously though, when he became England manager he seemed torn between pursuing football the right way – the West Ham way – or conforming to the national stereotype. At the start of his reign he picked both the elegant Brooking and the stylish Hoddle, but when they didn't deliver immediate results – only press criticism – he changed tack. So for one game he would pick Brooking, for the next Hoddle, for the next game neither, then both, then Hoddle, then Brooking, and so on. In spite of his apparent indecision, England qualified for the 1982 World Cup Finals and returned home head held high, undefeated, and unlucky not to progress into the later stages. Towards the end of his career, those who had urged Ron to abandon entertaining football and play to England's 'strengths' turned on him: they criticised him for playing, *boring football,* for, *being indecisive,* and for not giving Hoddle, *an extended run.* Ron resigned.

Bobby Robson was the next manager; he was also undecided about Glenn.

Whilst he recognised his undoubted talent, Bob didn't believe Hoddle could tackle or head the ball, and explained why he wasn't a regular,

Glenn doesn't have enough work-rate.

Aged 6, Glenn would sit on the front step of his house in Harlow clutching his football and patiently wait for his dad to come home from work. Then they would go straight to the park and practise until late into the starry night. Aged 12, Glenn told his friends that he would play for England and that one day he would manage his country. Aged 18, he was playing for Spurs but niggling injuries were hampering his progress. His girlfriend, Michelle Drewery, said that her mum could cure his dodgy knee with *faith*. Sceptical but curious, Glenn met Michelle's mother, Eileen, and she explained that Love could – not only mend a broken heart – it could mend a wounded knee.

Aged 32, Hoddle became the player/manager at Swindon Town. He was successful, got them promoted and caught the eye of the Chelsea chairman, Ken Bates, moved to Stamford Bridge and did well, so well in fact that he was offered the England job:

They have changed in Europe and if we don't open our minds and innovate then we will be left behind. That's where Hoddle comes in – he can transform English football.
Bert Millichip (FA)

Under Hoddle's direction England qualified for the 1998 World Cup Finals, and on the way he gave second chances to Tony Adams (Sun Libra), Matt Le Tissier (Sun Libra), and Paul Gascoigne (Mars Libra). England progressed comfortably into the second round. Now old rivals would be re-engaged: Argentina. The game got off to an explosive start: Seaman (Mars Scorpio) gave away a penalty...Owen struck back... England went ahead...Beckham flicked out at Simeone...Argentina equalised. England's 10 men were resolute in defence and dangerous on the counter-attack. Deadlocked at the end of extra time, the contest went to a penalty shoot–out...Batty missed his kick...England were knocked out. Beckham was blamed: Hoddle, acclaimed. In November 1998, Glenn's religious views were published in the *Times* and his beliefs broadcast on TV – beliefs that the soul survives death and we reap what we sow – he was ridiculed, leading politicians took potshots at him, and on the 2nd February 1999 England's best manager since Ramsey was hounded out of office.

In 2007 Glenn was inducted into the Football Hall of Fame. In 2008 he established the Glenn Hoddle Academy: a football school offering second chances to talented lads, who, through no fault of their own, have fallen by the football wayside.

Roman Abramovich, Luis Felipe Scolari

In 2003 Bates sold Chelsea to a Russian plutocrat: Roman Abramovic (Sun Scorpio Mars Virgo). Abramovic had amassed billions in the USSR as the former state owned industries were broken up in the 1990s. He transformed his one-man-business into one of the biggest and most powerful companies in the world. He was appointed Governor of Chukotka and gifted the remote, poverty-stricken province over £100M from his personal fortune to build schools and housing. He sponsored a national Academy of Football with the aim of constructing pitches across Russia, and organised a series of youth sports programmes; he was awarded the 'Order of Honour'.

His aim at Chelsea was to establish them as a global brand to rival Manchester United: between 2003 and '09 he invested around £700M in the project. He lifted the ban imposed by the previous chairman on Chelsea favourite 'chopper' Harris. He bought world-class players, at inflated prices, and was accused of distorting the transfer market. He appointed the European Cup winning manager, Jose Mourinho, and in 3 years Chelsea won 5 major trophies. Nevertheless, in spite of finishing ahead of Manchester United, his relationship with Mourinho was fraught and it ended with the sack. Avram Grant reigned briefly, despite Chelsea finishing runners-up in both the Champions League and Premier League. There were rumours that Grant's replacement would be the Reds' former deadly finisher Mark Hughes (Sun Scorpio Mars Sagittarius), but in the summer of 2008 Luis Felipe Scolari (Sun Scorpio Mars Sagittarius) was appointed on a salary of £5.5M – only Jose, now at Inter Milan, was earning more. At the time Scolari – a World Cup winner with Brazil, successful with Portugal, and twice winner of the Copa Libertadores – was, probably, the best manager around, but...

I'm not Mourinho – I'm more modest. I don't say that I will win 10 titles – I say I will try. Throughout the world if you ask the players about me, they say 'I like Scolari because he is a true man'. I will remain so until my last day in Chelsea. If I need to criticise a player, I will do it face-to-face; I am not afraid to upset players and, have no doubt, I will upset some Chelsea players.

What were you like as a player?

I was tough. I was an uncompromising defender in the Brazilian league. Although I am from Brazil I put defence first; I am not against the beautiful game, don't misunderstand me, but if it was necessary to play ugly to win, I did.

And as a coach?

I am disciplined and organised. I am practical, logical, and mystical. I was the most successful coach in South America; when Brazil were struggling to qualify for the 2002 World Cup Finals they asked for my help: not only did we qualify – we won it!

Mystical?

I am a devout Roman Catholic. Every time we play my backroom-staff carry a statue of Our Lady of Fatima to the game. I take a sports psychologist with us. I consult astrologers. I am a student of ancient Chinese warfare.

Warfare?

Football is war: the team is my army, the pitch is the battlefield. 2,500 years ago Sun Tzu, a Chinese general, wrote 'the Art of Warfare'; he summed it up: 'if you know yourself and your enemy, you will come out of a hundred battles victorious.'

And your relationship with Mr Abramovic?

We are on the same wavelength: we respect each other and discuss the players.

But there were unconfirmed reports that key players were unhappy with the new regime, that they didn't like the strict discipline and that a delegation went to the chairman to complain and undermine Scolari's authority. There was disunity and results were suffering – after 36 games he was sacked. There was speculation that Hughes would be the new manager, but Guus Hiddink (Sun Scorpio Mars Sagittarius) got the job:

How do you feel about working for Mr Abramovic, combining the Russia job with managing Chelsea?

We are on the same wavelength: we respect each other, and speak a lot. We discuss the players: who should play, what is their best positions and so on. It will only be until the end of the season; we have started well, so, we will see.

Ron Harris, Johnny Giles, Ron Yeats, Dave Mackay, Norman Hunter

In the 1960s and 70s Ron – chopper – Harris (Sun Scorpio Mars Scorpio) was the captain of Chelsea and, arguably, the hardest player in the Football League: at a time when, arguably, the English League was the toughest in the world. Every leading team had their brutal streak: Leeds United had an intimidating midfield, including Norman – bites yer legs – Hunter (Sun Scorpio Mars Gemini), Johnny Giles (Sun Scorpio Mars Libra), and Billy Bremner (Mars Scorpio). Liverpool had the colossus, Ron Yeats (Sun Scorpio Mars Aquarius), whilst Spurs had mighty Dave Mackay (Sun Scorpio Mars Virgo).

Perhaps the dirtiest match in English history was the 1970 FA Cup final between Leeds and Chelsea. Billed as a 'battle royal' it did not disappoint. Following a combative draw at Wembley, the game was replayed at a muddy Old Trafford. Leeds started brightly. They were capable of playing entertaining football and were crisply into their stylish stride. Elusive wing-play from Eddie Gray was causing havoc in the Chelsea ranks and Leeds forged into a 2-1 lead. They were coasting to victory – or so we thought – as Gray received the ball wide on the left...crrrunccchhhhhhh...the Old Trafford timbers shivered...Eddie was felled: 'chopper' had turned the tie.

Jean-Marc Bosman

It wasn't only the English sides who fielded brutal tacklers, Standard Liege had their own hard man: Jean-Marc Bosman (Sun Scorpio Mars

Leo). Although his most destructive tackle wasn't made on the football pitch, but on the football 'establishment'. It was Bosman who challenged the legality of the transfer system and after a long and expensive battle in the European courts, secured a victory that changed football: now players would no longer be possessions of a club – kept on minimum wages or bought and sold at the whim of a chairman – they would have the opportunity to move freely and become millionaires. The best players did just that, but Jean-Marc wasn't one of the best players and retired a year after his historic battle, persecuted, unemployable, penniless, and without a family life after his wife left him because of the stress:

It took courage and determination to win player freedoms; in those days players were earning a few hundred pounds a week, now they can earn a few hundred pounds an hour, but I paid the price and now that I'm broke they don't want to know. I can't get a job in football because I made enemies in every boardroom. I am bitter and resentful; my bitterness runs so deep it has affected my dog – when we walk down the Liege High Street and she sees a selfish footballer, she bites his legs.

Marco Van Basten

Maradona scored the best goal of the 20th century and two years later another Scorpio scored, probably, the second best goal. Marcel van Basten (Sun Scorpio Mars Sagittarius), a Dutch goalscoring legend, struck a volley from an impossible angle in the European Championship final, v Russia.

Born on Halloween 1964 in Utrecht, in what his mother described as, *a life and death struggle*. The 3 times 'European Footballer of the Year', 'World Player of the Year', and top scorer for Ajax 4 seasons running with 117 goals in 112, obsessed about football from the age of 6. He needed to know everything: every night young Marcel demanded a bedtime story from his dad and it had to be about football or he refused to sleep. Aged 10, he was bought a blackboard and chalks for Christmas and bedtime stories had a tactical context. He demanded that dad draw a real match scenario on the board and take questions...

What should I do if it comes to me with my back to goal? Where should I go if I lose possession? How do you create time and space?

They contemplated shots that tested the quantum world. They visualised fantasy moves and imagined how to manifest them. Having mentally achieved the impossible he cuddled his favourite Ajax ball and nodded off. As a child he suffered for football: he endured unbearable growing pains but continued to play hard. When he wasn't playing, he was studying the masters and copied their tricks: the Ruud Krol feint, the Cruyff turn, the Waddle step-over. The doctors warned him that if he didn't stop, he would spend his middle-age crippled, but he carried on regardless. He battled on but the injuries came more frequently and the burning pain seared deeper into his joints forcing his early retirement.

Although as a player he always said that he would never manage, when the chance came to coach Holland, he took it and led them in a successful Euro 2008 campaign.

SAGITTARIUS

Lucky breaks make all the difference.
Steve Perryman

Mancini has been blessed.
Inter Milan fans

I'm a very lucky guy.
Andy Gray

Sagittarius is a FIRE sign ruled by the benevolent god of thunder, Jupiter. Jupiter is the biggest planet in the solar system, more than 1,000 times the volume of Earth. It is the strongest planet with a magnetic field 20,000 times that of Earth's and, for its size, it is deceptively quick, rotating more than twice as fast as we are.

When Galileo landed on Jupiter in 1995, the probe had 1 hour to gather whatever evidence it could before it was wrecked by heat and pressure; just long enough to confirm the huge planet's mythical power and nobility: detecting large quantities of krypton and photographing titanic streaks of lightning – 1,000 times more brilliant than the brightest on Earth – flashing through the skies.

Jupiter is the planet of plenty, the bringer of abundance and good fortune, the inspirer of optimism and faith. Jupiter expands the mind and impulses the Sagittarian to seek higher knowledge and understanding. Sagittarians love the great outdoors and are freedom-loving adventurers who enjoy flights of fancy, but not just in the mind, they also like to travel and enjoy experiencing all cultures. They are honest, frank and forthright; they are warm, kind, generous, and philosophical. Everything they do seems to turn out well, and everything they touch seems to turn to gold. If there is such a thing as a lucky star sign to be born under, then this is it.

THE ARCHERS

CHAIRMEN
KEN BATES Leeds United
DAVE WHELAN Wigan Athletic

COACHES
ROBERTO MANCINI Manchester City
NEIL WARNOCK Crystal Palace
GEORGE GRAHAM Arsenal
DENNIS WISE Leeds United
KEVIN BLACKWELL Sheffield United
SIMON GRAYSON Leeds United

GOALKEEPER
PAUL COOPER Ipswich Town

DEFENDERS
ASHLEY COLE Chelsea
JOHN TERRY Chelsea
PAUL McGRATH Aston Villa
STEVEN WARNOCK Blackburn Rovers
LEIGHTON BAINES Everton

MIDFIELD
ALAN MULLERY Spurs
STEVE PERRYMAN Spurs
DAVID BATTY Leeds United
BILLY BREMNER Leeds United
TIM CAHILL Everton
MICHAEL ESSIEN Chelsea

FORWARDS
GEOFF HURST West Ham United
PETER LORIMER Leeds United
MICHAEL OWEN Liverpool
JOE JORDAN Leeds United
GARY LINEKER Spurs
ANDY GRAY Everton
BRIAN LITTLE Aston Villa
CHRIS WADDLE Spurs
MICK CHANNON Southampton
DEAN ASHTON West Ham United
JERMAINE BECKFORD Leeds United
RYAN GIGGS Manchester United
DAVID HIRST Sheffield Wednesday

INSPIRATIONS
FREDDIE FLINTOFF
NIJINSKI
FRANKIE DETTORI
MARK TWAIN
WRECKLESS ERIC
ROBIN HOOD

Is it too good to be true? There is of course another side to the sign. One of the symbols of Sagittarius is the centaur, the mythic half man / half horse. Chiron, the king of the centaurs, gives us a deeper insight into the Sagittarian. He was an astrologer, healer, and coach to the heroes: Achilles, Jason, and Hercules. However, he was injury prone and following an accident in training – hit by an arrow above the knee – he became known as *the wounded healer*. Although lucky in everything else, the Sagittarian, therefore, needs to be on his guard against the slings and arrows of pulls and leg strains. Hopefully, he can find a coach who understands him and guides him to his full potential, which is of course – HUGE. When their playing days are over, and if they don't become coaches or physios, they make opinionated pundits and engaging free spirits – though, sometimes, they would do better to hold their horses.

Geoff Hurst

When Alf Ramsey was appointed England manager, Geoff Hurst (Sun Sagittarius Mars Aries) was a mediocre wing half at West Ham United. Hurst made his debut for the Hammers in February 1960, but only made 2 appearances that season. The following year he only played in 6 matches and was struggling to make any impact at all in first class football. However, Geoff was fortunate to have Ron Greenwood as his manager: Ron saw something special, something perhaps no-one else could see, but it meant his game had to undergo a complete transformation. It started with a new shirt and a more appropriate number – 10 – and a new Geoff beckoned. He was detailed to support the clinical finisher, Budgie Byrne, and encouraged to learn all he could from the more accomplished striker, but as a partnership it didn't work: they had contrasting styles and didn't gel. Regardless, Geoff was keen, and Greenwood, patient. On the training pitch Ron worked hard to hone his technique and teach him the striker's craft:

How to sustain offensive momentum: how to create space: how to slow time: how to receive the ball, swivel-and-shoot in one movement: and, how to volley.

Geoff improved – 13 goals, then a 14 goal season – by Christmas 1965 he was prolific, including a 6 goal haul against the Black Cats of Sunderland. When he was interviewed by the national press, honest Geoff admitted that he had knocked one in with his hand. He was blasted in the newspapers the following day; when his dad read the reports, he was blasted again. So what, he had caught the eye of Alf Ramsey and next year was World Cup year. On New Year's Eve Geoff made his resolution – *to score a hat-trick in the World Cup final.* Hang on, Hursty, you haven't even made your England debut yet! In February he did, and did, *quite well.* Ramsey included him in his World Cup squad as cover for the legendary Jimmy Greaves. England started the World Cup campaign reasonably well and progressed, without too many difficulties, to the second stage, however, there were worries about Jimmy's injury. He certainly wouldn't be fit to play in the quarter-final against Argentina, but hopefully he would be back for the semis, if England got through. Hurst was in and, unbelievably, scored the winner. England were through, but Jimmy was still nursing his injured leg so Hurst kept his place. Thankfully, Greavsie was declared fit for the final and all England expected him to return: it seemed inconceivable that Alf would leave him out and favour his understudy. Whatever, Geoff was optimistic, after all he knew Ramsey, *liked horses for courses,* he also knew that Alf, *never changed a winning team.* What Geoff didn't know was what Alf saw in the crystal ball as he pondered his starting team for England's biggest game – he was back in 1964 at the FA Cup final: West Ham v Preston North End. At half time the Hammers were losing 2-1, Greenwood had to make tactical changes to combat the attacking menace of Preston's Black Prince and contain their 19-year-old midfield starlet, Howard Kendall: he reorganised midfield and pushed Hurst further forward. 15 minutes later, Geoff burst into the penalty area...banged a header goalward...it rattled the underside of the crossbar...came straight down...on the line...or was it over...was it in, Ref? 2-2. As extra time seemed certain Geoff collected the ball near half way...galloped into space...hit a long diagonal to Brabrook...Brabrook crossed to Boycey...3-2. It was all over; Hurst was in: Greavsie, sacrificed.

The final started badly. English hearts sank as Helmut Haller shot West Germany ahead, then the Wembley 'roof' lifted as Hurst banged in the equaliser, hearts fluttered as his West Ham colleague ghosted in to put England in front, and just when victory seemed certain Germany scrambled an equaliser. With extra time to be played, Ramsey urged his men on but they were deflated and the Germans, resurgent. England needed more than Alf's inspiring words, they needed a stroke of luck: half turning – half falling...Geoff rifled a shot goalward...it rattled the underside of the crossbar...came straight down...on the line...or was it over...was it over, Linesman? 3-2. With seconds remaining Hurst received the ball near half way...galloped into space...volley...goal...World Cup.

In September 2000, Sir Geoff's shirt fetched a record £91,750 at auction.

Andy Gray

There's no doubt about it, my friends tell me that I'm hugely lucky. Just look at how Everton signed me when my career was going nowhere, then look at how television signed me just when my playing career was finishing. Yes, I am a very lucky guy.

Andrew Mullen Gray (Sun Sagittarius Mars Scorpio) was born into a fanatical football family in Glasgow on the 30th November 1955. He was a teenage prodigy at Dundee United. At Aston Villa he scored 69 goals in 141 appearances; he won the League, the FA Cup, and the European

Cup Winners Cup with Everton. He is the only player to have won the 'PFA Player of the Year' and the 'Young Player of the Year' awards in the same year.

His childhood wish came true when he was part of Glasgow Rangers' record-breaking side that dominated Scottish football for a decade. As a player, he was a strong running, inspirational centre forward who would boldly put his head where other, more cautious, strikers wouldn't. He was a charismatic leader of the forward line. When he arrived at Aston Villa, he struck up an immediate understanding with Brian Little (Sun Sagittarius Mars Libra), their skilful, if under-rated, injury-prone inside forward whose promising career ended prematurely: in their first full season together they scored 55. But off the pitch Andy's relationship with the manager was difficult – it was affecting his game. Fortunately, Wolverhampton Wanderers were looking for a strike-partner for John Richards (Sun Scorpio) and their manager, John Barnwell, believed Gray was ideal. He was right: they gelled. Gray scored on his debut – at Goodison Park – and got on well with the manager. Wolves climbed the League table, qualified for Europe, and reached the League Cup final where they met Brian Clough's formidable Forest. Wolves rode their luck. Forest were relentless. Wolves were hanging on, then against the run of play – a chance – and Gray took it. Apart from a few niggling injuries, first the knee and then the thigh, life was, *going great*, but with Andy injured, results suffered. Wolves slipped down the table and, to make matters worse, they were in a financial mess: in order to survive they had to sell their prize asset – Gray.

In 1983-84, Everton were struggling near the bottom of the First Division and the fans were howling for the head of their former star and novice manager, Howard Kendall. Press criticism, poor results, and barracking from the home fans had brought the former rock of Everton's holy trinity to his knees. He had tried everything and nothing had worked. On a grainy autumn evening with a cold wind blowing off the Mersey, Kendall stood outside St Domingo's remembering their history, realising – he had to do the right thing. The next day he offered his resignation, but the Board refused and instead gave him some cash to buy a much needed goalscorer: he put his trust in Andy. Gray not only scored the goals, he lifted the dressing room: his optimism and enthusiasm rubbed off and the atmosphere around Goodison was transformed. Performances improved and Howard began to see things differently – injuries to key players were opportunities to give young talent a chance: he discovered a formidable centre back partnership in the reserves and Everton went on a winning run to Wembley. As the emotional anthem 'Abide with Me' echoed around the Empire stadium, Howard stared up at the sky in wonderment, whilst Elton John's eyes filled up with tears.

From the kick-off Watford were buzzing: their rising star John Barnes and his strike partner, Mo Johnson, were pushing back the Toffees, but with only Southall to beat Barnes stumbled and...missed his kick. Everton were unsettled, slow to find their rhythm, but, fortunately, they were still in the contest. Gradually their passing became crisper; nonetheless, it was against the run of play when Sharp shot from the edge of the penalty box to put them ahead. The Hornets hit straight back, then, with the game in the balance, Everton surged forward...swung the ball high and hopeful into the Watford area...the keeper got there first...wrapped his hands around – Gray arrived – head...bang...wallop...FA Cup.

Throughout his distinguished career, the robust, larger-than-life and sometimes reckless Gray was only sent off 3 times: twice for dissent and once for retaliation. He was rarely booked and when he was it was for offering forthright opinions to referees when none were wanted, anyway, some said that put him in good stead for a successful career in television.

Gary Lineker, Chris Waddle

As one Sagittarian striker, future broadcaster and opinion former left Everton, another Sagittarian striker, future broadcaster and opinion former – Gary Winston Lineker (Sun Sagittarius Mars Cancer) – arrived. Not only does Gary share his birthday with Churchill, he shares it with Andy. When the lucky goal-poacher arrived from Leicester City, however, he wasn't welcomed: the fans were still pining for Gray, and Gary had to prove himself. Of course he fitted seamlessly into the side, and Everton continued their winning streak all the way to Wembley again. That summer, the free-scoring Lineker established himself as an automatic choice for England's World Cup squad. Indeed, as good fortune would have it, in the space of 11 days and 3 games, Gary became world famous: he scored the first World Cup hat-trick since Geoff Hurst to put England into the second phase, he scored 2 against Paraguay in the first knock-out round, scored against Argentina in the quarter-finals, and without the intervention of the 'Hand of God' he would surely have scored more. Despite that, he won the 'Golden Boot' award to join former goalscoring greats: Just Fontaine (1958), Eusebio (1966), and Gerd Muller (1970). He was officially the best striker in the World Cup and one of the most sought after players on the planet: by late summer he was enrolling for Spanish lessons. What was his secret? Apart from being in the right place at the right time, he needed a supplier of crosses and a creator of chances. Bobby Robson found both: from the wing the fleet-footed Chris Waddle (Sun Sagittarius Mars Cancer) with his long striding step-overs did the trick, whilst through the channels beavered the selfless creator, Peter Beardsley (Mars Cancer). Peter and Gary had an uncanny understanding, *Beardsley is the best partner I could ever have*. In the 1990 World Cup, England were playing their best football since 1966; Lineker was on fire and England reached the semis, only to find themselves in another penalty shoot-out (when Sagittarians take pens they hit and hope), on this most vital occasion Chris hit it hard and...over.

The incoming manager, Graham Taylor, was a different proposition and, unfortunately for Gary and Chris, he wasn't on the Sagittarian wavelength. Whilst Waddle was setting France alight with his mazy runs for Olympique Marseille and helping them climb to the pinnacle of European football, he was being consigned to the England substitutes' bench. In the 1992 European Championships, and needing to beat Sweden to progress, England – without Waddle – were awarded a vital penalty: Lineker – England's second highest goalscorer, now ahead of Jimmy Greaves and only one behind Bobby Charlton – bravely stepped forward...placed it carefully on the spot...stepped back...hit it hard and...was substituted never to play for England again – still one goal short.

His home town forgave him, made him a 'Freeman', and he helped save their football club. In his long and distinguished career the benevolent, and sporting, Lineker was never sent off nor in trouble for foul play; only occasionally was he reprimanded for shooting off opinions when they weren't wanted. Anyway, some said that would help him forge a successful career in television.

Neil Warnock, Kevin Blackwell, Ken Bates

I first hit the headlines by getting a Gary Lineker hat-trick struck off the record books.

Neil Warnock was the manager of non-league Burton Albion at the time. Burton had reached the 3rd Round of the FA Cup and were lucky to draw a big club: Leicester City. They started brightly. It was 1-1 after about half an hour and then the Albion keeper was seeing stars – hit on the head by a block of wood thrown from the crowd – but carried on regardless. At half time Warnock pleaded with the ref to call the match off – *no, Neil, no* – and by the end it was 6-1 to City. Warnock thundered across the back pages; on Monday morning it was national news; he wanted justice and he wouldn't let it drop. On Tuesday the FA investigated and, following an 'official hearing', ordered the match to be replayed.

Neil (Sun Sagittarius Mars Capricorn) was born on the 1st December 1948 in Sheffield. A lifelong United fan – and speedy right winger – his dream was to play for the Blades; he came close: Chesterfield, Scunthorpe, Barnsley and closer still, Rotherham. The irrepressible, forthright Tyke went on to manage Scarborough but things weren't going too well on the east coast, well, not until a chance encounter in London,

I first met my keeper, and future partner, when we played Stan Flashman's and Barry Fry's Barnet; he was banging a ball against the wall while he explained why he'd been dropped – for being too flashy. Nevertheless, I signed him. His first game, against Kettering, could have been my last: we were sliding down the Table and it seemed that if we didn't win, my career would be over before it got started. We did win – 1-0 – and Blackie (Kevin Blackwell: Sun Sagittarius Mars Taurus) was magnificent: by Christmas we were top of the League.

Changes in the Boardroom brought Neil's successful adventure at Scarborough to an abrupt end. He joined Notts County and took the Meadow Lane club on a rollercoaster ride from the Third to the First Division. He was so high profile, and successful, that the Chelsea chairman, Ken Bates (Sun Sagittarius Mars Sagittarius), saw him as his ideal man for Stamford Bridge. They looked around the ground together; it was dilapidated but Bates had big plans, and he wanted Neil to help take them forward; they liked each other, they saw football the same way, but Neil decided to stay loyal to County. A year later they sacked him. He joined Sheffield United and built a formidable unit. The Blades were entertaining and hard to beat and won promotion to the Premiership. However, in May 2007 Warnock was being tested both on and off the pitch: United had slipped into the relegation zone, along with West Ham who, allegedly, were fielding an ineligible player – Carlos Tevez. Warnock complained to the FA, but they took no action. On the last day of the season Neil was anxious: he needed a win or West Ham to lose, but the Hammers were playing a weakened Manchester United, and Tevez. Nevertheless, Neil was comforted in the knowledge that the future was still in his hands, all he had to do was beat Wigan.

There was still something else though; something was nagging him – penalties! Really? He was still disappointed that David Unsworth had missed that vital penalty against Blackburn earlier in the season, those dropped points would have made all the difference and then to go and sell him to – of all clubs – Wigan. As if written in the stars, they were awarded a vital penalty...Unsworth bravely stepped forward,

I just knew he would score. I knew Dave had come back to haunt me. The injustice of it all drove me mad. Perhaps I should have taken the Chelsea job; at least Ken would have stood by me, and after all, he is lucky.

The following year Warnock did take a job in London, he joined Simon Jordan (Mars Sagittarius) at Crystal Palace. But as Fate would have it, on the final day of the season Palace were hosting Sheffield United, now under the management of Blackwell, and all Kevin had to do to win promotion was beat his former partner. He didn't. Whatever, he was optimistic for the new season: *we started well, but then we hit massive injuries and results have been poor since (November 2009).* They picked up after Christmas, whereas Palace injured themselves by over-stretching financially, going into administration, and having 10 points deducted.

Michael Owen

Some people have this false idea that I'm injury prone. When I was seriously injured for the first time, I was devastated because I was on the brink of winning the 'Golden Boot'. When I ripped my hamstring for the second time, I was sent for all the medical tests, consulted all the experts, got second opinions, and they all said the same thing – 'there is nothing wrong with you.'

On the 30th June 1998, in St Etienne, Michael Owen (Sun Sagittarius Mars Virgo) made his name. Before, he was an unknown talent trying to get in the Liverpool team, Glenn Hoddle saw his potential, gave him his England debut, and this huge game – Argentina in the second round of the World Cup Finals – was only his second. The game got off to an explosive start...penalty...1-0 to Argentina. 4 minutes later England were awarded a penalty...Shearer blasted the equaliser. 6 minutes later, Owen received the ball from Beckham close to half way, knocked it forward and looked around....

Ayalla is retreating...Chamot is holding off...I am galloping into space...10 yards...20 yards. Ayalla is still backing off....30 yards. Unbelievable: Ayalla is still backing off...flashhhh...hard and high...goooooaaalllllll
    I was over the moon, but not for long:

Beckham was sent off, Argentina equalised and the game went to a penalty shoot-out...

Shearer bangs his into the top corner. Now it is my turn. I'm walking forward. I put the ball on the spot, but for some reason I'm laughing – my mind has jumped out of my body. I want to hit it to the right side of the goal, I am running up...I just want it to go to the right, anywhere low on that side will do...I look down and see the ball going high...it's going over...my stomach is churning...it isn't going where I want...it strikes the woodwork...I am running away overcome with joy. Suddenly my mind jumps back – David Batty (Sun Sagittarius Mars Libra) is preparing to take the vital kick. Batts mans-up: he hits it hard and...I feel his sorrow.

Owen went on to establish himself as England's most prolific striker since Gary Lineker. In a World Cup qualifier in Munich, he became the first Englishman to score a hat-trick against Germany since Geoff Hurst. In 2002, he was voted 'European Footballer of the Year' and was soon enrolling for Spanish classes. In 85 games for England he scored 40; he was on track to overtake Lineker's tally leading up to the 2006 World Cup Finals. At one stage it seemed he would be helped in his quest by having the ideal strike partner – the prolific, injury-prone West Ham centre forward, Dean Ashton (Sun Sagittarius Mars Libra) – but at the last minute, young Dean was unfortunately denied (a few seasons later he was forced into early-retirement following an accident in training). Nevertheless, Michael looked in good shape and was optimistic; 74 seconds into the match against Sweden, he received the ball wide on the right...unmarked...with time to bring it under control and look around...half turning...falling...clutching his knee...writhing in agony...hit by an invisible arrow!

A year later he was on the road to recovery, but was struggling to re-establish himself – he was out of the England squad and out of favour at Newcastle United. In 2009, Newcastle were relegated and just when Michael needed a stroke of luck, Sir Alex Ferguson signed him. He did well: scored a hat-trick in the Champions League, and scored in United's Carling Cup Final victory before pulling up with a hamstring on half time. When he decides to hang his boots up he can look forward to success with the horses.

Alan Mullery, Steve Perryman, David Hirst

Talking of luck, when Hunter Davies was researching 'The Glory Game' (1972), he prepared a questionnaire for the Spurs players and asked – *What was the most important factor in your success?* Captain Alan Mullery (Sun Sagittarius Mars Aries) put luck top of his list. Hang on Mullers, don't you just mean that you were in the right place at the right time? And future captain Steve Perryman (Sun Sagittarius Mars Libra) put luck top of his list. Hang on Stevie, don't you just mean that you were at the right club, with the right coach, and had the right captain? *Wasn't that lucky?*

After his success in Marseille where he had helped his strike partner,

Jean-Pierre Papin (Mars Sagittarius), to an onion-bag-full of goals and the 'European Footballer of the Year' award, and although still out of favour with Taylor, Chris was in demand back home. 'Tricky' Trevor Francis appreciated top quality wing play and needed Waddle to provide accurate crosses for his strong running, hard hitting, injury-prone striker, David Hirst (Sun Sagittarius Mars Aquarius). Waddle proved to be the catalyst, igniting Hirst and propelling Wednesday to the FA Cup and League Cup finals (there may have been another reason why Chris chose to live in Sheffield: it was a long throw in from Taylor's house). Both Chris and Dave excelled at Wembley, they both scored, but not enough, and the Owls were beaten. Anyway, Waddle impressed the nation and was voted the 'Football Writers Footballer of the Year' – even Graham couldn't ignore him any longer. When Francis left, Hirst clashed with the new manager, David Pleat, and was soon on the M1 south.

John Terry, Dennis Wise, Ashley Cole, Michael Essien

In the 1970s White Hart Lane was a lucky place for Sagittarians – it was just as lucky for Waddle and Lineker in the 1980s. Whilst Stamford Bridge proved just as lucky for Ken Bates, captain Dennis Wise (Sun Sagittarius Mars Libra), for future captain John Terry (Sun Sagittarius Mars Capricorn), England teammate Ashley Cole (Sun Sagittarius Mars Capricorn), and for Michael Essien (Sun Sagittarius Mars Capricorn). Unluckily, for Felipe Scolari (Mars Sagittarius), Essien was injured for most of his time at the club, but when Guus Hiddink (Mars Sagittarius) arrived, Michael had recovered and Chelsea were much better; when Ancelotti arrived, he was better still – until an unfortunate injury at the African Cup.

After a disappointing 2006 World Cup campaign, Steve McLaren was appointed England manager. Steve appointed the former Chelsea and England coach Terry Venables (Mars Sagittarius) as his right-hand-man, and John Terry, captain.

Born in Barking in 1980, the inspirational, and sometimes reckless tower of strength, combines the defensive solidity of Mars in Capricorn with the adventure and burning desire of Sagittarius. As a young lad he started as a ball-playing midfielder at Stamford Bridge, but was struggling to make any impression: his youth team coach was undecided – *hmmm...can JT make it*? Fortunately, for John, the regular centre back didn't turn up for the next match, Terry was drafted in, did well, was lucky to be on the same wavelength as club captain Dennis Wise – *Dennis was a great captain and inspiration* – and never looked back. Even though a succession of foreign players were signed, even though he was behind 2 World Cup winning centre halves – Marcel Desailly and Frank Leboeuf – in the pecking order, he never lost faith. Despite one season going by, two, three, and even when Chelsea fielded 11 foreigners (Boxing Day 1999), he remained positive. Then Bates sacked Vialli, Claudio Ranieri arrived and Terry was blessed. John played well, kept his place, went on to become club captain, and England captain – until his reputation was injured by press allegations about his private life. The following week, the injured Ashley Cole (broken ankle) was confronted by press allegations about his private life.

Joe Jordan, Billy Bremner, Peter Lorimer

England may have qualified for the 2010 World Cup Finals but Scotland hadn't. Not since Andy Gray and their powerful, strong running, prolific, centre forward Joe Jordan (Sun Sagittarius Mars Libra), had they threatened to contest a major trophy. Gray won 20 caps for Scotland and it could have been more if he hadn't been in competition with Jordan, who was the apex of an attacking triangle for club and country. At Leeds United he had developed uncanny partnerships with his inspirational captain Billy Bremner (Sun Sagittarius Mars Scorpio), and the straight-talking, sharp-shooting Peter Lorimer (Sun Sagittarius Mars Sagittarius). Jordan still holds a Scotland record, having played in 3 World Cup Finals: 1974, 1978, and 1982, scoring in all 3.

Peter Lorimer was born in Dundee on the 14th December 1946. He joined Leeds as a 16-year-old and spent most of his career at Elland Road. He made 449 appearances and scored 151 goals. As an attacking half back, he would drift out to the wing before cutting inside to volley, or slide a pass into Jordan's path. Always relaxed and optimistic, he often gave the impression that his mind was somewhere else: perhaps Wetherby or Pontefract races, but it never hindered his career. When the club was facing bankruptcy his support was invaluable to new chairman, Ken Bates. He became Bates' trusted spokesman and honest broker. The Leeds faithful had total belief in Lorimer's integrity and never blamed him for anything; not even for tempting Fate against Sunderland before the 1973 FA Cup final. Pardon? Leeds were, probably, the best team in Europe and the firm favourites to beat Second Division Sunderland. On the morning of the game the BBC interviewed Lorimer; David Coleman asked for his prediction, Peter was confident about Leeds' prospects, *a racing certainty*.

As the teams came out of the Wembley tunnel, they were greeted by thousands of flashing cameras and a thunderous 'Roker Roar' from the Black Cats' 20,000 travelling fans and deafening cheers for the underdogs from the 60,000 'neutrals'. The Roar seemed to unnerve Leeds: from the start their play was tentative and lacked conviction, they were struggling to impose themselves. They couldn't come to terms with the elements as the ball zipped around on the wet surface. Against all the odds, the early chances fell to Sunderland, but luckily for Leeds, they failed to capitalise – until the 13th minute – sorry, 31st. Sunderland won a corner, the ball was swung in high...Hughes rose to head it...missed...the ball bounced off Vic Halom's knee – it could have gone anywhere – it didn't, it dropped invitingly to Ian Porterfield. Ian whacked it home. At half time, Revie settled his side down and they returned for the second half composed, playing expansive football...stretching the Sunderland back 4. It seemed just a matter of time...but chances came and went...time was running out...then the golden opportunity – Reaney crossed from wide on the right...Cherry dived full-length, made firm contact...the ball flew goalwards...the crowd roared...goaaa...Hang on! Jim Montgomery pulls off an instinctive save and palms the ball away, it falls invitingly to Lorimer...6 yards out Hotshot lashes it...the crowd roar...Coleman screams...gooooaaaaalllllllll. Hang on, Dave! Monty flashes across to make the save of the century.

Nowadays, Peter has the greatest respect for black cats.*

---

*Strange, black cat story (Argentina 1967): Argentine players are just as superstitious as the English, so, when the fans of Independiente told their rivals and reigning champions – Racing Club – that they had buried 5 black cats at their ground (1 black cat = 7 years bad luck) they didn't win the title again until 2002.

HERBERT
CHAPMAN.

CAPRICORN

A club create their own public.
Herbert Chapman

*I had a feeling that night in Barcelona
that there was fate attached to it.*
Alex Chapman Ferguson

Capricorn is an EARTH sign ruled by Old Father Time, Saturn. Saturn is perhaps the most easily recognised of the planets with its iconic bands of twinkling crystal, ice coated rocks and giant snowballs. Tilted at a jaunty angle, the sparkling rings add a fascinating lustre to the grey old man. The rings travel at great speed and – with a width of over 180,000 miles, but a height less than the main stand at Old Trafford – the boulders bump and grind together and, occasionally, one tries to break away from the orderly procession, though not for long, because the wayward rock is soon whipped back into shape by the power of its boss's gravitational force.

All the Earth signs are associated with aspects of the landscape;

Taurus with lowlands: Virgo, rolling hills: Capricorn with the highlands' rocky peaks and dangerous passes. It seems appropriate, therefore, that – having the mountain goat for a symbol – Capricornians are ambitious and aim for the top. However, they do not rush ahead: they are deliberate, sensible, and take care to find firm footholds. They are serious, hard working, responsible, and in the end achieve their goals. They are football's empire builders, but no sooner have they built one dynasty than they set out to build another – only bigger and better. Always providing that they remember to start at the bottom again, they do, otherwise they can slip up and be the scapegoat.

As players and managers they are professional, disciplined, and well organised. Capricornians make paternalistic, long-serving chairmen and, although Saturn is the bringer of old age; they age gracefully – becoming more relaxed, more humorous and, spontaneous as they get older.

A DYNASTY

CHAIRMAN
DOUG ELLIS Aston Villa

COACHES
HERBERT CHAPMAN Arsenal
GEORGE RAYNOR Sweden
ALEX FERGUSON Manchester United
OTTMAR HITZFELD Bayern Munich
TERRY VENABLES Spurs
STEVE BRUCE Sunderland
PEP GUARDIOLA Barcelona
TONY PULIS Stoke City
MARK ROBINS Barnsley
VICENTE DEL BOSQUE Spain

GOALKEEPERS
GORDON BANKS Leicester City
FELIX Fluminense
HUGO LLORIS Lyon
ROBERT GREEN West Ham United

DEFENDERS
LILIAN THURAM Juventus
TERRY BUTCHER Ipswich Town
JOHN CHARLES Leeds United
BILL FOULKES Manchester United

MIDFIELD
BRYAN ROBSON Manchester United
GENNARO GATTUSO AC Milan

JACK WILSHERE Arsenal
LEE BOWYER Birmingham City
JAIRZINHO Botafogo
VINNIE JONES Wimbledon

FORWARDS
EDDIE GRAY Leeds United
JAMES MILNER Aston Villa
EMILE HESKEY Aston Villa
PETER BEARDSLEY Newcastle United
MALCOLM MACDONALD Newcastle United
DUNCAN FERGUSON Rangers
CHARLIE NICHOLAS Arsenal

ADMINISTRATOR
GORDON SMITH SFA

INSPIRATIONS
MUHAMMAD ALI
JOE FRAZIER
LEWIS HAMILTON
JENSON BUTTON
DAVID BELLAMY

The first match I went to was the Owls v Man United; my dad was a Blade and granddad, a Wednesdayite, and he – they say it skips a generation – took me to see his team play Matt Busby's. It was 1963; Hillsborough was packed to the rafters. I remember Bronco Layne (Mars Capricorn) marauding forward with Johnny Fantham, but they made no impression on the rock that was Bill Foulkes (Sun Capricorn Mars Capricorn) at the heart of the United defence, whilst at the other end Bobby Charlton (Mars Capricorn) rattled a couple of goals past Ron Springett. On the bus back home, granddad and the other old fellas were discussing what went wrong, what should have been done, what wasn't, and what would never be. As we went through Kiveton Park one old tyke sighed:

We should have had him who lived ov'r there as our manager: he was the best, better than yon Busby.
Oh aye...who was that, old lad?
Bert Chapman!

Herbert Chapman

Herbert Chapman (Sun Capricorn Mars Aries) was born in Sheffield on the 16th January 1878. He was a hard-working family man and a thoughtful inside forward, but never quite played at the highest level: although he did get close to the top – turning out for Sheffield in their annual fixture with Glasgow. It was a match of contrasting styles with the Glaswegians playing a quicker tempo, intricate passing game, whilst Sheffield were more direct and robust. Chapman was impressed with the tricky inside forward play of the nippy Scots and as a manager he tried to blend Glasgow guile with Sheffield steel. He started as he meant to go on, first, at lowly Northampton Town where he imposed a rigid organisational structure, disciplined the players and turned them into a clever, winning machine: 7-0 v Watford, 10-0 v Southend, 5-1 v Luton. When the Cobblers were off-form they ground out a boring draw. They didn't get beat and in 1909 were Southern League champions, but they didn't get promoted either, because in those days the lower rungs of the football ladder didn't reach to the top. To get there a manager had to catch the eye of a bigger club. The following season his opportunity came in the FA Cup, v Sheffield Wednesday. Bert was *Yorkshire Post* news: *could he cobble together a victory over the high-flying Owls or would he be, prey?*

He wasn't, and conjured a surprise, was the toast of West Yorkshire and signed for Sheffield rivals, Leeds City. It was progress, but Leeds were a club in debt and Chapman's first priority was to keep the wolf from the door. He struggled on and off the pitch. His first indignity was defeat by his brother Harry's Hull City, whilst in the courts his name was being dragged through the mud for making illegal payments to players. Although the prosecution provided no hard evidence, he was found guilty and banned for the rest of his life. Out of the game and out of work, Herbert found a position at the Selby Oil and Coke works, and in his spare time prepared a legal defence; his case was that during the Great War – when the illegal payments were made – he was working long hours in the local munitions factory, was out of touch with day-to-day matters and uninvolved with the financial side. With the help of friends attached to Huddersfield Town his appeal was successful and he returned from the football wilderness to become their assistant coach. His first impression of the Terriers was that they had, *good players but no focus.* He took it upon himself to create that *focus* and persuaded the manager to buy Aston Villa's star, Clem Stephenson, but, *what about the brass?* Herbert then persuaded the directors to part with their hard earned cash – OK – but how would he persuade the reigning FA Cup holders to part with their best player, and why would Clem want to join the Terriers anyway? He did though, and Clem was an immediate success. The owners were impressed with Bert's vision and determination, and promoted him. He proceeded to build a fortress in the Pennine foothills; within 5 years Chapman had established Town as the best team in England: winning the FA Cup twice and the First Division title twice. How? He picked self-disciplined characters with natural skill; he always had a tricky playmaker alongside a powerful centre forward, and he always had a 'rock' at the heart of defence. He also instilled discipline: if anyone let Chapman's high standards slip he was out of the team for good. So when Ernie Islip was clattered by the 6ft 5in Notts County goalkeeper, Albert Ironmonger, and chinned him, Ernie was ordered to pack his bags and never return.

Herbert's football wisdom was much sought after: aspiring continental coaches consulted him, he became the unofficial England coach, and from St Valentine's Day 1925 – when the Terriers drubbed the Gunners 5-0 – he was the target for the Arsenal. That summer he surprised everyone and moved to Highbury. A doubling of his wages may have helped, but it was the prospect of founding a lasting dynasty that really attracted him to London. Although, in his first season he struggled to avoid relegation; in his second season, nothing changed. He had made one or two signings but they hadn't been effective – or so it seemed. The best schemer in England at the time was Sunderland's Charlie Buchan, and Chapman had identified him as the key to release Arsenal's potential, but it took time to get the directors to agree to part with their cash, and it took longer to persuade Sunderland to part with their star player. However, somehow, they did. With Charlie in the side everything clicked into place, and they went on a winning streak all the way to Wembley, where ironically, Chapman faced his protégé, Stephenson, and the team Bert had built in his own image. Arsenal's subsequent victory signalled the start of a successful era for the Gunners, and the beginning of the end for Huddersfield. Nonetheless, Chapman didn't rest on his laurels and signed the tricky Scots inside forward, Alex James, and moulded him into Buchan's successor. The winning machine rolled on: they won the League and then the FA Cup again. Chapman was the best manager in England going into the winter of 1934, unfortunately, he caught a heavy cold, it turned nasty and he passed away – leaving his great legacy and unfinished business...

George Raynor

Chapman was one of the top 3 managers in the world in the1930s and one of the top 3 managers in the world in the 1950s was the irascible tyke, George Raynor (Sun Capricorn Mars Scorpio). Born on the other side of town from Herbert on the 13th January 1907, Raynor started with Sheffield United. He never quite reached the top as a player – spending most of his career wandering through the lower divisions and then through non-league football – but he was determined to reach the top in management.

By the end of the 1950s he was the best coach in Europe, nevertheless, he couldn't get a job in England. Really? At the start of his managerial career, the short-tempered Raynor couldn't find a home posting and was forced to ply his trade abroad. He coached the Iraq national side and developed a method of team-building that brought results way above and beyond expectations. Not only did he impress the Persian Empire, his achievements drew the attention of the British and Sir Stanley Rous in particular. So when Sweden were looking for a new coach, and asked the FA for advice, Sir Stan suggested George. Although, when Raynor arrived in Sweden he wasn't welcome: nobody had heard of him for a start, and it didn't help his cause when a pre-season touring party from Birmingham City was interviewed:

How good is Raynor then, boys?
Ray who?
George Raynor our new coach, how good is he?
Never heard of him, mate.

Going into the 1948 Olympics, Raynor was on trial, anything less than the quarter-finals and he would be sacked, but Sweden were the surprise of the tournament, they played well, they were cohesive, well organised and beat Yugoslavia 3-1 in the final. They were welcomed back by the people, however, the real test of his abilities would be the 1950 World Cup. Anything less than the quarter-finals would be seen as failure, but Sweden were the surprise of the competition, they played well and went further than any Swedish side had gone before. Raynor was a hero. *How good were they then?* In 1953 they were the best and were unlucky to be held 2-2 by the great Hungarians. Juventus swooped to sign their mastermind, whilst AC Milan signed his star player, Nils Liedholm (Mars Capricorn). In the meantime, Sweden were awarded the honour of hosting the 1958 World Cup, but without Raynor the national team spiralled into decline. As the World Cup approached, and the downward spiral continued, the Swedish FA asked George for help. He responded to their call and rebuilt the side around old Nils, the aging Gunnar Gren (Mars Capricorn), and Nacka Skoglund (Sun Capricorn Mars Sagittarius), and surprised everybody by reaching the final. The following year, Raynor brought his side to Wembley and gave England a football lesson. In the 1960s he came home looking for work, hoping to finish his career at a top club. He did get a job at Doncaster Rovers, but they thought he had crazy ideas and sacked him after 7 months. He drifted along the east coast, found work in a factory warehouse, and spent his spare time coaching Skegness Town.

Alex Ferguson, Steve Bruce, Mark Robins, Ottmar Hitzfeld

On Hogmanay 1941 in Glasgow, arguably, Scotland's best manager was being welcomed into a war-torn world. Almost 7 years after

Herbert's untimely death, Alexander Chapman Ferguson (Sun Capricorn Mars Aries) – a boy destined to win a hat-trick of League titles with two different clubs – arrived. He started his football practice playing in the local bomb craters. Aged 15, he was apprenticed to a toolmaker in a nearby factory, became an active union shop steward, and joined the amateurs of Queens Park. Aged 19, he joined St Johnstone as a professional and in the next 4 years played 45 times and scored 22 goals as an abrasive centre forward with a hot temper, a powerful header, and an eye for goal. He progressed steadily up the Scottish football ladder and eventually caught the attention of Glasgow Rangers – by scoring a hat-trick against them. Aged 26, his dream came true when he signed for his boyhood favourites, Rangers. He was a local hero – until the 1969 Cup final, v Celtic – it was the biggest day of his football life, but what should have been fulfilment turned into disappointment. Detailed to mark Billy McNeill at corners, McNeill slipped his marker, soared, and put Celtic ahead. Determined to make amends, Ferguson drove himself hard and eventually his tireless effort paid off: the ball fell at his feet with the open goal at his mercy, but at the moment of truth his legs entangled, then Celtic scored another, and another, and again. He didn't know it, but his Rangers career was over. At the post-match inquest he was blamed and snubbed. He languished in the reserves never to play for the first team again. He contemplated his future and determined that he would get to the top in management.

He got his chance at East Stirlingshire. He brought them discipline and organisation. He was professional and diligent: results followed. He was also ambitious, and when St Mirren offered him a job, he welcomed the challenge of a bigger club. He made steady progress and when Aberdeen came in for him, he moved to the granite city. They were made for each other. Alex brought discipline, organisation, and grit to the Grampians. He challenged the supremacy of the 'Old Firm', won the League title 3 times, the Cup 4 times, and then beat Bayern Munich and Real Madrid on the way to the European Cup Winners Cup. When Manchester United offered him the opportunity to conquer world football, he jumped at the chance. He brought his former coach Archie Knox (Mars Aries), and his keeper, Jim Leighton, with him. Archie worked on getting the players physically fit, whilst Alex worked on their heads. He introduced boundaries for his players and demanded personal and collective responsibility. He appointed Bryan Robson (Sun Capricorn Mars Aries) captain, and spent £13M on new players, but nothing changed. 3 years later he was struggling to make an impression in the Pennine foothills, the team looked disjointed, they were playing drab football, and most worrying of all, attendances at Old Trafford had dipped below 35,000. The fans were voting with their feet and, worse still, a United fanzine was also putting its influential boot in:

When will Mr Ferguson realise he doesn't know what he is doing and go back to the Highlands?

Ferguson was isolated and it seemed that in January 1990 he was one bad result away from the sack. There was speculation that United's 3rd Round FA Cup tie against Brian Clough's Nottingham Forest would be his last, but then something clicked into place; maybe, the spine of the team: solid Steve Bruce (Sun Capricorn Mars Cancer) at centre half, Robson in midfield, and Brian McClair (Mars Capricorn) in attack: or maybe, Cloughie really was jinxed in the FA Cup: or maybe it was Mark Robins' (Sun Capricorn Mars Pisces) fateful glancing header. Whatever, from then on United were on the up-and-up. They rose from the relegation zone, got to the FA Cup final and were hot favourites to beat Steve Coppell's Crystal Palace. But it was Palace who got off to the better start: after 18 minutes Palace won a free kick wide on the right, Phil Barber bent a tempting ball into the United penalty area, Jim Leighton was undecided: should he come out and catch it, or go back? In that split second, Reilly looped the ball over Jim's head and his career was over. Regardless, the Reds responded...McClair crossed...Robson equalised...extra time beckoned...Ian Wright put Palace ahead again, but with seconds remaining...Hughes struck back. At the post-match inquest Leighton was blamed, snubbed, and banished to the reserves. United ground out a boring 1-0 win in the replay, and so 4 years after taking charge Ferguson had won his first trophy.

The following season he built a team around the mercurial French genius, Eric Cantona. Now they were exciting, the crowds flocked back to Old Trafford and the foundations of the empire were consolidated. The winning streak continued – Alex won the League and in 1999 won the Treble: the FA Cup, the Premier League, and surpassed his namesake.

In the Champions League final, Ferguson faced the wily old fox's, Ottmar Hitzfeld's (Sun Capricorn Mars Aquarius), Bayern Munich. The omens were good: at Aberdeen, Alex had beaten Bayern 2-1 on the way to winning the Cup Winners Cup. Nevertheless, he had his problems: captain Roy Keane was injured and so was his partner, and clinical finisher, Paul Scholes. Beckham and Butt were drafted into midfield, but they didn't click. Matthaus took control and Bayern were leading 1-0 with time running out: with 5 minutes to go George Best couldn't bear to watch anymore and left the stadium: 3 minutes to go...substitutes Gunnar Solskjaer (Mars Capricorn) and Teddy Sheringham (Sun Aries) were sent on – was it too late, would they even get a kick? 30 seconds left...*bloody hell*...2-1. At the post-match interview:

I want to go on and build a dynasty at Old Trafford.

10 years later United were 'World Club Champions'. In 25 years Sir Alex had won 26 trophies, including – the Premiership three times running twice and the Champions League again:

I have no intention of retiring, none whatsoever. Let's just pray that my health is still good in five years time.

Bryan Robson

When Ferguson's captain marvel's, Bryan Robson's, playing career came to the end, he followed in his mentor's footsteps and became a manager. Bryan was born in his grandmother's house in County Durham on the 11th January 1957. He was an exceptionally talented youngster and, aged 15, was spoilt for choice: should he sign for Sheffield Wednesday, Burnley, West Bromwich Albion, or his favourites – Newcastle United? St James Park didn't feel right, West Brom did, and so, standing barely 5 foot 2 in his stocking feet and weighing less than 7 stones, he signed for the Baggies. He was put straight onto a special mashed potato diet with a secret ingredient and a drink formula that helped greyhounds run faster; he shot up to 5 ft 10 in, was stronger, and quicker out of the traps. His mother said there were two Bryan Robsons; the responsible and serious-at-home Bryan, and the rampaging Robbo: on the 12th April 1975 Robbo was given his chance in the first team. He did quite well, and was making steady progress until he broke his leg in October. After 5 weeks of intensive treatment and muscle-building exercises he returned to the fray, and broke it again. 6 months later he broke his ankle. He began to wonder whether the secret ingredient had done him any good. Regardless, he battled on and was fighting fit for the 1982 World Cup Finals, and duly made his international name by scoring the fastest goal in World Cup history: 27 seconds against France, and then he scored another to set England up for a famous victory. Fellow north-easterner, Bobby Robson, made him England captain and he went to the 1986 World Cup Finals with high hopes, anyhow, he dislocated his shoulder and missed most of the tournament. In total he won 90 caps, captained his country 65 times and scored 26 goals; he also scored the fastest Wembley goal: 38 seconds, against Yugoslavia.

Having enjoyed a good start in management at Middlesbrough, the 2000-01 season brought serious challenges. Boro dropped into the relegation zone, key players were injured and Bryan was struggling to stop the downward spiral, so he asked his friend and former England manager, Terry Venables, for help. Results improved and relegation was avoided, but at the end of the season he was sacked. Fortunately, Alex was looking for an assistant:

Hi, boss...I hear you are looking for an assistant?
Aye.
Well....I'd like to be considered.
You aren't an assistant, Robbo, you are a leader: just like me.

He applied to Bradford City, had a good interview, got the manager's job, made a good start, formed a promising partnership with his assistant, Colin Todd (Mars Capricorn), but then the club went into administration and he had to start again. He managed the Baggies, then the Blades, and then in 2008 he returned to his spiritual home, Old Trafford, to work behind the scenes. But then again, he would probably climb Everest for another crack at management.

Terry Venables

Terry Venables (Sun Capricorn Mars Sagittarius) was born in Dagenham on the 6th January 1943.

He is the only player to have represented his country on each step of the football ladder: schoolboy, youth, amateur, Under 23, and full-international. He signed for Chelsea in 1957 and quickly established himself as an astute, outspoken, inside forward. He was tactically minded and a natural leader and, therefore, almost inevitably clashed with his manager Tommy Docherty. He transferred to Spurs and, ironically, helped them beat Chelsea in the 1967 FA Cup final. When he finished playing he joined Crystal Palace and coached them to promotion at the first attempt. He joined Second Division QPR in 1980 and 2 seasons later took them to the FA Cup final, curiously, v Spurs. The following season he won promotion, joined Barcelona and won the Spanish League and Cup. He returned to Spurs – they say you should never go back – won the Cup and was appointed chief executive, but a personality clash with his chairman led to a parting of the ways and a lengthy legal action. In 1994 he was appointed England coach, reached the semi-finals of the European Championships but, distracted by on-going legalities, stepped down.

John Charles

Bobby Robson said that he was as good as George Best and Pele. Sir Alex Ferguson picked him twice for his all time World X1: he was a rock at centre half and a towering centre forward. He inspired Wales to their best ever achievements and was an inspiration at Leeds United and Juventus. He was a star wherever he went.

John Charles (Sun Capricorn Mars Capricorn) was born in Swansea. He possessed great physical strength and willpower; he was dominant in the air and commanding on the floor; he was deadly in front of goal and never lost control in defence. He was a sportsman, a model professional and was never sent off or cautioned.

In 1957 he was at his peak, living in the foothills of his adopted Italian Alps, loved in Leeds, adored in the Welsh valleys, and idolised in Turin: scoring an amazing 93 goals in 155 games, the Juve' fans voted him their best foreign player ever – ahead of Zidane and Platini.

Vinnie Jones

In contrast to the hard-but-fair image of John the gentle giant, fellow

Wales international Vinnie Jones (Sun Capricorn Mars Virgo) had a reputation as hard-and-unforgiving. Vinnie started late in football – on leaving school he took a job hod-carrying up building site ladders during the day whilst in the evenings he was training with Wealdstone. He helped them win their League and Cup double, was signed by Wimbledon and scored the winner against Manchester United on his debut – even though his role was marking, restricting, and squeezing the opposition's star player until his pips squeaked. In the 1988 FA Cup final, v Liverpool, he helped upset the odds; he was on a high but, in spite of his success, in the evenings he was building a new career – in films. Pardon? Playing the role of hard-man enforcer on the mean streets of gangland, his debut film was a great success. He moved to America, set up home in the Hollywood hills and gave lessons to John Travolta in how to pass and move.

Gordon Banks, Jairzinho, Felix

Some say the best save of the 20th century was made by Jim Montgomery in the 1973 FA Cup final, others say that the best save was made by Gordon Banks (Sun Capricorn Mars Pisces) in the 1970 World Cup, against the best team in the world, from the best player in the world.

Gordon was born in Sheffield on the 30th December 1937. He played for Chesterfield and his early highlight was reaching the final of the FA Youth Cup against the Busby Babes. Dedicated, single minded and well organised, he first came to prominence at Leicester City. Ramsey was impressed with his form and selected him for his first England international in April 1963, v Scotland, at Wembley in front of 98,606. England lost: Banks let 2 goals in but he didn't make a mistake and was selected for the next match. He was reliable and inspired confidence in the defenders around him. By 1965 he was firmly established as England's first choice goalkeeper and yet, strangely, couldn't command a place at Leicester City. Really? A teenage prodigy – Peter Shilton – had put Banks first team position in jeopardy; ironically, Gordon had recommended Peter in the first place. Anyway, Banks remained one of the key figures for England. Ramsey kept faith with him through the 1970 World Cup Finals and was rewarded; Beckenbauer even went so far as to say that if Banks had played against Germany, England would have gone on to the final – a stomach problem before the game forced him to withdraw.

However, it was in an earlier round that he made the greatest save: Jairzinho (Sun Capricorn Mars Sagittarius) received the ball near halfway and galloped into space...raced down the right wing...slipped past Cooper...Gordon covered the near post...Jairzinho crossed...Pele rose above Tommy Wright at the far post...Banks scrambled across...Pele timed his leap to perfection, made firm contact and powered the ball towards the bottom corner...the crowd roarrrrred...Pele shouted GOAAALLL...Gordon: full-length...cat-like...stretching...twisting...extending a telescopic thumb...clawing the ball up...over...and away. Around the world millions watched in amazement, even the great 'black cat' Felix (Sun Capricorn Mars Pisces) in the other goal was transfixed. In 1972 Gordon crashed his car into a ditch, lost the sight of one eye, and was forced into early retirement. Shilton took his place for the next game.

Banks was voted one of the best 2 goalkeepers of the 20th century.

RAYMOND
DOMENECH.

AQUARIUS

Never change a winning team.
Alf Ramsey

*All parameters have to be considered
and I have added one by saying,
there is astrology involved.*
Raymond Domenech

Aquarius is an AIR sign ruled by Uranus. Uranus was discovered by William Herschel in 1781 and 6 years later he spotted its 2 moons, Oberon and Titania – king and queen of the fairies in Shakespeare's 'Midsummer Night's Dream'. Curiously, Herschel was so in tune with Uranus that he lived for one Uranus orbit – 83.7 years. In the sky, Uranus appears as a pearlescent pale green-blue light; under its glowing hydrogen-helium skies, in 1986, the Voyager 2 spacecraft found no solid ground, only a swirling molten cauldron generating powerful electromagnetic currents around the planet.

In myth, Uranus is known as the Awakener and the Lightening bringer, and is associated with the enlightenment of humanity. An interesting feature of Uranus is that its movement is different to that of the other planets as it rolls like a ball rather than spinning on its axis like a top and, curiously, those born under this sign also feel that they have to be different. They are independent and seem incapable of conforming: they are contrary loners and community spirited humanitarians. They believe in individual freedom and creative self expression but not at another's expense. They are detached but feel deeply for their teammates; they are rational and intuitive; they are radical traditionalists who rarely change their minds, but welcome new ideas and innovation.

There is no agreement on when the Age of Aquarius began. Some say it started in 1781, others say it started in February 1962 when the Sun, Moon, Mercury, Venus, Mars, Jupiter, and Saturn were all in Aquarius and in a powerful aspect to Uranus and Alf Ramsey. Others say that it will start in February 2013.

THE LIGHTENING

PRESIDENT
LORD HAREWOOD Leeds United

COACHES:
ALF RAMSEY England
BOBBY ROBSON England
RAYMOND DOMENECH France
SVEN-GORAN ERIKSSON England
BILL NICHOLSON Spurs
JOSE MOURINHO Inter Milan
ALEX McLEISH Birmingham City
MICK McCARTHY Wolves
GUSZTAV SEBES Hungary
BOB PAISLEY Liverpool
KEVIN KEEGAN Newcastle United

GOALKEEPERS
LUIGI BUFFON Juventus
DAVID HARVEY Leeds United

DEFENDERS
GARY NEVILLE Manchester United
PHIL NEVILLE Everton
PHIL THOMPSON Liverpool
JAMIE CARRAGHER Liverpool
BILLY WRIGHT Wolves

MIDFIELD
BARRY FERGUSON Birmingham City
DARREN FLETCHER Manchester United
DANNY BLANCHFLOWER Spurs

ROMARIO Vasco da Gama
LIAM BRADY Arsenal
XAVI Barcelona

FORWARDS
EUSEBIO Benfica
ROBERTO BAGGIO Fiorentina
CRISTIANO RONALDO Real Madrid
STANLEY MATTHEWS Blackpool
STAN COLLYMORE Liverpool
LUTHER BLISSETT Watford
DIMITAR BERBATOV Manchester United
CARLOS TEVEZ Manchester City
PETER CROUCH Spurs

INSPIRATIONS
MOZART
JULES VERNE
JAMES DEAN
EDDIE IZZARD
FRANCIS BACON
BOB MARLEY

Aquarians want to leave the world a better place than they found it; they have an interest in politics and would have agreed with Nye Bevan when he admonished the House of Commons during the 1950s Middle East crisis:

In resorting to epic weapons for squalid reasons it is no use honourable Members consoling themselves because they have more support in the country than they feared, of course they have, not all adults have grown up yet.

Many would also empathise with the Italian doctors Mauro and Rullo and their community football initiatives; one mental-health patient found himself on their project:

I felt like an island, all the people I met seemed too far away – I couldn't reach them – but the football team provided a bridge back to society.

Rullo explained that for a man isolated by mental illness football brings him into a community of creativity, movement, and cooperation. It helps him re-discover who he is through making his unique contribution to the common goal.

Alf Ramsey

In February 1962, Alf Ramsey (Sun Aquarius Mars Libra) was riding the crest of a wave at Ipswich and was about to take charge of England. Alf, nicknamed 'the general' because of his strategic mind and military gait and 'darkie' because of his jet-black hair and romany roots, was born into straitened circumstances in 1920s rural Dagenham. There was no electricity, hot water, or amenities in the Ramsey's humble home; his dad eked out a living rearing a few pigs, growing organic vegetables, totting, and making a few 'bob' racing greyhounds. When Alf was not helping with the weeding or polishing the crystal, he was mastering the rag ball. His natural authority, balance, strong shot and accurate pass marked him out as captain material for the school team. Although small in stature, 2-3 years younger than the other lads and lacking sprinting speed, he was a commanding centre half with an eye for the counter-attack. He was selected for Essex schoolboys and was invited to trial with the London Schools, but was barged about by a burly centre forward and rejected. He seemed to lose interest in the competitive game, left school with no qualifications and joined the Cooperative society as a delivery boy. Cycling around Dagenham 6 days a week gave him time to think about his future whilst building his leg muscles. On Sundays he played for 5 Elms United and then, out of the blue, was invited for trials with Pompey and Southampton. He impressed the Saints but it wasn't until he joined Spurs, and formed a telepathic partnership with wing half Bill Nicholson, that he really began to make progress. He captained their famous 1951 title winning push-and-run side, was capped by England and enjoyed a good understanding with captain Billy Wright (Sun Aquarius Mars Sagittarius). He also had an uncanny partnership with wing-wizard Stanley Mathews:

To my surprise Stanley played football the way I believe it should be played. He was the ideal right winger for my style of play.

And Billy appreciated playing alongside Alf,

I soon learned that nothing could disturb Alf's perfect balance or force him to abandon his immaculate style.

However, Alf's reign at White Hart Lane was coming to a natural conclusion as the ice-cool playmaker, Danny Blanchflower, stood on his toes and took his peg; somewhat bemused, Alf asked his friend Eddy Baily,

Who does he think he is?
You. That's the way you used to carry on, Alf, he's exactly the same.

In 1955 Ramsey was appointed manager of Third Division South side, Ipswich Town, by the Corinthian spirited Cobbold family. The set-up though was ramshackle: goats and donkeys wandered about the grounds and the corrugated roof flapped in the gentlest sea breeze. The players he inherited were of, *modest ability*, although the fans claimed that the donkeys were better. At the start, Mr Cobbold's only instructions to Alf were that he played the game the right way and kept the club out of administration.

In Alf's first match they were outclassed by Torquay. The players said that when they walked off they were expecting a rocket from the new manager, but Alf surprised them – saying nothing. He surprised them the following week by picking the same team, and even though they got hammered again, he picked the same 11 for the following week. In training he encouraged them to talk to each other; he drilled them in passing and moving and, after 6 weeks, they won their first match. The players began to look forward to training and helping – they mended the roof, built some fences, and moved the donkeys. They climbed the table, challenged for the title, and were unlucky not to gain promotion. Next season, though, they did win the title and Cobbold released some cash; Alf spent it wisely – in came Ray Crawford (Sun Cancer), Jimmy Leadbetter (Sun Cancer), and future captain Andy Nelson (Sun Cancer Mars Libra): the 3 incomers balanced the team and, in 1961, Ipswich were promoted to the First Division. Nevertheless, nothing was expected of them: they were the bookies' favourites for relegation. Yet in May 1962 they were crowned First Division champions: a BBC reporter put the feat in context,

Here we have Mr Ramsey, the architect of this miracle. How on Earth did you do it, Alf?

I have been fortunate at Ipswich in that although we do not have any great players, we have men of very high character and that shows in the way they play.

Following the 1962 World Cup the FA offered the England job to Bill Nicholson, but Bill declined and the post was advertised. There were 59 applications, but not one from Ramsey. Anyhow, the FA offered the post to Alf and, after obtaining assurances from them that he would be in sole charge of the team, he accepted. Straight away he predicted that he would win the World Cup and when he did, and as the players were jigging around the pitch in front of an ecstatic crowd, a reporter caught him off-guard:

How does it feel to have achieved the impossible?

Well...errmmm...I too feel very emotional, but my feelings are tied up inside. Maybe it is a mistake to be like this, but I cannot govern it. There is nothing wrong with being emotional in public, but it is something I can never be.

Gusztav Sebes

In 1953 Alf was one of the unfortunates to be humiliated by Gusztav Sebes' (Sun Aquarius Mars Pisces) men from 'outer space'; on the other hand he received a valuable lesson in team-building. Sebes was ahead of his time. He came up with a method of play based on the insights of Jimmy Hogan; it was a cohesive system with collective interchange: quick, accurate passing: intuitive partnerships, and with no focal point in attack the opposing central defender – with no one to mark – was thrown into confusion.

Born on the 22nd January 1906, in Budapest, Sebes coached Hungary between 1949 and 1957. The late 1940s was a time of power struggles and military conscription in Hungary and Sebes had been issued orders to create world-beaters; he had also been given extensive powers to achieve his goal. He set about his commission with enthusiasm and belief: he read all the coaching manuals and became expert at tactics and psychology. He befriended the great Vittorio Pozzo, the two-time World Cup winning manager of Italy; he studied the outstanding work of Herbert Chapman, and the brilliant Hugo Meisl. Following his research Sebes devised a plan to recruit the nation's best players to 3 teams. His idea was that if the best players were concentrated in 3 teams they would be spurred on to get even better by their teammates, and they would have 2 other top quality sides to test themselves against. Occasionally a player would politely decline Sebes invitation, but Gus would not take, *no,* for an answer and using his negotiating powers – *either you can volunteer to play for MTK, or patrol the border* – implemented his plan.

His methods, both on and off the pitch, brought immediate results. Between 1950 and 1954 Hungary went 31 games without defeat. They scored 139 goals and conceded 33. When they came to Wembley in 1953 they gave England a football lesson and then gave them a 7-1 thrashing in the return fixture.

Bill Nicholson, Danny Blanchflower

In February 1962 Bill Nicholson (Sun Aquarius Mars Aquarius) was riding high. He was the best manager in England, his Spurs were virtually unbeatable, and he was widely expected to be the next England manager.

Bill was born in Scarborough on the 26th January 1919, one of 5 brothers and 4 sisters. He was a bright boy and passed the scholarship exams to Scarborough High, however, the Great Depression meant that he had to leave early, get a job, and help the family income. He found work in a communal laundry but his dream was to earn a living playing professional football. Aged 16, he was playing for Scarborough's Young Liberals, aged 17, he was playing for Spurs. He moved into lodgings on Farringham Road, near White Hart Lane, and fell in love with Grace ('darkie') the raven-haired beauty living three doors away. When he returned from the War, Bill and Grace were married, and he also teamed up with Alf. Ramsey was the constructive defender; Bill was the defensive wing half covering Alf's forward runs.

In 1956, with his playing career ending, he was offered the manager's post. He accepted, made Danny Blanchflower (Sun Aquarius Mars Capricorn) captain, and so began the most glorious era in Spurs' history. In 1961 he led them to the League title and the FA Cup. They won the Cup again the following season, only narrowly missing out on doing the double. In 1963 Spurs were the first English club to win a major European trophy, beating Atletico Madrid 5-0 in the European Cup Winners Cup final, but not without drama: just before the game, the ever-dependable Dave Mackay failed a fitness test. Bill took it badly. He was already worried about breaking through the European psychological barrier as well as the quality of the opposition but without his midfield-destroyer, and protector of Blanchflower, it would be too much. He was downcast, his pre-match team talk was dull and he was beginning to depress the players. Blanchflower interjected: cool, calm, collected, polite, *let me say a few words boss...*

*So, lads, they may have the goal-threat Chuzo, but we have Jimmy – the goal machine – Greaves. So, they may have the elusive Mendoza, but we have John – the ghost – White. Yes, they are a good team, but we are better. Remember: we are more resolute in defence, more inventive in midfield, and more deadly in attack – we are the team that is going to **win** the Cup!*

But it wasn't about winning – *no* – there was something more important than that, they were the Hotspurs and they would go out and play with style and grace for Tottenham – *for* **glory,**

The great fallacy is that the game is first and last about winning. It is nothing of the kind. The game is about glory, it is about doing things in style and with a flourish, about going out and beating the other lot, not waiting for them to die of boredom.

Nicholson and Blanchflower were on the same wavelength. Nick believed in flair, skill and style. He also believed that coaching, practice and more practice was vital, but above all he needed the right characters. He thought about the game all the time: combinations, tactics, partnerships and inventive training regimes. Darkie complained that he never switched off: he couldn't relax. When he wasn't planning for the next game, he was thinking about the mistakes he had made. When he wasn't thinking, he was researching, reading scouting reports and analysing the opposition. There was a purpose behind everything he did and meaning in everything he said. He discouraged chit-chat, moaning, defeatism and he didn't entertain time wasters. When asked what the key to his success was, he answered:

Apart from skill, what I want is – character.

Sven-Goran Eriksson, Roberto Baggio

The architect of the best England performance since 1966 (Germany 1-5 England, in a 2002 World Cup qualifier),was Sven-Goran Eriksson (Sun Aquarius Mars Virgo). The cool, calm and collected Swede had swept Germany aside with a passionate display of inventive, enterprising, and innovative football. He brought a new approach: in the 1990s Eriksson had developed his philosophy whilst working closely with sports psychologists:

It is not enough to simply pick the best players and hope that they will produce the best team; a good team has some players who are leaders and others who take a supporting role; a good team has players that are disciplined and responsible and others who take risks and express themselves freely; a good team has players who complement each other. I pick players with character, with no mental barriers, with no upper limits: men who dare to fail.

A good coach creates mental, emotional and physical energy in his players and is forward thinking. A good coach picks the right captain; when he is picking the captain he isn't necessarily choosing the best player, he isn't necessarily choosing a natural leader – he is choosing a symbol.

Sven admires natural talent and is a deep-thinking student of the game; in 1987 he got his chance to put his ideas into practice at Fiorentina. When he arrived their great hope was the mystical playmaker, Roberto Baggio (Sun Aquarius Mars Scorpio), but Roberto was struggling to fulfil his potential. He was plagued by injuries and was the almost-forgotten-man of Italian football, but that was about to change. From now on Baggio's individuality, idiosyncrasies, and creativity were appreciated. His appearance started to change. He grew his hair long and tied it in a pony tail. He meditated. He began to look the way he felt inside. He read Japanese philosophy and was moved by the life story of Soka Gakkai, a Buddhist who had been imprisoned and died for his ideals. Soka encouraged people to think for themselves: to resist divisive consumerist propaganda and political brainwashing. He promoted brotherhood and advocated international peace and cooperation.

On the pitch Baggio radiated skill, sportsmanship, enlightenment and on occasions, did magic. Wherever he went his name was chanted by lovers of grace and beauty; he signed for Juventus and in his first season scored 27 goals in 37. In 1993 he starred as they won the UEFA Cup; in the 1994 World Cup – lining up in the Giants stadium New York against Bulgaria in front of 77,094 fans: most of them with Italian roots – he reached new heights. Receiving the ball wide on the left, he brought it under control...beat his marker with the gentlest touch...glided along the edge of the penalty area...skirted an iron curtain of destructive tacklers, and without looking...drifted the ball on a zephyr into the net. 10 minutes later he bounced the ball to Albertini, spun onto the return and volleyed the second. In 1995, he signed for AC Milan, didn't hit it off with Capello, moved to Bologna, scored 22 goals in 30 and won a sentimental recall – from Cesare Maldini (Sun Aquarius Mars Aquarius) – to the national side.

His last game in football was for Brescia in the San Siro. In the 84th minute he was substituted; as he jogged off he was hugged by Paulo Maldini and then 70,000 spectators, realising it was the end, started chanting his name. He embraced both benches and with cheers still ringing around the stadium, disappeared. In retirement the inspirational footballer inspired an opera: Mario Marisi, a French-born Italian musician, received a Stendhal grant (Stendhal syndrome: being mentally and emotionally overcome by sublime beauty) to write and perform an operatic tribute to Roberto. The opera compares Orpheus the musician, who enchanted with the lyre, with Baggio the player, who enchanted with the football.

Eriksson went on to manage Lazio of Rome where he won the Scudetto. He succeeded in taking England to the World Cup quarter-finals in 2002 and then again in 2006. There was a widespread belief that England should have done better second time around, and so, after being knocked out by Cristiano Ronaldo's Portugal, he resigned.

Raymond Domenech

Portugal were favourites to beat France in the semi-final, with Les Bleus under the management of the eccentric Raymond Domenech (Sun Aquarius Mars Scorpio). Domenech was born on the 24th January 1952 in Lyon. The former defender at Olympique and Paris St Germain was appointed France coach in July 2004, and given the task of taking them to the semi-finals. From the start, the contrary, amateur astrologer was controversial. He was accused of being tactically naive and out of his depth by the French media: he was using the wrong system, selected the wrong players, and his substitutions never worked. He persuaded Claude Makelele (Sun Aquarius Mars Capricorn) to come out of international retirement; he included Pascal Chimbonda (Mars Aquarius) in the squad, and mysteriously excluded the Arsenal star, Robert Pires (Sun Scorpio). When he was asked to explain himself, he said that he was wary of Scorpios and on his guard against Leos. Anyway, he included Thierry Henry (Sun Leo), William Gallas (Sun Leo), and Patrick Vieira (Sun Cancer Mars Leo), exceeded all expectations, beat Portugal, and reached the 2006 World Cup final. Indeed, if Zidane (Moon Scorpio) hadn't, ironically, been sent off, then he would surely have won the Cup.

With Makelele, Thuram, and Zidane all retired, France struggled to qualify for the 2010 World Cup Finals: they were second in their Group and had to play-off against Ireland. In the lead up to the first leg in Dublin, Domenech was accused of being tactically naive and criticised for choosing Alou Diarra (Sun Cancer) instead of Vieira, for leaving the £35M Real Madrid striker Karim Benzema (Mars Scorpio) on the substitutes' bench, for using the wrong system, and for making ineffective substitutions. A lucky deflected goal gave them a 1-0 advantage going into the second leg in Paris – *c'est la vie* – but injury to Abidal meant Ray needed to make a change: he brought Julien Escude (Sun Leo) into the back 4 alongside Gallas. He got his tactics hopelessly wrong. Giovanni Trapattoni out-manoeuvred him, Robbie Keane shot Ireland into a 1-0 lead forcing extra time – a penalty shoot-out loomed – to have any hope Domenech needed to enliven the attack: he got the subs ready. The whole of France was hoping that he would bring on Benzema – but no – on came Sidney Govou (Sun Leo), and, nothing changed. Defeat was imminent, then the ball broke to Henry to the left of Shay Given's goal: Gallas charged forward....the ball bounced too high for Henry....he couldn't control it....he couldn't keep it in play...he couldn't cross it....or could he, he wouldn't would he? Would he uphold the spirit of football or be a rascal, would the great Henry choose to be greater or diminish himself? With sleight of hand he guided the ball to Gallas....William bundled it in...1-1. France celebrated. Henry slumped on the grass with a black cloud where joy should have been. At the Press conference, Trapattoni called on FIFA to explain their choice of referee. Was he suggesting foul play? Inspector Clouseau was commissioned:

Monsieur Domenech, je travail for le Force International de Frappe Astral. Je investigating your conduct dans le World Cup et demand your confession!
Comment?
Confess!!!
Comment?
How can you use le wrong system, pick le wrong players, make le wrong substitutions, et keep winning....without mal-practice?
Parlez avec Thierry Henry.

Monsieur Henry, je travail pour le Force International de Frappe Astral. Je demand your confession!!!
Je confess. Moi sorry, Irlande!
Bon bon. Now let's just hope that les petite peoples *don't drop you.*

Alex McLeish, Barry Ferguson, Darren Fletcher, Mick McCarthy

Domenech's only loss in his first 17 home games was delivered by Alex McLeish's (Sun Aquarius Mars Taurus) Scotland: he was undone by a shock James McFadden rasper, and commanding performances from

Barry Ferguson (Sun Aquarius Mars Cancer) and Darren Fletcher (Sun Aquarius Mars Scorpio). In 2008-09 McLeish joined Birmingham City, signed Ferguson and won promotion to the Premiership – coming second to Mick McCarthy's (Sun Aquarius Mars Taurus) Wolves. With Scott Dann (Sun Aquarius) at centre back alongside Johnson (Sun Taurus) Alex' side went on a winning streak – 17 games and only one defeat – and on the 7th February 2010 (Mick's birthday) Birmingham entertained Wolves (who were looking for their first victory against the Blues, in the top flight, since the days of Andy Gray). With 20 minutes to go it looked like many happy returns for Mick...1-0. 17 minutes to go: Alex sent on his 36-year-old sub (ironically, Mick's former Sunderland star striker) Kevin Phillips: 1-2. Both scored by – Kev: *it's a cruel old game*.

Bobby Robson

Bobby Robson (Sun Aquarius Mars Virgo) was born on the 18th February 1933 in County Durham. Aged 15, he followed his dad down Langley Park pit whilst at the weekends he was a hard working, technical wing half with a dream of playing for Newcastle United. Although when his chance came he turned it down in favour of Fulham. Pardon? He liked their manager Bill Dodgin (Mars Aquarius); he warmed to Bill's philosophy, *be happy when you win, Bob, and smile when you lose.* He also felt that Dodgin would give him a fair chance. He did, and Bobby thrived going on to play for West Brom and England, but as the end of his playing career drew near he dreamed of managing Newcastle, or perhaps West Brom, or even Fulham, but he had a good interview with Mr Cobbold. There was chemistry between them and Bob liked his philosophy, *love the game more than the prize, Bob.* Bobby soon showed that he was a good judge of character, and a good coach, as he led Ipswich to the UEFA Cup and beat Arsenal in the FA Cup final.

In 1982 he took charge of England; he had a mixed start to his reign: he drew his first game and lost the next, he chopped and changed the players. He tried his Ipswich centre half, Osman (Sun Aquarius Mars Gemini), he tried Luther Blisset (Sun Aquarius Mars Sagittarius), he tried Cyrille Regis (Sun Aquarius Mars Capricorn), but the side was still unbalanced, and disappointed with himself, offered his resignation. The FA refused to accept. He soldiered on. He tried different formations and more players: Cowans, Morley, Walsh, Chamberlain, Allen and Stein. Results improved, but going into the 1986 World Cup Finals, he was still anxious that he hadn't found the right blend.

He lost the first game to Portugal then drew with Mexico. Now he had to beat Poland or be eliminated, and to make matters worse he was beset with injuries to key players. He was forced to play Peter Beardsley (Mars Cancer) alongside Lineker (Mars Cancer), even though Beardsley had only made his England debut in January: he had no option. As Bob walked down the tunnel he had an awful vision of 1973: in his mind's eye he saw a dejected Alf making that long lonely walk back to the dressing room. He needn't have worried, Beardsley and Lineker clicked, Gary scored a hat-trick, England progressed.

In the 1990 World Cup, he led England to the semi-finals and was unlucky to lose in a penalty shoot-out. He joined PSV Eindhoven. He moved to Portugal and managed Sporting Lisbon, where he was met at the airport by chairman Sousa Sintra, but because of the language barrier Sintra had brought along an interpreter: Jose Mourinho. Bobby and Jose got on so well that Bobby asked him to help with the coaching, but they struggled to find the right blend and Bob was sacked. That seemed to be the end of their partnership, however, when Robson was appointed manager of FC Porto he called on Jose again and in 1995 they won the League title. They joined Barcelona and had a successful season, but not successful enough: Bob was sacked and Mourinho returned to Portugal to continue his research.

Jose Mourinho

Jose Mourinho (Sun Aquarius Mars Leo) was born on the 26th January 1963 in Setubal. He wasn't unemployed for long: after turning down an offer to manage Newcastle United, he accepted the challenge of bringing the glory days of Eusebio back to Benfica. Aged 37 he became the youngest Portuguese manager of the club, and the second youngest, curiously, to Sven-Goran. After the disappointment of being knocked out of the UEFA Cup by Halmstads, Jose called the players together and put his cards on the table:

We must have character and those players who don't have it offer me nothing.

He was sacked at the end of the season. He reflected on lessons learnt, continued his research, and refined his coaching philosophy; he gave it a name: *The Path of Guided Discovery*. The *Path* required players to develop their imagination and intuition, to accept Jose's general approach to tactics and apply their own interpretation on where those tactics should lead in practice. They played out various scenarios on the training pitch, then reflected and discussed the outcomes. They anticipated the next moves, they looked beyond the next twist on the *Path* and played out the appropriate scenario. They stopped, drank, reflected, discussed, felt, imagined, predicted, and executed. It is an inclusive and exclusive *Path*: it is a special path leading – *inwards* – to victory. In 2002 he became manager of FC Porto and in 2003 won the UEFA Cup, but he felt that the club should do better and demanded greater humility, and more detachment, from his players:

We must always keep our emotions under control otherwise we'll be half way down the path to defeat.

In 2004 Porto were Champions League winners; the following season

Mourinho moved to Chelsea and won the Premier League title twice, before being sacked. Whilst unemployed he continued his research and promoted community football initiatives in Africa. In 2008 he became Inter Milan coach and the highest paid manager in the world.

Eusebio

Eusebio (Sun Aquarius Mars Taurus) was born in Mozambique on the 25th January 1942. He was the first African to be voted 'European Footballer of the Year'.

In the Spring of 1961 the Benfica president was in need of a haircut and a striker; in the barber's chair he listened to the story of an African, *black pearl, who plays football as no other. This boy is the best player I've ever seen: better even than di Stefano. Are you joking me? Believe me, senor!* The president caught the next flight to Mozambique.

Eusebio played 715 times for Benfica and scored 727 goals, an all-time club record – if it hadn't been for Nobby Stiles, he would have scored a few more. He scored twice to inspire Benfica's European Cup victory over Real Madrid in 1962; he helped them win the League title 7 times and the Cup twice. He was the jewel in the crown of Portuguese football and became their ambassador for sportsmanship and fair play. He led Benfica in their European Cup final defeat against Manchester United; in the dying moments of normal time he was through on goal, with the chance to win the Cup, but Alex Stepney made a brave save, Eusebio shrugged his shoulders and congratulated him. Humble in victory, he could smile in defeat. His statue now stands at the gates to the Estadio da Luz. However, if it hadn't been for Stanley Matthews it may never have been: it was Matthews' custom and pleasure to spend the close-season coaching on community football initiatives in Africa. It was at one such summer camp that Eusebio was inspired by the wizard.

Stanley Matthews

Stanley Matthews (Sun Aquarius Mars Aquarius) was born in Hanley, Stoke-on-Trent, on the 1st of February 1915. His dad was a fitness fanatic boxer, and barber, and encouraged young Stanley to live a clean-cut life, eat the right food, avoid excess, and train hard. A vegetarian, teetotaller, advocate of vitamins and food supplements, Stan was still playing top class football at 50. He was voted the first 'European Footballer of the Year' and had the 1953 FA Cup final named after him. The enigmatic Matthews was widely believed to be the best player in the world – Pele said that Stan showed the world the right way to play the game – yet in 23 years he only made 54 appearances for England. After his first representative game, one in which England won and he scored, the *Daily Mail* questioned whether Matthews, *had the big-match temperament*. In the 1953 final Matthews' Blackpool faced Bolton Wanderers. The 38-year-old, high cheek-boned, slightly stooping Matthews was the people's sentimental choice: all the neutrals wanted him to have a winner's medal, but within 2 minutes Blackpool were behind. Nat 'The Lion of Vienna' Lofthouse roared into the area, the keeper froze and the ball bobbled into the net for the first goal. After an hour the Trotters were 3-1 ahead, Matthews had hardly touched the ball and it seemed to be the same old story: the ultimate prize was out of reach – or was it? In the 68th minute the 'wizard of the dribble' received the ball wide on the right, dropped his left shoulder...tricked his marker...raced to the bye-line...crossed into the 6 yard box, the ball spun out of the keeper's grasp and fell to Mortensen...Stan steered it into the net. With 2 minutes left Blackpool were awarded a free kick on the edge of the penalty area, Morty rifled the ball home to equalise. Deep into injury time Matthews received the ball wide on the right...turned inside...dropped the other shoulder...went past Ralph Banks....wrong-footed the centre half and...swivelling on the whitewash...guided the ball into Bill Perry's path for the South African to hammer in the winner. Pandemonium.

Those who were there said it was more emotional than the World Cup final. Stan Mortensen scored a hat-trick, Perry got the winner, but it was Matthews who was chaired around Wembley.

Cristiano Ronaldo

Ronaldo (Sun Aquarius Mars Aries) is the best winger since Matthews and better than George Best and Denis Law, according to Johan Cruyff. He was voted 'World Footballer of the Year' in 2008, and is the most photographed Portuguese player since Eusebio.

Cristiano Ronaldo was born in Funchal, off the north coast of Africa, on the 5th February 1985. As a boy Cristiano was never interested in television or computer games, he was only interested in football. He practised 6 hours a day every day and, aged 11, was invited to join Sporting Lisbon – he found it difficult to adjust and only settled when his mother moved to join him – aged 18, Manchester United paid £12M for his signature. He more than repaid them with his wing-wizardry and explosive shooting; he helped them conquer world football and on the way broke George Best's goalscoring record. In 2009 Real Madrid paid £80M for him, even though some diehard English newspapers still maintained that Ronaldo, *didn't have the big-match temperament.*

PISCES

I played several positions which demanded
sacrifice for the team.
Samuel Eto'o

It's a funny old game.
Jimmy Greaves

Pisces is a WATER sign ruled by Neptune – the 'king of the seas'. Neptune, with its artistic pattern of azure blue stripes and navy / aquamarine spots, was first sighted in 1846. Like Uranus, it has no solid surface and its atmospheric gases gradually compress into churning waves of 'rock-ice' at its core. Of its two major moons the larger one, Triton, strangely orbits backwards, hinting at an origin beyond the solar system. As well as being king of the seas, Neptune is the king of magic and illusion, making Pisces the most mysterious of all the signs. What seems to be is often not the case where Neptune is concerned: appearances can indeed be deceptive.

The Piscean's sixth sense is usually well developed, instinctively tuning them into the shifting moods and emotions of their teammates, family, friends, and fans. They are compassionate and sensitive; they long for peace and security, and often feel the need to get away from the hustle and bustle of daily life to recharge their batteries and reset their internal compass.

The symbol for Pisces is two fish trying to swim in opposite directions, but they can't because they are tied together by a silver cord; there are two sides to the Piscean: one side longs for action, excitement, involvement and adventure, whilst the other would prefer to escape to a fantasy island with a favourite book, film, or music. Of course, they love to be beside the sea.

There are two types of Piscean player; one is nimble, elusive and leaps like a salmon: the other is more robust and rides the amethyst waves like a dolphin. One is a Denis Law (Sun Pisces Mars Taurus) or Eto'o (Sun Pisces Mars Pisces): the other is a Didier Drogba (Sun Pisces Mars Cancer) or Adebayor (Sun Pisces Mars Aries).

THE DOLPHINS

DIRECTOR
PETER RIDSDALE Leeds United

COACHES
KENNY DALGLISH Liverpool
MARTIN O'NEILL Aston Villa
HARRY REDKNAPP Spurs
NIGEL CLOUGH Derby County
GIOVANNI TRAPATTONI Ireland
RON ATKINSON Manchester United
IAN HOLLOWAY Blackpool
ALLY MACLEOD Scotland

GOALKEEPERS
DINO ZOFF Juventus
STEVE HARPER Newcastle United

DEFENDERS
LEE DIXON Arsenal
BILLY McNEILL Celtic
ALESSANDRO NESTA AC Milan
KOLO TOURE Manchester City
BRANISLAV IVANOVIC Chelsea

MIDFIELD
COLIN BELL Manchester City
NANDOR HIDEGKUTI MTK Budapest
GARETH BARRY Manchester City
JACK RODWELL Everton

FORWARDS
JIMMY GREAVES Spurs
BOBBY SMITH Spurs
JOHN RADFORD Arsenal
DENIS LAW Manchester United
SAMUEL ETO'O Inter Milan
DIDIER DROGBA Chelsea
LANDON DONOVAN LA Galaxy
THEO WALCOTT Arsenal
PETER OSGOOD Chelsea
NICOLAS ANELKA Chelsea
EDUARDO Arsenal
EMMANUEL ADEBAYOR Manchester City
TERRY CURRAN Sheffield Wednesday
PARK JI-SUNG Manchester United
OLE-GUNNAR SOLSKJAER Manchester United
PETER MARINELLO Arsenal

INSPIRATIONS
ALBERT EINSTEIN
TITUS OATES
HAROLD WILSON
FRANCIS DRAKE
EDGAR CAYCE
MARY MAGDALENE

When Alf Ramsey said, *I don't always pick the best players,* most of the players he had in mind were Pisceans; the Spurs goal-machine, Jimmy Greaves (Sun Pisces Mars Taurus): the prolific Arsenal striker, John Radford (Sun Pisces Mars Aquarius): the king of the Kings Road, Peter Osgood (Sun Pisces Mars Aquarius): and the best of Manchester City, Colin Bell (Sun Pisces Mars Cancer).

Denis Law

According to Denis Law (Sun Pisces Mars Taurus), Greavsie was the best striker he ever saw and if it had been down to him, Jim would have played in the 1966 World Cup final.

The son of a North Sea fisherman, Denis was born to play football, but all bar one of the Laws had a squint – Denis' manifested when he was 4 – which made playing difficult. To compensate for the distortion to his vision he played with one eye shut, which, understandably, threatened to thwart his ambition of getting into the school team:

It's true that seemingly trivial actions can have unimaginable effects: when Mr Durno moved me from full back to inside left, not only did the school team want me, so did Matt Busby (Mars Pisces).

However, in 1955 Denis signed for Huddersfield Town:

I was used to fresh air, kittiwakes and pink granite buildings, but when I got to Huddersfield (for a trial) it was full of sooty chimneys, black sparrows, and smog. I was 5ft 3inches, 8 stones, had a throbbing boil on my cheek, and when the coach clapped eyes on me he called me a freak – I felt sick.

Anyhow, Denis was a different proposition on the pitch: the Terriers were impressed with the wee imp and signed him. The following year, Busby wanted him to join his Babes and made a record bid for a junior. Fortunately, for Denis, Huddersfield turned it down. The following year Arsenal made a bid, Huddersfield accepted, but when they sent their assistant manager to negotiate terms Denis felt slighted and lost interest. He signed for Manchester City instead, but Maine Road was run-down, training was dispiriting, and Denis was unhappy. Nevertheless, he was playing well and being selected for Scotland. In 1961 he was picked for the big clash with England – in those days internationals were played on the same day as League games – but City wanted him to play for them, however, Denis insisted on playing for his country. He wished he hadn't: Scotland suffered their worst defeat ever and at the post-match inquest he got the blame, along with the hapless keeper, Haffey. It wasn't until Matt took temporary charge of Scotland that Law was reinstated. In July 1961 he signed for Torino:

Big money tempted me to Italy – I did love the place, I loved everything about it – but I didn't like the football. I didn't like the defensive style, neither did I care for the violent tackling, nor the manager – he wouldn't release me for internationals and when we lost he refused to pay my wages. I soon realised that I'd made the wrong move – but I was trapped.

When Dennis Viollet left, Busby turned again to Law. Ironically, in his first year at United he helped get City relegated: it was May 1963, the Sky Blues needed a win to stay up, they were leading 1-0 with a few minutes to go...Law received the ball with his back to goal...there appeared to be no danger – *I didn't want to score* – he didn't want to be the one to send his old club down and he didn't want anything to spoil the upcoming FA Cup final...he meandered around...going nowhere...then, strangely, the City keeper rushed out and pulled him – and City – down.

Leicester City were their opponents in the final. City had finished above United in the League and with Banks in goal, and Frank McLintock at centre half, the Foxes were slight favourites. That is until

Banks threw the ball to Gibson...Crerand intercepted...broke forward...crossed...Law darted into the box...trapped the ball... wriggled...slipped two markers...swivelled...snap-shot...goal. He was uncontainable. At the end, the BBC interviewed the 'man of the match'...

How does it feel, Denis, to win the Cup?
I'm delighted – delighted to have been in the final, delighted to have scored and delighted to have won. Now I don't care if I never get to another FA Cup final.

He never did. In 1964 United won the First Division title and Law was voted 'European Footballer of the Year'; everything was perfect in his world, apart from an old knee injury that kept flaring up and apart from being sent off every December, and banned – without pay – over Xmas. In 1966 he boldly asked Matt Busby for a pay rise, Busby took exception and made a statement to the *Manchester Guardian, not even my best player can hold United to ransom: Law will not play for us again.* After making a public apology, and withdrawing his pay claim, he signed an extension to his contract. He was disappointed with the terms but more disappointed when his knee flared up again. However, the 1967-68 season started well, his knee was OK, but by Xmas he was playing under cortisone injections, and between hot and cold kaolin poultices; he carried on regardless, until the Gornik match: his knee burst and he was out for 4 months. He started his come-back just in time for the biggest game of his career – the European Cup final – unfortunately, he aggravated the old injury and missed out.

When Matt Busby retired there were many upsetting changes for Denis: in came Wilf McGuinness, then Frank O'Farrell, and then Tommy Docherty ended his reign – transferring him to City. Denis gelled with Colin Bell and Francis Lee (Sun Taurus), had a good season, was enjoying his football again, and then, fatefully, with his last kick in professional football he scored the crucial goal to relegate United. Revenge? *No – I didn't want to, I didn't mean to – I felt sick.* The United fans were desolate, but they didn't blame Denis, there were no hard feelings: they knew Law couldn't help scoring.

Colin Bell

Colin Bell was, arguably, the finest all-round English midfield player of his era. He was fast, skilful, graceful and the star of Manchester City's greatest side. But even so, he was never a favourite of Alf Ramsey. When Alf finally gave Colin his chance he was blamed for England being knocked out of the World Cup (1970). Ramsey had selected Bell for his squad and put him on the subs' bench for the quarter-final against West Germany, whilst on the pitch Bobby Charlton was inspiring England to a comfortable 2-0 lead. Seemingly cruising into the semi-final, Alf decided to rest Bobby and bring Bell on, and England were knocked out. Everybody blamed Bell: he had failed to hold midfield and allowed Beckenbauer to take control. He had let the side down. At least that was the image created in the public eye. His reputation was in tatters. But what really happened? Hadn't Franz scored the crucial goal, the goal that turned the game upside down, whilst Charlton was **on** the field? As a matter of fact he had, and didn't Alf really take the 32-year-old Bobby off because he was flagging in the Mexican heat and thin air? Yes, but that didn't seem to make any difference. When Joe Mercer took temporary charge, Bell was the first name on his team sheet.

Jimmy Greaves

Jimmy Greaves was born in bombed-out Manor Park, London, in 1940. His dad was the Treasurer at Fanshaw Old Boys FC and Jimmy was brought up on football. When he played for Southampton Lane Junior school he found that goal scoring came naturally; he was prolific for Essex Boys and was scouted by Jimmy Thompson, alias Mr Pope, and signed by Ted Drake's Ducklings (Chelsea). The Ducklings were supposed to eclipse the Babes and with Jim dancing his goal-scoring way through all the youth league's defences, they had the potential. He signed professional in 1957, scored on his debut against Spurs, and was Chelsea's top scorer in his first season – a season in which he hoped he would be included in England's World Cup squad. However, disappointingly, he was told that he wasn't selected because at only 18 years old, he was too young to make a contribution, ironically, one of the stars of the tournament was 17 (Pele). Back at Chelsea Jimmy wasn't sure whether Ted Drake thought he could make a contribution either; after being dropped for the FA Cup tie he watched his teammates take a beating from Darlington. When he arrived at the post-match inquest he found Ted telling the players some home truths:

One by one each player was demeaned and then Ted turned to me and said, 'as for you Greaves, some bloody player you are, you can't even get in this shower.'

Nevertheless, he was back in the side the following week and by the end of the season was the First Division's joint-topscorer with Spurs' Bobby Smith (Sun Pisces Mars Virgo). Aged 21, he became the youngest player to score 100 goals in the First Division, but he was unhappy. He was scoring plenty, but constantly had to bale-out a leaky defence; he was working his socks off, breaking records, draining himself physically and emotionally just to help an average side stay mid-table. In his quiet moments he thought about all the other, unknown, people who had sacrificed themselves: *who's ever heard of the last-but-one Mohican?* He didn't want that and asked for a transfer; Spurs were interested but Chelsea wouldn't sell to their London rivals. So in the summer of 1961 he followed Denis to Italy and signed a lucrative deal with AC Milan; playing alongside the 'golden boy' of Italian football, Giovanni Rivera (Mars Taurus), he was prolific – 9 goals in 14 games – and back home to celebrate Christmas. On holiday, Jim? *No, for good.* He didn't like the Italian style of play, he didn't like the violent tackling or the man-to-man marking, and communications with management were not good;

he was fined regularly for being in the wrong place at the right time, or in the right place at the wrong time:

Big money tempted me to Italy, but from the start the place was ill-fated: as soon as I landed they told me the manager had died of a heart attack, and then the new coach, Nero, hated me, and things were about to get worse. We were playing Sampdoria: I scored and made the other – I was tackling, tracking back, pressing, sacrificing myself for the team, then one of their players spat in my face – I kicked out, the ref gave them a free kick, they scored, and all hell broke loose...Nero went mad: he said I was a disgrace – I wasn't fit to wear the red and black. At that point I knew I had to leave, but I was trapped. There was only one crumb of comfort – Denis – in a funny sort of way knowing that he was trapped too made me feel better. However, unlike Denis I managed to slip through the net (Jim signed for Bill Nicholson's Spurs for a British record £99,999), but never received a single lira.

A hat-trick on his debut helped him settle and by March Spurs were in contention for 3 trophies, but by the end of the month 'Ramsey's Rustics' had done the double over them, whilst Eusebio's Benfica had put them out of the European Cup. However, the FA Cup final promised better:

Nick didn't say much before the game, 'you are all good players, you have been good enough to get us here, and you are good enough to win the Cup. Now go out and do your jobs: Greavsie, it's your job to score.'

Before the game Jimmy had joked that he would score inside 5 minutes. The official version...

Almost inevitably it was Greaves who had the first say in deciding the destination of the FA Cup. Beforehand, he had boasted that he would score in the 4th minute, however, in the event he opened his account with 60 seconds to spare and in a decidedly bizarre fashion. Goalkeeper Bill Brown punted downfield, Bobby Smith nodded the ball into Jimmy's path, but as the ace goal-

226

poacher moved into the penalty area he over-ran it and fell. With the chance seemingly having eluded him he somehow managed to half-hit a shot into Blacklaw's net.

Jimmy's version...

I darted into the box, Bobby Smith nodded it into my path. I had a clear run on goal but the defence was quick to cover and forced me away, but sensing an opening I swivelled and fired a snap-shot past Adam Blacklaw.

At Spurs, at last, Jimmy had found his spiritual home. Winterbottom (Mars Pisces) selected him for his World Cup squad (1962), but injuries deprived England of key players: centre half Peter Swan was out, wing half Robson was out, and the barrel-chested scourge of Europe with the happy knack of finding Jimmy with his deft flicks, Bobby Smith, was also injured and, unluckily, England didn't make it to the later stages.

In the 1962-63 season the football world was changing; Spurs were conquering Europe and Alf Ramsey was appointed England manager: between 1963 and the World Cup, England played 36 internationals and Greaves played in 24 – scoring 21 – but his big day was about to be ruined...

*Contrary to popular belief I got on well with Alf; he was a Dagenham lad and had a profound knowledge of the game. He knew the character of every player and he treated us as individuals. Even though our attitudes to football were different – he was technical and I played off the cuff – I liked him. There is a myth that I didn't like him because he dropped me for the biggest game of my life. Let me say now – once and for all – that is **not** true. Alf did not deny me that opportunity, Joseph Bonnel did when he scraped his studs down my shin; I knew Alf wouldn't change a winning team, even so, I was bitterly disappointed to miss out, but I never blamed him. He was a great manager.*

Anything else you want to get off your chest?

*Since you ask, 'it's a funny old game' is **not** my quote.*

Sure, Jim.

In all, Jimmy Greaves scored 357 goals in 516 First Division games and 44 goals in 57 England appearances. Denis scored 300 goals in 587 and a record 30 goals for Scotland. They were the goalscoring kings of the 1960s.

Kenny Dalglish

The goalscoring king of the 1970s was Kenny Dalglish (Sun Pisces Mars Aries). The 'king of the Kop' had already made his name at Celtic before joining Liverpool. In 1975, Billy 'the Lion of Lisbon' McNeill (Sun Pisces Mars Taurus) hung his boots up and handed the club captaincy to the 24-year-old Dalglish. They won everything together, except the European Cup. Not wanting to finish his career without winning the lot, Kenny signed for Liverpool. He believed that the Reds had the right players and the right backroom staff to help him achieve his goal. His timing was perfect: in 1977 Kevin Keegan (Mars Pisces) was transferred to Hamburg and Liverpool saw Dalglish as the perfect replacement. They were right. It was on Merseyside that Dalglish established himself as the most successful footballer in Britain. He set a record with 102 international caps for Scotland and won the League title managing Blackburn Rovers and Liverpool. Curiously, he had been rejected by Liverpool as a schoolboy: the timing was wrong then but it was right now and with the help of coaches Joe Fagan (Sun Pisces Mars Aries) and Ronnie Moran (Sun Pisces Mars Pisces), he fitted in seamlessly. Kenny was also an automatic choice for a very strong Scotland World Cup squad (1978).

Ally MacLeod

Dalglish was highly regarded by the Scots romantic, pied-piper of a manager, Ally MacLeod (Sun Pisces Mars Cancer). After success at Ayr and Aberdeen, Ally was now looking forward to success playing his brand of cavalier football in Argentina. His infectious enthusiasm had so inspired the Scottish fans that the squad was cheered off by a swirling sea of kilted flag wavers and bagpipers. Ally responded with a pledge to bring back the World Cup. In his estimation the main obstacle to realising his dream was a star-studded Holland. But the Dutch were the last opponents in Scotland's Group and they both would have qualified for the next stage by then, *nae bother.*

First up was unfancied Peru; they surprised the Scots with their fine ball skills, with their speed and organisation. Cubillas (Sun Pisces Mars Pisces), their rollicking centre forward with a rifle shot and a subtle touch, struck a wonder goal to help them win. Second up were the rank outsiders Iran; they surprised Scotland with their technique and silky skills, with their energy and their determination. Now, adrift on the del Plata, MacLeod needed a big win against the Group favourites to progress. He threw caution to the wind, played with flair and bold adventure, and won. Archie Gemmel (Mars Pisces) scored a memorable goal, but, not having scored enough, they were out. When MacLeod looked back on his career he said:

I was a good manager who just happened to have a few disastrous days in Argentina.

Martin O'Neill

As a football crazy boy growing up with a Republican view of the

United Kingdom, Martin O'Neill (Sun Pisces Mars Scorpio) was an ardent Glasgow Celtic supporter. Martin was born into a deeply religious Irish family on the 1st March 1952. Intelligent, articulate, and a natural athlete, he was also lucky: having feared the worst when baby Martin toddled out of the bedroom window – fell two storeys and survived without a scratch – his family believed that the *Little People* had broken his fall. In 1971 his lucky break in football came at Nottingham Forest. Although, when new manager Allan Brown arrived, it looked as though the *Little People* had dropped him in it. Brown and O'Neill saw football differently and Martin was about to languish in the reserves with his pal, John Robertson (Mars Pisces).

In 1975 Brian Clough arrived at the City ground and everything changed. Up to then Martin had thought of himself as a winger and John had thought of himself as a midfielder, but now they had to think of themselves the other way around. Cloughie was a great admirer of Martin, but didn't show it, and Martin never felt it. Quite the reverse: in 1979 Forest reached the European Cup final and, having helped the team get there, Martin was looking forward to playing in the biggest game of his life, but he was dropped. What should have been the happiest day turned into the worst; seeing his disappointment Cloughie promised that he would be in the 1980 European Cup final side – *empty words*. Overcome with emotion, and believing that his one and only chance had gone, O'Neill was full of resentment. Whatever, the following year Forest did get to the final again and Old Big 'ead kept his promise.

When his successful playing career ended he made countless applications to get into football management. Eventually he did secure a post at Grantham; they were heavily in debt and struggling to survive on weekly attendances of around 200. They improved slightly, but the real silver lining was teaming up with Robertson again: they found that they were a good pair. They had a brief spell at Shepshed, and then a chance encounter with Alan Parry, TV presenter, and chairman of Wycombe Wanderers proved to be the turning point. Alan was looking for a manager and Martin was in the right place at the right time, and in 1990, signed. Success at Wycombe was followed by a brief spell at Norwich and then success at Leicester City, but the magnetic attraction of Celtic proved too much. The Bhoys saw both sides of him: the cool, calm, studious, intellectual O'Neill and the romantic, emotionally frantic Martin. On match days he was so animated that many referees had cause to send him to the Stands to calm down. When reporters asked if he thought his pitch-side antics made him look crazy:

When you look at the way I behave at matches, I suppose I am.

At the height of his success he resigned to care for his sick wife. In 2007 he returned to football as manager of Aston Villa, made Gareth Barry (Sun Pisces Mars Pisces) captain, and began to re-launch the Villains.

Nigel Clough

Having practised with Dave Mackay, Kevin Hector, and John O'Hare at Derby and played 317 games scoring 102 goals for Forest, Nigel Clough (Sun Pisces Mars Aries) was appointed Derby County manager in January 2009. When Brian took charge in 1967 the Rams were lying in 17th place in the old Second Division; he steered them out of the relegation zone and within 5 years turned them into First Division champions. When Nigel took charge they were lying in 18th place, in the equivalent Division, and in his first season steered them out of the relegation zone. He arrived at Derby having served a 10 year apprenticeship with Burton Albion – ready for the challenge. As a Forest youth player, his dad played him under a pseudonym so that the other lads wouldn't hack him, and so the supporters wouldn't abuse him:

The sins of the father shouldn't be visited on the son, but they are no matter what I say. What the hell, our Nige is brave and brainy – he will cope.

His first League game was against Peter Ridsdale's Cardiff City, and curiously, his first FA Cup tie was against Forest:

It's as if someone upstairs has been a bit mischievous when they made the draw!

Peter Ridsdale

At one stage it had looked as though Peter Ridsdale (Sun Pisces Mars Scorpio) – Leeds United chairman – would sign his ideal manager: Martin O'Neill. Anyway, as the bells rang in the Millennium, Peter's Leeds were sitting on top of the Premiership, but there were troubled waters ahead, and 7 years later – after Leeds had spiralled into debt and down the Leagues – Ridsdale re-emerged: taking Cardiff City to the FA Cup final where he was narrowly beaten by Harry Redknapp's Pompey.

Reflecting back on his time at Leeds – Peter was a lifelong fan having grown up in the Elland Road 'cow shed' – he was still at a loss: he had done all he could to bring back the halcyon days, so why did they blame him for everything? *Why did they hate me? Why did they call me traitor? Why did they spit on me?* Wasn't it because of the sea of debt and the, alleged, misuse of funds, Peter? *Wait a minute! Didn't the DTI conclude their 'in-depth' investigation and report, 'no wrong-doing on Ridsdale's part'?* Well, yes, as a matter of fact they did – 'everything chairman Ridsdale did, he did with the best of intentions for Leeds United' – but that didn't seem to make any difference to the fans.

Harry Redknapp

Harry James Redknapp (Sun Pisces Mars Aquarius) was born in Poplar, London, on the 2nd March 1947. He was an Arsenal supporter and followed Spurs: as an 11-year-old he trained at White Hart Lane. Aged 17 he signed for West Ham United and enjoyed a long and successful career there. In 1976 he was a player/assistant coach with Seattle Sounders. In 1982 he coached Bournemouth. In 1994 he managed the Hammers and helped mould the careers of future England stars: Frank Lampard, Rio Ferdinand, Michael Carrick, and Joe Cole. In 2000 he left in curious circumstances: some speculated that his chairman took exception to 'off the cuff' remarks Harry made to a fanzine. In 2002 he joined Portsmouth and won promotion; he didn't stay long: some speculated that disputes with his chairman caused him to take the Southampton job. A brief, unhappy, spell with the Saints saw him return to Pompey and take them to their first FA Cup trophy in over 60 years. Shrewd acquisitions in the transfer market, the ability to get the best out of players, and a happy knack of blending disparate characters into a cohesive unit helped him establish Portsmouth as a top Premiership club.* So when Steve McLaren was sacked, there was a bandwagon rolling for Harry. Unfortunately, allegations of improper payments to Pompey players, with reports of a Police raid on his home, stopped the bandwagon before it gathered sufficient momentum. In 2007, the 'Stephens Inquiry' found, *no wrongdoing on Redknapp's part*; there was a curious reference to his horse, 'Double Fantasy', never having won a race but that **isn't** a crime. No charges were brought, and yet, damage was done. In May 2008 the City of London Magistrates ruled that the raid on his Poole home was illegal and ordered the Police to pay compensation. In football, as in life, timing is everything:

However, on the 26th February 2010, Portsmouth became the first Premier League club to go into administration.

It was like someone up above had said: Hang on! He's getting a bit too popular we'd better hit him over the head with a bloody great sledge hammer. It would have been a great time to get the England job...what with all that talent around: Lampard, Ferdinand, Carrick, the Coles, Rooney, and Walcott (Sun Pisces Mars Gemini).

In October 2008 Redknapp agreed to join Spurs on condition that he would be in sole charge of team affairs – ironically 2 days later he was made a 'Freeman of Portsmouth'. Spurs were bottom of the Premiership at the time, but by 4th January 2010 they were challenging for the title. 10 days later he was charged on 2 counts of tax evasion – he pleaded *not guilty*.

PART
2

The zodiac and team-building

PARTNERSHIPS

Partnerships create success.
Charlie Nicholas

In Part 1, we considered the 12 signs of the zodiac as expressed through the characters and careers of some of the football world's leading figures, each one of those considered made his mark in the game by, *doing what fitted his personality.* Now we will look at how doing what fits your personality is just the beginning on the path that leads to fulfilling your potential: being at the right club at the right time is important, being with the right players is just as important, and having the right coach is vital. Indeed, success is built on having effective partnerships throughout a club.

CHAIRMAN / MANAGER

Your best time as a manager is when
you have got a relationship
with your chairman.
Neil Warnock

The fortunes of a football club rest on the shoulders of the owner / chairman. His or her business acumen and knowledge of the game is important, but having the ability to select the right manager is crucial. If the chairman / manager relationship is fraught then their tensions can damage the club. Therefore, at successful clubs, the manager reflects the attitude, ambition, and values of the chairman: they understand each other and are on the same wavelength.**

Let's look at some examples:

When Simon Jordan took control of Crystal Palace, Steve Coppell was enjoying some success as their manager, but they didn't get on and Coppell's contract was terminated by mutual consent. Coppell said that they couldn't work together; Jordan said there was a personality clash:

JORDAN SUN Libra (AIR) MARS Sagittarius (FIRE)
COPPELL SUN Cancer (WATER) MARS Cancer (WATER)

Simon appointed Steve Bruce: 4 months later Steve left of his own accord…

BRUCE SUN Capricorn (EARTH) MARS Cancer (WATER)

They probably saw things very differently. Simon appointed Iain Dowie next. Things started brightly and in 2004 they won promotion, then, curiously, Iain resigned for *personal reasons*. They parted amicably. Soon afterwards, impressively, Dowie bounced back into management with Charlton Athletic. Jordan, somewhat less than impressed, claimed that Dowie had misrepresented his intentions when leaving Palace and sued for compensation. It came out in evidence that Simon didn't like Iain's tactics, moreover, he didn't like his teams; Dowie said that he found Jordan *difficult to work with*:

DOWIE SUN Capricorn (EARTH) MARS Virgo (EARTH)

** *The Sun/Mars in the AIR/FIRE signs have a natural affinity, whilst the Sun/Mars in the WATER/EARTH signs also get along well, but when AIR or FIRE is mixed with WATER or EARTH, special care needs to be taken.*

Simon appointed Peter Taylor next. Taylor had done well in charge of Gillingham, Brighton and Hull, and was doing well in his part-time coaching role with the England Under 21's. But he got off to a poor start at Palace, was encouraged to give up his part-time job and, with the team dropping to 19th place, was sacked:

TAYLOR SUN Capricorn (EARTH) MARS Scorpio (WATER)

On the 11th October 2007, Neil Warnock came out of retirement to take charge. At the press conference, Simon said,

He represents everything I want in a manager. He is a winner: confrontational... fiery...charismatic...passionate – sparks will fly between us. It's a dream ticket (going into administration generated unwanted sparks).

WARNOCK SUN Sagittarius (FIRE)

Milan Mandaric is the chairman of Leicester City. Following the departure of former managers Ian Holloway and Martin Allen – Mandaric spoke highly of both, but results hadn't been good enough – Milan introduced his new manager, Nigel Pearson. At the Press conference,

When I met Nigel I immediately knew he was the right man. There is no agenda: he is honest, has integrity and manages people straight with a certain discipline. He is a man of presence.

I am delighted to have the opportunity to manage Leicester City, and work with Milan. It feels right.

MILAN MANDARIC MARS Leo
NIGEL PEARSON SUN Leo
IAN HOLLOWAY MARS Leo
MARTIN ALLEN SUN Leo

Pearson took them on a record 21 game winning run to the top of the table and promotion in 2009.

Astrologically, Roman Abramovic, the Chelsea chairman, and his manager Jose Mourinho were an unlikely partnership. Nevertheless, it was very successful while it lasted.

ABRAMOVIC SUN Scorpio (WATER) MARS Virgo (EARTH)
MOURINHO SUN Aquarius (AIR) MARS Leo (FIRE)

The end was signalled in September 2007 by defeat at Aston Villa – but would Jose come back to haunt the Bridge? Avram Grant was promoted: he was unknown in England but had been a successful manager with Maccabi Haifa and Israel.

I don't think that he can do well at Chelsea I am sure of it.
He's got what it takes. He is a top manager.
Yossi Benayoun (Sun Taurus)

GRANT SUN Taurus (EARTH) MARS Gemini (AIR)

Chelsea had quite a good year – apart from being knocked out of the FA Cup by Barnsley – coming second in the Premier League and runners-up in the Champions League. After mega-investment, that wasn't a good enough return for the chairman. On the 1st July Mr. Abramovic appointed Luis Felipe Scolari (fresh from his Euro 2008 success with Portugal); at the Press conference Felipe was asked what his relationship was like with the chairman:

Fantastic: we respect each other: we discuss the players – who should play, what are their best positions, and so on.

He confirmed that John Terry would be captain:

SCOLARI SUN Scorpio MARS Sagittarius
TERRY SUN Sagittarius

After a poor run of results and a reported players' delegation (excluding Terry) of complainants to the chairman, Scolari was sacked. Abramovic turned to the Russia manager, Guus Hiddink, to take temporary charge:

HIDDINK SUN Scorpio MARS Sagittarius

Hiddink confirmed Terry as captain.

In 1996 the Chelsea chairman, Ken Bates, appointed Ruud Gullit to succeed Glenn Hoddle. In their first season Chelsea won the FA Cup for the first time in 26 years: the following season they continued the good form, but, sitting in 2nd place in the League, Gullit was sacked. Then there were spells for Luca Vialli and Claudio Ranieri. When Bates became chairman of stricken Leeds United he appointed Kevin Blackwell, kept faith with him as they struggled, and eventually had to replace him. In came Ken's former Chelsea captain, Dennis Wise; Ken was supportive of Dennis as they continued to struggle and were relegated. When Wise joined Newcastle, former Leeds' star Gary McAllister arrived, 5 games without a win and Gary was out. Then Ken appointed Simon Grayson and went on a winning run:

BATES SUN Sagittarius MARS Sagittarius
GULLIT SUN Virgo
VIALLI SUN Cancer
RANIERI SUN Libra
BLACKWELL SUN Sagittarius
WISE SUN Sagittarius
McALLISTER SUN Capricorn
GRAYSON SUN Sagittarius

Bates tried to appoint Neil Warnock but, according to hearsay, his ideal manager was George Graham:

WARNOCK SUN Sagittarius
GRAHAM SUN Sagittarius MARS Sagittarius

Peter Ridsdale regrets not signing his ideal manager, Martin O'Neill. Regardless, things went well with David O'Leary – for a while they were *the real deal*. Following the financial collapse at Elland Road, and a spell in the football wilderness, Peter re-emerged in South Wales leading resurgent Cardiff City to their first FA Cup final in living memory, with manager Dave Jones:

RIDSDALE SUN Pisces MARS Scorpio
O'NEILL SUN Pisces MARS Scorpio
O'LEARY MARS Pisces
JONES MARS Pisces

MANAGERS / ASSISTANTS

Without a capable assistant even the best managers fail; one of the most successful combinations was Brian Clough and Peter Taylor. As Cloughie once said to Pete, *I'm nothing without you*. Although they were very different characters, they learnt to value their differences and came to understand that together they were better than apart, even though, *we fought like cat and dog*:

CLOUGH SUN Aries (FIRE) MARS Libra (AIR)
TAYLOR SUN Cancer (WATER) MARS Taurus (EARTH)

In his later years Brian spoke highly of the management potential of his former players, Martin O'Neill and John Robertson:

O'NEILL SUN Pisces
ROBERTSON MARS Pisces

Rafa Benitez is sometimes accused of not having a good rapport with his players, but his assistant Pako Ayesteran did and together they enjoyed great success in Valencia and at Liverpool. When Pako returned to Spain at the start of the 2007-08 season the assistant's post remained vacant. At the end of a disappointing season Benitez signed a new assistant, former Liverpool midfielder Sammy Lee:

AYESTERAN SUN Aquarius
LEE SUN Aquarius

Jose Mourinho was not exactly Bobby Robson's assistant manager, but he played his part in Robson's success. As interpreter and tactical go-between, Jose was vital in conveying Bobby's message at Sporting Lisbon, FC Porto, and then at Barcelona:

ROBSON SUN Aquarius
MOURINHO SUN Aquarius

MANAGERS / CAPTAINS

The captain should be an extension of the manager.
Glenn Hoddle

Usually, successful sides have a captain who leads the team and plays the game in the way that the manager has envisioned it should be played. Arguably, the best team the visionary Jimmy Hogan coached was the Austrian Wunderteam. His captain became a national legend and was voted 'Austrian player of the 20th Century'. Hogan described Matthias Sindelar as the Mozart of football:

HOGAN SUN Libra
SINDELAR MARS Libra

Hogan's German protégé, Helmut Schoen, went on to become the most successful World Cup coach ever. He had the perfect help:

SCHOEN SUN Virgo MARS Cancer
BECKENBAUER SUN Virgo MARS Cancer

The most successful Sweden manager was George Raynor. An admirer of Jimmy Hogan, he too understood the importance of having the right captain:

RAYNOR SUN Capricorn
LIEDHOLM MARS Capricorn

England's most successful manager, Alf Ramsey, also had the right man:

RAMSEY SUN Aquarius
MOORE MARS Aquarius

At Spurs the 'Double' winning Bill Nicholson had Danny Blanchflower's help on and off the pitch:

NICHOLSON SUN Aquarius
BLANCHFLOWER SUN Aquarius

After only 4 months in charge, Tony Barton won the European Cup (1982) with Aston Villa. Tony was lucky to take over from Ron Saunders (Sun Scorpio) and have the right captain:

BARTON SUN Aries
MORTIMER SUN Aries MARS Scorpio

In his early years at Manchester United Alex Ferguson had the right captains:

FERGUSON SUN Capricorn MARS Aries
ROBSON SUN Capricorn MARS Aries
BRUCE SUN Capricorn
G NEVILLE MARS Capricorn

Whilst at Arsenal, so did Arsene Wenger:

WENGER SUN Libra MARS Leo
ADAMS SUN Libra MARS Leo
VIEIRA MARS Leo
HENRY SUN Leo
GALLAS SUN Leo

When no one understood him; when no one supported him; when the media persecuted him for using 78 players in Argentina's struggle to qualify for the 2010 World Cup Finals, it was just Diego and his captain:

MARADONA SUN Scorpio MARS Cancer
MASCHERANO MARS Scorpio

and 2 more. Diego also said, *my team is Mascherano, Messi, Jonas (Gutierrez), and the others:*

MESSI SUN Cancer MARS Cancer
GUTIERREZ SUN Cancer MARS Cancer

PLAYERS

The foundations of most successful teams are built on telepathic, defensive partnerships. Chelsea's success, under Mourinho, was founded on the understanding between their keeper, Petr Cech, and centre back, Ricardo Carvalho:

CECH SUN Taurus
CARVALHO SUN Taurus

Manchester United's solid foundation was the good understanding between goalie, Edwin van der Sar, and centre back, Rio Ferdinand:

VAN DER SAR SUN Scorpio
FERDINAND SUN Scorpio

In 2006, Paul Robinson was enjoying a purple patch for Spurs and England. At the time Ledley King, his club captain and centre half, was also enjoying a good run of form and fitness:

ROBINSON SUN Libra
KING SUN Libra

It could be a strange coincidence, but a period of prolonged injury to King was accompanied by a run of bad luck, loss of confidence, and poor form for Paul, resulting in him being transferred by Spurs and dropped by England.

The Arsenal, of the 1980s and 90s, was legendary for its miserly defence. With Tony Adams and Martin Keown at the heart, the Gunners did the League and FA Cup double:

ADAMS SUN Libra MARS Leo
KEOWN SUN Leo

Arsenal also did well when Adams was partnered by Steve Bould or Sol Campbell:

BOULD MARS Leo
CAMPBELL MARS Libra

However, his partnership with Steve Morrow ended in tears: although they won the FA Cup together their lack of understanding finally showed itself in their victory lap of honour, Adams lifted Morrow shoulder high in celebration and...whoops...Steve slipped and broke his collar-bone:

MORROW SUN Cancer MARS Cancer.

Clearly, Morrow's ideal defensive partner wasn't Adams. He would have been much safer alongside Gary Pallister, Steve Bruce, or Paulo Maldini. Indeed, it was Gary and Steve who formed a watertight defensive unit in a formidable Manchester United (1994):

PALLISTER SUN Cancer
BRUCE MARS Cancer

They weren't Alex Ferguson's first or last intuitive central defensive foundation though, it all started at Aberdeen – on granite:

MILLER SUN Taurus
McLEISH MARS Taurus

Perhaps the best ever defensive partnership was Franco Baresi and 'Billy' Costacurta at AC Milan. Instinctively they knew where the other would be, and what he would do. They helped Milan win the European Cup in 1989 and 1990:

BARESI SUN Taurus
COSTACURTA SUN Taurus MARS Taurus

In 2007, AC Milan beat Liverpool in the European Cup final with another accomplished defensive pairing, Paulo Maldini and Alessandro Nesta:

MALDINI SUN Cancer
NESTA MARS Cancer

In the 1980s, Alan Hansen and Mark Lawrenson were on the same wavelength at the centre of Liverpool's European Cup winning side:

HANSEN SUN Gemini MARS Cancer
LAWRENSON SUN Gemini MARS Cancer

Hansen and Lawrenson were so 'in tune' they could have been twins. Born 20 minutes apart, defenders Aleksei and Vasili Berezutsky – appropriately Sun Geminis – are 'real life' twins and helped CSKA Moscow to the UEFA Cup in 2005.

In Sheffield United's, and Neil Warnock's, battle against relegation (2007), the Blades' fight was carried by centre backs Chris Morgan and Phil Jagielka:

MORGAN SUN Scorpio MARS Leo
JAGIELKA SUN Leo MARS Scorpio

The following season Jagielka signed for Everton and picked up where he left off, in a promising partnership with Joleon Lescott:

LESCOTT SUN Leo MARS Scorpio

However, Mark Hughes (Sun Scorpio) at Manchester City had money to spend (£200M in 18 months) and was team-building; he signed Lescott to partner former Gunner, Kolo Toure, unfortunately it didn't work; he signed former Gunner, Adebayor, to partner Robinho, unfortunately that didn't work either. In his farewell game, on the 19th

December 2009 – although he didn't know it at the time – with Adebayor and Robinho dropped, Lescott injured, and Roque Santa Cruz, Tevez, and Shaun Wright-Phillips in attack, he beat Sunderland 4-3 to go 6th in the Premiership:

SANTA CRUZ SUN Scorpio
TEVEZ MARS Scorpio
WRIGHT-PHILLIPS SUN Scorpio

The backbone in Bobby Robson's World Cup campaign (1990) was the partnership between centre backs Terry Butcher and Des Walker. They were well supported from midfield by the rock, Bryan Robson:

BUTCHER SUN Capricorn
WALKER MARS Capricorn
ROBSON SUN Capricorn

Fabio Capello stuck with England's tried and tested partnership of Rio Ferdinand and John Terry:

TERRY SUN Sagittarius
FERDINAND MARS Sagittarius

In 1960 Real Madrid won the European Cup with a display of sublime football; at their intuitive hub was Alfredo di Stefano, Ferenc Puskas, and Luis del Sol:

DI STEFANO MARS Aries
PUSKAS SUN Aries
DEL SOL SUN Aries

Del Sol was the replacement for Didi – who featured briefly, clashed with Di Stefano, and was transferred mid-season. Anyhow, Didi did enjoy a perfect understanding with his Brazil teammates:

DIDI SUN Libra MARS Scorpio
PELE SUN Libra
ZAGALLO MARS Libra
VAVA SUN Scorpio
GARRINCHA SUN Scorpio

Don Revie's legendary Leeds side had a strong sense of togetherness: they hunted in packs and attacked in waves. At the hub was captain Billy Bremner, Johnny Giles, and Norman Hunter:

GILES SUN Scorpio
BREMNER MARS Scorpio
HUNTER SUN Scorpio

Brian Clough built his successful Derby side on similar lines; there was an uncanny connection through the spine of the team – from Dave Mackay in central defence, to John McGovern in midfield, to the trojan Kevin Hector in attack:

MACKAY SUN Scorpio
McGOVERN SUN Scorpio
HECTOR SUN Scorpio

When Clough went to Forest, he took McGovern with him. John enjoyed a good relationship with striker, Tony Woodcock:

WOODCOCK MARS Scorpio

The 'silver fox' Schoen, preferred to pair a hard tackler alongside a playmaker in midfield. In his 1974 World Cup winning side, Helmut partnered rock solid Uli Hoeness with the scheming playmaker, Wolfgang Overath:

OVERATH SUN Libra
HOENESS MARS Libra

In the 1970s Manchester City's success was founded on the flowing inter-play between Colin Bell, Francis Lee, and Mike Summerbee:

BELL SUN Pisces MARS Cancer
LEE MARS Cancer
SUMMERBEE MARS Pisces

When Rodney Marsh was signed to secure the First Division title, the flowing football stopped:

MARSH SUN Libra MARS Libra

At the heart of the flawless French diamond (1984) was Michel Platini and his partner Jean Tigana. Tigana's career had been going nowhere until Aime Jacquet paired him with Platini. France went on to win the European Championships:

TIGANA SUN Cancer
PLATINI MARS Cancer

In 2008 -09 Wigan Athletic made a surprising assault on the top of the Premiership. The key to their rise was their central midfield partnership of Wilson Palacios and Valencia. Palacios had been signed the season before for around £1M; in the January 'transfer window' he moved to struggling Spurs for £15M:

VALENCIA SUN Leo MARS Leo
PALACIOS SUN Leo

Would he settle as quickly at White Hart Lane? He made a promising start alongside Luca Modric:

MODRIC MARS Leo

Curiously, Wigan slipped down the table whilst Spurs were transformed.

In the same 'transfer window' Spurs arch-rivals, Arsenal, signed the diminutive Russian midfielder Andrei Arshavin. On the 4th April 2009 Arsenal played Manchester City. It was Arshavin's first game and he was playing alongside Cesc Fabregas and Theo Walcott. They clicked. After 8 minutes Arsenal went ahead. Fabregas was in command, whilst Theo and Andrei inter-changed on either side; in the end, Arsenal won more comfortably than the 2-0 scoreline suggests:

FABREGAS SUN Taurus MARS Gemini
ARSHAVIN MARS Taurus SUN Gemini
WALCOTT MARS Gemini

Perhaps the key signing that transformed Bill Shankly's Liverpool was Ian St John. Before St John, Roger Hunt was a reliable goalscorer: after, he was prolific:

HUNT SUN Cancer
St JOHN MARS Cancer

In the 1980s Napoli won Serie A, twice, and they also won the UEFA Cup. Some said Napoli was a one-man-team: Diego Maradona, but Maradona gave credit to his teammates, in particular to his fellow striker Careca:

MARADONA MARS Cancer
CARECA MARS Cancer

When Maradona left, his understudy, Gianfranco Zola, took his place in the first team and formed an immediate bond with Careca:

ZOLA SUN Cancer

At the 1986 World Cup, Maradona, Careca (Brazil), and Emilio Butragueno (Spain) were pipped for the 'Golden Boot' by Gary Lineker, who was greatly helped by his strike partner Peter Beardsley:

LINEKER MARS Cancer
BEARDSLEY MARS Cancer

One of Sunderland's most prolific partnerships was Niall Quinn and Kevin Phillips:

PHILLIPS SUN Leo
QUINN MARS Leo

In the 1990s, Nottingham Forest were bidding for promotion and in that bid they gambled on the rebel striker, Pierre van Hooijdonk, partnering him with the veteran centre forward, Kevin Campbell. They clicked. Pierre scored 34 goals and Kevin hit 23 in a successful season:

VAN HOOIJDONK MARS Aquarius
CAMPBELL SUN Aquarius

In 2008 Manchester United were the World Club champions. One of their midfield stars was Scottish international Darren Fletcher. On the 28th March 2009, Fletcher played for Scotland in their crucial World Cup qualifier against Holland, but the omens were not good – Scotland had not won in Holland for 50 years. Nonetheless, George Burley was quietly confident; his preferred midfield pairing of Fletcher (Sun Aquarius) and Barry Ferguson (Sun Aquarius) were on form. Holland were at full-strength with Klaas Jan Huntelaar – *in the box he is the best player in the world:* Louis van Gaal – leading the attack, with Arsenal's Robin van Persie alongside, and Liverpool's Dirk Kuyt in support – 3-0 at half-time – all 3 scored and Holland won comfortably (despite Fletcher and Ferguson doing well):

HUNTELAAR SUN Leo MARS Cancer
VAN PERSIE SUN Leo MARS Cancer
KUYT SUN Cancer
VAN GAAL SUN Leo MARS Cancer

In the summer of 2009 Manchester United sold their best strikers: Carlos Tevez and Cristiano Ronaldo, and didn't replace them. So who would score the goals now? Sir Alex moved Wayne Rooney to centre forward and provided him with plenty of the right type of support.

ROONEY SUN Scorpio
SCHOLES SUN Scorpio
FLETCHER MARS Scorpio
NANI SUN Scorpio
GIBSON SUN Scorpio

Wayne was prolific.

SOLAR SYSTEMS

I don't think that a manager should have just one system of play.
Fabio Capello

Good partnerships are the building blocks of successful clubs. Having the right chairman and manager is important, having the right captain is also important and having telepathic player partnerships is ideal. However, in addition to tactical formations and a host of off-field preparations there is something just as important – having the right *system*. Many systems have been used over the past 100 years or so but they can all be reduced to two basic types. One is based on a structured formation with a balance between players with a constructive mindset and those with a defensive attitude. In this system roles and responsibilities are clearly defined and when it is working well such a team is extremely difficult to beat. The other is more fluid: the players interchange positions, they defend as a unit and attack in waves, and when this system is working well, it is irresistible.

For ease of reference we will name the first system, *Balanced,* and the other, *Cohesive.* If we were to compare team-building with composing a piece of fine Art, we could say that one follows the golden rules of proportion, harmony, and structure to create a realistic image. Whereas the other painting flows across the canvas in broad, vibrant sweeps that merge, separate, and merge again to produce an abstract beauty.

Which system is better? What happens when the irresistible force meets the immovable object? Both systems are effective in the right hands, or to paraphrase an ancient Chinese text:

When the right manager uses the wrong system, the wrong system works in the right way. When the wrong manager uses the right system, the right system works in the wrong way, but when the right manager uses the right system he comes through a hundred matches victorious.

What do the systems look like astrologically? Let's consider the *Balanced* system in detail.

Balance is the goal of Chinese philosophy and a life that achieves balance between the two forces in the universe – yin and yang – that together make the whole, is not wasted. The concept of balance is linked to harmony and timing and without it there is no good fortune. In the football context, *balance* is derived from the elements: the ideal *balanced* side has 5 players from the yin elements, and 5 players from the yang elements in the outfield.** Pardon?

Let's look at some examples of how balancing the elements creates winning teams:

** *The yin Elements are EARTH and WATER, the yang Elements are FIRE and AIR. To determine whether a player's natural disposition is yin or yang, consider the position of the Sun in the horoscope.*

WINNING TEAMS

No man is an island entire of itself, everyman is a part of the team,
a member of the squad. Therefore never send to know for whom
the whistle blows. It blows for thee.
John Donne (with apologies)

SOUTHAMPTON 1976

Over a decade after Tommy Docherty's Chelsea were pipped for the
Second Division title by Stoke City, he was still wondering how it had
happened when lightning struck again. In 1976, Docherty's Manchester
United were hot favourites to beat the 7-1 Second Division outsiders,
Southampton, in the FA Cup final. Bobby Stokes' Saints, like Tony
Waddington's Stoke of the 1960s, were a team of talented veterans
mixed with young, selfless athletes.

After riding their luck for the first 20 minutes, Southampton settled
into their game and began to look dangerous. With 7 minutes
remaining, Jim McCalliog fed the ball through for Stokes to run on to
and slot the winner. United fought back but couldn't break through.
McMenemy's Southampton had pulled it off; Tommy was bemused:
how?

Ask the local gentry, Doc – it's ELEMENTARY!

TURNER SUN Capricorn
RODRIGUES SUN Aquarius (AIR)

HOLMES SUN Scorpio (WATER)
PEACH SUN Aquarius (AIR)
BLYTH SUN Leo (FIRE)
STEELE SUN Pisces (WATER)
GILCHRIST SUN Capricorn (EARTH)
McCALLIOG SUN Virgo (EARTH)
OSGOOD SUN Pisces (WATER)
STOKES SUN Aquarius (AIR)
CHANNON SUN Sagittarius (FIRE)

BALANCE OF ELEMENTS IN THE OUTFIELD:
AIR 3 / FIRE 2 (5 YANG) – WATER 3 / EARTH 2 (5 YIN)

Southampton are not the only 'giant killers'; over the years there have been many Cup upsets when the club with the better players was not the better team: including Barnsley 2008. When the Tykes beat Chelsea in the semi-finals of the FA Cup, they also fielded a well balanced – 3/2/3/2 – system.

LIVERPOOL 1979

Bill Shankly laid the foundations and built the walls at Anfield, but according to Ian St John, *Bob Paisley (Sun Aquarius) put the roof on*. In 1974 Paisley took charge of Liverpool: he brought continuity, made very few changes, and yet won 3 European Cups!

His 1979 team, according to Alan Hansen, was the best Liverpool team: it not only had ability, *it was how the players blended together that was special*. In 42 First Division matches, the Reds conceded 16 goals and scored 85: winning 30. They were unbeaten at home; they finished the season 8 points clear of 2nd placed Nottingham Forest. So what were the few changes? Paisley made Phil Thompson captain and signed a couple to, *add balance*.

CLEMENCE Leo
NEAL Pisces (WATER)
A KENNEDY Virgo (EARTH)
THOMPSON Aquarius (AIR)
HANSEN Gemini (AIR)
CASE Taurus (EARTH)
SOUNESS Taurus (EARTH)
McDERMOTT Sagittarius (FIRE)
R KENNEDY Leo (FIRE)
DALGLISH Pisces (WATER)
HEIGHWAY Sagittarius (FIRE)

ELEMENTS
FIRE 3 / AIR 2 / EARTH 3 / WATER 2

BLACKBURN ROVERS 1995

After a successful managerial spell at Liverpool, where he won the First Division title, Kenny Dalglish (Sun Pisces Mars Aries) became the manager of Blackburn Rovers. With the help of owner Jack Walker's millions and coach, Ray Harford (Mars Aries), Dalglish led newly promoted Rovers to 4th in the League; the following season they were runners-up and in 1995 they won it. Dalglish is one of only 3 managers to win the top League in England with different clubs: joining Herbert Chapman and Brian Clough. Rovers broke the British transfer record twice on the way: signing Alan Shearer from Southampton for £3.6M, then paying Norwich £5M for Chris Sutton. The team that won the Premiership cost a total of £17.65M: proving that you can buy the title, providing that your manager buys the right players:

FLOWERS Aquarius
BERG Virgo (EARTH)
PEARCE Taurus (EARTH)

HENDRY Sagittarius (FIRE)
Le SAUX Libra (AIR)
RIPLEY Scorpio (WATER)
SHERWOOD Aquarius (AIR)
BATTY Sagittarius (FIRE)
WILCOX Cancer (WATER)
SHEARER Leo (FIRE)
SUTTON Pisces (WATER)

ELEMENTS
FIRE 3 / AIR 2 / WATER 3 / EARTH 2

MANCHESTER UNITED 2007

In 2003-04, in 2004-05, and 2005-06, Alex Ferguson's Manchester United won nothing. In 2006-07 they were the outsiders of the big 4 Premiership clubs – Arsenal were invincible in 2004, Chelsea were unbeatable in '05 and '06, and Liverpool had won the Champions League – early matches confirmed the bookies' odds: United were disjointed and results were poor. In September / October 2006, the starting line-up was…

VAN DER SAR Scorpio
G NEVILLE Aquarius (AIR)
FERDINAND Scorpio (WATER)
VIDIC Libra (AIR)
HEINZE Aries (FIRE)
RONALDO Aquarius (AIR)
CARRICK Leo (FIRE)
SCHOLES Scorpio (WATER)
GIGGS Sagittarius (FIRE)
ROONEY Scorpio (WATER)
SAHA Leo (FIRE)

ELEMENTS
AIR 3 / FIRE 4 / WATER 3 / EARTH 0

It was going to be another disappointing, trophy-less season. Hang on! United have plenty of world-class players! What is going wrong? Ferguson sprang into action – made an emergency short-term signing, Henrik Larsson, and brought in France international, Patrice Evra. They clicked. United went on a winning streak and by the end of February were 9 points clear at the top.

However, on the 3rd March they had a crucial away game at Liverpool, United needed to win to keep up the momentum. At 0-0 with time running out, Alex made a decisive substitution – Evra off, John O'Shea on. It did the trick. John scored and United went on to become champions. The starting line-up at Anfield:

VAN DER SAR Scorpio
G NEVILLE Aquarius (AIR)
FERDINAND Scorpio (WATER)
VIDIC Libra (AIR)
EVRA Taurus (EARTH) (sub O'SHEA Taurus)
RONALDO Aquarius (AIR)
SCHOLES Scorpio (WATER)
CARRICK Leo (FIRE)
GIGGS Sagittarius (FIRE)
ROONEY Scorpio (WATER)
LARSSON Virgo (EARTH)

ELEMENTS
AIR 3 / FIRE 2 / WATER 3 / EARTH 2

In addition to being well balanced, the partnership between Larsson and Rooney (Mars Virgo) was vital.

261

ENGLAND 1966 WORLD CUP WINNERS

In 1963 Alf Ramsey became England manager. From the start he was confident: even though England had never won the World Cup, he boldly predicted that they would. Why so confident, Alf?

The eccentric, and secretive, Ramsey believed that he had discovered a pattern of play that transformed good players into invincibles. Alf was a lifelong student of the game: he lived and breathed football. As a player he admired Brazil: he thought that their 1958 team was the best. When he was a lad, he admired the Uruguayans: they were the best team in the 1920s. When he went into coaching his research was exhaustive and – Eureka! – he discovered the secret. He tried it out in the footballing backwater of Ipswich and won promotion, then won promotion again, and again, and then, unbelievably, won the First Division title. When he became England manager he made some curious selections, prompting Jack Charlton to enquire:

Why did you pick me, Alf?

Well, I have a pattern of play in my mind and I pick the best players to fit the pattern, I don't necessarily always pick the best players. I've watched you play, Jack, and you are quite good. You are a strong tackler and good in the air and I need those things. I also know that you do not trust Bobby Moore: you and he are different characters. If Gordon gives the ball to you on the edge of the penalty box you will pass it back, but if Gordon gives it to Bobby he will play it through midfield, all the way forward if he can. I've watched you play, Jack, and I know that as soon as Bobby goes up field you will fill in behind so that if Bobby does make a mistake, you will always be there to cover.

As hosts England didn't have to qualify for the tournament. They had a difficult draw in the Group Stage: France, Mexico, and Uruguay. In the first match he showed Uruguay great respect, the teams cancelled each other out in a boring, goalless draw. Both teams progressed to the knock-out stages, and England progressed to the final. To fulfil his prophecy Alf had to beat his arch-rival, Helmut Schoen, at the Empire Stadium. England started brightly, but hearts sank as Haller opened the scoring for the white-shirted Germans. England hit back with 2 goals from lucky Geoff Hurst, and Martin Peters ghosted in for another. With seconds remaining Hurst galloped into space...volley...goal...4-2: the crowd erupted, fog horns blasted on the Thames, and spontaneous street parties were thrown.

The Germans complained for years that the linesman cost them.

BANKS Capricorn
COHEN Libra (AIR)
WILSON Sagittarius (FIRE)
MOORE Aries (FIRE)
J CHARLTON Taurus (EARTH)
BALL Taurus (EARTH)
STILES Taurus (EARTH)
HUNT Cancer (WATER)
R CHARLTON Libra (AIR)
HURST Sagittarius (FIRE)
PETERS Scorpio (WATER)

ELEMENTS
FIRE 3 / AIR 2 / EARTH 3 / WATER 2

URUGUAY 1930 WORLD CUP WINNERS

Uruguay were the first World Cup winners beating their arch-rivals Argentina 4-2 in the 1930 final. In the run-up to the match the media stirred up public passions, arousing old hostilities between the nations. By final-day nationalistic blood was up: referee John Langenus was rattled. He made a worried call to the Chief of Police, *protection... protection, I need protection!* He demanded that the Authorities guarantee his personal safety or the match would be abandoned before it got started: a brigade of armed guards was dispatched to the Centenary Stadium and the game got underway.

After a bright start, Uruguayan hearts sank as Argentina took control and went into the interval 2-1 ahead. The captain of the guard expected the worst as the referee headed for the tunnel, but the crowd was strangely silent. In the Uruguayan dressing room, manager Suppicci was calm, confident, inspired – he reminded his players that they were, *The Invincibles,* and sent them out to prove it. The second half began with a brilliant dribbling run from Pedro Cea…2-2. The excitement was unbearable as left winger, Santos Iriarte, ghosted into the penalty box to put Uruguay ahead. With Montevideo praying for the final whistle, the one-armed Sagittarian striker Castro galloped into space…volley… goal…4-2. The stadium erupted, fog horns blasted in the Bay, spontaneous street parties were thrown, and a national holiday was declared.

The Argentinians complained for years that one-sided refereeing cost them.

BALLESTEROS Capricorn
NASAZZI Gemini (AIR)
MASCHERONI Scorpio (WATER)
ANDRADE Libra (AIR)
FERNANDEZ Taurus (EARTH)
GESTIDO Taurus (EARTH)
DORADO Cancer (WATER)
SCARONE Sagittarius (FIRE)
CEA Virgo (EARTH)
CASTRO Sagittarius (FIRE)
IRIARTE Scorpio (WATER)

ELEMENTS
EARTH 3 / FIRE 2 / WATER 3 / AIR 2

BRAZIL 1958 WORLD CUP WINNERS

Some say this was the best team ever. The manager was Vicente Feola (Sun Scorpio): he had the best player in the world, Didi (Sun Libra Mars Scorpio), and he had the future best player in the world, Pele. His team had flair, beauty, resilience and balance. In the final they were playing the hosts. Sweden had their best side ever and were quickly onto the attack. Liedholm put them ahead, Brazil were knocked out of their stride, but gradually Didi took control, brought Pele into the game and inspired Zagallo. Vava was outstanding and the flying winger, Garrincha, was on song...5-2.

GILMAR Leo
D SANTOS Pisces (WATER)
N SANTOS Taurus (EARTH)
ZITO Leo (FIRE)
BELLINI Gemini (AIR)
ORLANDO Virgo (EARTH)
GARRINCHA Scorpio (WATER)
VAVA Scorpio (WATER)
DIDI Libra (AIR)
PELE Libra (AIR)
ZAGALLO Leo (FIRE)

ELEMENTS
AIR 3 / FIRE 2 / WATER 3 / EARTH 2

BARCELONA 2009 CHAMPIONS LEAGUE WINNERS

In 2008 Manchester United won the Champions League. In 2009, the vastly experienced Ferguson was bidding to become the first manager to retain the trophy; in contrast, his opponent was in his first season of management. Nevertheless, Pep Guardiola (Sun Capricorn Mars Scorpio), a former Barcelona star, was about to make history (he had already won the Spanish League and Cup).

VALDES Capricorn
PUYOL Aries (FIRE)
SYLVINHO Aries (FIRE)
TOURE Taurus (EARTH)
INIESTA Taurus (EARTH)
PIQUE Aquarius (AIR)
XAVI Aquarius (AIR)
BUSQUETS Cancer (WATER)
MESSI Cancer (WATER)
ETO'O Pisces (WATER)
HENRY Leo (FIRE)

ELEMENTS
3 FIRE / 2 AIR / 3 WATER / 2 EARTH

ENGLAND 2009

When Fabio Capello took over from Steve McLaren, he inherited a side that was unbalanced, lacked cohesion, and had no confidence. There was no doubt, however, that England had plenty of world-class players including: John Terry, the Coles, Lampard, Gerrard, and Rooney. So football pundits were asking, *why are they hopeless?* In answer, some experts said that Lampard and Gerrard were so similar that they couldn't play together, some said Rooney was out of position, and others that Ashley Cole was good going forward, but not so good defending. Anyway, with the same key players England went on an 8 match winning streak and qualified for the 2010 World Cup Finals with 2 games to spare. How?

Fabio Capello is an avid art collector and he particularly appreciates abstracts, but first let's look at his blank canvas:

ENGLAND 0 – 0 MACEDONIA.
Wembley Stadium
October 2006.

ROBINSON Libra
G NEVILLE Aquarius (AIR)
KING Libra (AIR)
TERRY Sagittarius (FIRE)
A COLE Sagittarius (FIRE)
GERRARD Gemini (AIR)
LAMPARD Gemini (AIR)
CARRICK Leo (FIRE)
DOWNING Cancer (WATER)
ROONEY Scorpio (WATER)
CROUCH Aquarius (AIR)

ELEMENTS
5 AIR / 3 FIRE / 2 WATER / 0 EARTH

It was a disappointing performance. England lost the following European qualification match against Croatia 0-2, with the same – 5/3/2/0 – pattern, and in March 2007 they were ineffective against Israel with – 6/2/2/0. Anyhow, in September 2009 Capello's England beat Croatia 5–1. Gerrard scored twice, Lampard scored twice, Rooney scored, and Ashley Cole was the 'man of the match'. How had Fabio transformed them?

BIBLIOGRAPHY

In writing this book I have drawn on numerous website sources; newspaper articles and match reports; television programmes, shows and interviews; films; football journals and magazines (including: *FourFourTwo, Champions, and Shoot)*; and the following books:

Ball, Phil (2007). *White Storm: the story of Real Madrid*. Mainstream Publishing.

Barend, Frits and Henk Van Dorp (1999). *Ajax, Barcelona, Cruyff; the ABC of an obstinate maestro*. Bloomsbury.

Beckham, David with Tom Watt (2004). *David Beckham: my side*. Collins Willow.

Bell, Colin with Ian Cheeseman (2005). *Colin Bell: reluctant hero – the autobiography of a Manchester City and England legend*. Mainstream Publishing.

Brown, Craig (2003). *Craig Brown: the game of my life*. John Blake Publishing.

Burn, Gordon (2006). *Best and Edwards*. Faber & Faber.

Campion, Nicholas (1988). *The Book of World Horoscopes*. The Aquarian Press.

Chaisson, Eric J (2001). *Cosmic Evolution: the rise of complexity in nature*. Harvard University Press.

Charlton, Bobby with James Lawton (2007). *Sir Bobby Charlton: The Autobiography - My Manchester United Years*. Headline Publishing.

Clough, Brian with John Sadler (1994). *Clough: the Autobiography*. Partridge Press.

Darby, Tom (2001). *Talking Shankly*. Mainstream Publishing.

Davies, Hunter (1972). *The Glory Game*. Mainstream Publishing.

Derbyshire, Oliver (2006). *Thierry – the biography – Henry*. John Blake Publishing.

Derbyshire, Oliver (2007). *John Terry – captain marvel – the biography*. John Blake Publishing.

Docherty, Tommy (2006). *The Doc: my story – hallowed be thy game*. Headline Publishing.

Eriksson, Sven-Goran with Willi Railo and Hakan Matson (2002). *Sven-Goran Eriksson – the inner game : improving performance – on Football*. Carlton Books.

Finney, Tommy (2006). *Tom Finney: my autobiography*. Headline Publishing.

Fox, Norman (2003). *Prophet or Traitor: The Jimmy Hogan story*. The Parrs Wood

Press.

Gascoigne, Paul with Hunter Davies (2004). *Gazza: my story.* Headline Publishing.

Glanville, Brian and Jerry Weinstein (1958). *World Cup.* The Sportsman Book Club.

Glanville, Brian (2007). *England Managers: the toughest job in the world.* Headline Publishing.

Goldblatt, David (2007). *The ball is round – a global history of football.* Penguin Books.

Goldblatt, David and Johnny Acton (2009). *The Football Book.* Dorling Kindersley.

Graves, Robert (1992). *The Greek Myths: complete edition.* Penguin Books (first published by Pelican Books, in 2 editions, in 1955).

Gray, Andy (2004). *Gray matters – Andy Gray – the autobiography.* Pan Books.

Gray, Eddie with Jason Tomas (2001). *Eddie Gray: marching on together – my life with Leeds United.* Hodder & Stoughton.

Greaves, Jimmy (2006). *Greavsie; the autobiography.* Sphere.

Greaves, Jimmy with Norman Giller (2007). *Football's great heroes and entertainers.* Hodder & Stoughton.

Hamilton, Duncan (2008). *Provided you don't kiss me: 20 years with Brian Clough.* Harper Perennial.

Hansen, Alan with Jason Tomas (2000). *Alan Hansen: a matter of opinion.* Bantam Books.

Hodgson, Joan (1978). *Astrology the Sacred Science.* The White Eagle Publishing Trust.

Holt, Oliver (2006). *If you are second you are nothing: Ferguson and Shankly.* Macmillan.

Hopcraft, Arthur (2006). *The Football Man.* Aurum (first published in 1968).

Hurst, Geoff with Michael Hart (2006). *Geoff Hurst – my autobiography – 1966 and all that.* Headline Publishing (first published in 2001).

Inglis, Simon (2006). *The best of Charles Buchan's Football Monthly.* English Heritage & Football Monthly Ltd.

Jordan, Joe (2004). *My Autobiography.* Hodder & Stoughton.

Keane, Roy with Eamon Dunphy (2002). *The autobiography: Keane.* Michael Joseph.

Kelly, Stephen F (1997). *Fergie – the biography of Alex Ferguson.* Headline Publishing.

Law, Denis with Bob Harris (2003). *The King – my autobiography – Denis Law.*

Bantam Books.

Leatherhead, Clive (2006). *England's quest for the World Cup; 1950 – 2006.* Desert Island Books.

Lourenco, Luis (2004). *Jose Mourinho; made in Portugal.* Dewi Lewis Media.

Macpherson, Archie (2004). *Jock Stein: the definitive biography.* Highdown.

Maradona, Diego Armando with Daniel Arcuicci and Ernesto Bialo (2005). *El Diego.* Yellow Jersey Press.

Marcotti, Gabriele (2008). *Capello; portrait of a winner.* Bantam Press.

Matthews, Stanley (2001). *Stanley Matthews - my autobiography - the way it was.* Headline Publishing.

McKinstry, Leo (2007). *Sir Alf.* Harper Sport.

McNeill, Billy (2004). *The Autobiography.* Headline Publishing.

Michelsen, Neil F (1992). *The American Ephemeris:1900-2000.* ACS Publications.

Montgomery, Alex (2007). *Martin O'Neill: the biography.* Virgin Books.

Mourant, Andrew (2003). *Don Revie: portrait of a footballing enigma.* Mainstream Publishing (first published in 1990).

Owen, Michael with Paul Hayward (2004). *Michael Owen - off the record – my autobiography.* Collins Willow.

Page, Simon (2006). *Herbert Chapman: the first great manager.* Heroes Publishing.

Palmer, Myles (2001). *The professor: Arsene Wenger.* Virgin Books.

Pele with Orlando Duarte and Alex Bellos (2006). *Pele: the autobiography.* Simon & Schuster.

Ponting, Ivan (1993). *The FA Cup final: a post war history.* Haynes Publishing.

Radnedge, Keir (2006). *The complete encyclopedia of football.* Carlton Books.

Reedie, Euan (2007). *Alan Shearer: portrait of a legend.* John Blake Publishing.

Ridpath, Ian and Wil Tirion (2004). *Gem Stars.* Harper Collins (first published as Gem Night Sky in 1985).

Ridsdale, Peter (2007). *United we Fall: boardroom truths about the beautiful game.* Macmillan.

Robson, Bobby with Paul Hayward (2005). *Bobby Robson – farewell but not goodbye – my autobiography.* Hodder & Stoughton.

Robson, Bryan with Derick Allsop (2007). *Robbo: my autobiography.* Hodder & Stoughton.

Robson, Vivian E (1997). *The fixed stars and constellations in astrology.* Ascella (first published in 1923).

Saffer, David (2004). *Bobby Collins.* Tempus Publishing.

Shaw, Phil (2008). *The book of football quotations.* Ebury Press.

Sleight, Andrew (2008). *Robbie Keane: the biography.* John Blake Publishing.

Sobel, Dava (2005). *The planets.* Fourth Estate.

Stiles, Nobby with James Lawton (2003). *Nobby Stiles after the ball: my autobiography.* Hodder &Stoughton.

Warnock, Neil with Oliver Holt (2007). *Neil Warnock – made in Sheffield – my story.* Hodder & Stoughton.

Wilhelm, Richard and CG Jung (1975). *The secret of the golden flower.* Causeway Books (first published in 1931).

Wilhelm, Richard (1992). *I Ching or book of changes.* Penguin Books (first published in 1951 by Routledge & Kegan Paul).

Williams, John and Ramon Llopis (2007). *Rafa: Liverpool FC, Benitez and the new Spanish fury.* Mainstream Publishing.

Williams, Richard (2007). *The Perfect 10.* Faber & Faber.

Woolnough, Brian (1998). *Glenn Hoddle: the man and the manager.* Virgin Books.